DIGITAL DEMOCRACY, SOCIAL MEDIA AND DISINFORMATION

Digital Democracy, Social Media and Disinformation discusses some of the political, regulatory and technological issues which arise from the increased power of internet intermediaries (such as *Facebook*, *Twitter* and *YouTube*) and the impact of the spread of digital disinformation, especially in the midst of a health pandemic.

The volume provides a detailed account of the main areas surrounding digital democracy, disinformation and fake news, freedom of expression and post-truth politics. It addresses the major theoretical and regulatory concepts of digital democracy and the 'network society' before offering potential socio-political and technological solutions to the fight against disinformation and fake news. These solutions include self-regulation, rebuttals and myth-busting, news literacy, policy recommendations, awareness and communication strategies and the potential of recent technologies such as the blockchain and public interest algorithms to counter disinformation.

After addressing what has currently been done to combat disinformation and fake news, the volume argues that digital disinformation needs to be identified as a multifaceted problem, one that requires multiple approaches to resolve. Governments, regulators, think tanks, the academy and technology providers need to take more steps to better shape the next internet with as little digital disinformation as possible by means of a regional analysis. In this context, two cases concerning Russia and Ukraine are presented regarding disinformation and the ways it was handled.

Written in a clear and direct style, this volume will appeal to students and researchers within the social sciences, computer science, law and business studies, as well as policy makers engaged in combating what constitutes one of the most pressing issues of the digital age.

Petros Iosifidis is professor in Sociology and Media Policy at City, University of London, UK.

Nicholas Nicoli is associate professor of Communication at the University of Nicosia, Cyprus.

DIGITAL DEMOCRACY, SOCIAL MEDIA AND DISINFORMATION

Petros Iosifidis and Nicholas Nicoli

LONDON AND NEW YORK

First published 2021
by Routledge
2 Park Square, Milton Park, Abingdon, Oxon OX14 4RN

and by Routledge
52 Vanderbilt Avenue, New York, NY 10017

Routledge is an imprint of the Taylor & Francis Group, an informa business

© 2021 Petros Iosifidis and Nicholas Nicoli

British Library Cataloguing-in-Publication Data
A catalogue record for this book is available from the British Library

Library of Congress Cataloging-in-Publication Data
A catalog record has been requested for this book

ISBN: 978-0-367-33208-2 (hbk)
ISBN: 978-0-367-33210-5 (pbk)
ISBN: 978-0-429-31848-1 (ebk)

Typeset in Bembo
by Deanta Global Publishing Services, Chennai, India

Our deepest thanks as ever to our families for their love, support and patience, without which this book would not have been written.

CONTENTS

TABLE

ABOUT THE AUTHORS

Petros Iosifidis is professor in Sociology and Media Policy at City, University of London, UK. He has acknowledged expertise in the realms of communications policy, public service media, regulation of social media, and media coverage of sport. He is author of eight books, including *Reinventing Public Service Communication* (2010), *Public Television in the Digital Era* (2012), *Global Media and Communication Policy* (2013), *Public Sphere and Mediated Social Networks* (2016, with M. Wheeler), and *Global Media & National Policies* (2016, with T. Flew and J. Steemers). He has contributed numerous book chapters and has published extensively in peer-review journals. He has served as an ESRC Peer Review College reviewer, as principal editor of the *Journal of Digital Media & Policy* and co-editor of the *Palgrave Global Media Policy and Business*. He is vice-chair of *IAMCR Global Media Policy* group and has acted as national expert on European projects.

Nicholas Nicoli is associate professor of Communication at the University of Nicosia, Cyprus. His research focuses on communications policy and creative industry institutions. His initial research sought to deconstruct creativity management policies within public service broadcasters such as the BBC. Thereafter he focused his attention on the impact of communications policy upon strategic communication. His current research explores the intersection of communications policy, digital disinformation and the public interest. He has contributed book chapters and has published extensively in peer-review journals. He is a co-founder of the Institute for Mass Media, Cyprus and is on the editorial boards of Journal of Digital Media & Policy and Journal of Media Business Studies and has acted as a national expert and science communications manager on European projects.

GUEST FOREWORD

Since the late 1990s in the West, supporters of liberal democracy have been experiencing an evolution of sorts – on one level historical and, on the other, emotional. Those of us of sufficient age can recall our initial enthusiasm for the internet as a utility promising new potential for democracy. And certainly we saw some of this potential fulfilled, not least with the new ways of doing citizenship with the aid of online tools – building civic interconnectivity, promoting civic identities, coordinating political action. We cheered. Then we began to notice considerable uncivil activity on the net: many individuals refused to listen to others; they engaged in insults and other forms of communicative nastiness in discussion forums and other online settings of interaction. We found these un-Habermasian modes of communication troublesome.

With the emergence of Web 2.0 and social media came further encouraging possibilities for democratic communication. Yet our jubilation was tempered by the realisation that social and political groups were now systematically using the new media ecosystem in highly unethical ways, including gross lies, harassment, and even dire threats. We gritted our teeth as we were forced to acknowledge that the online environment could also be truly baleful. Mainstream journalism, meanwhile, was going through deep crises, trying to find its way in the new media ecosystem. It had not only gone online but was also now in various ways merging with social media – with ambivalent consequences.

With the emergence of strong right-wing populist movements and parties and their at times vicious use of social media, it became clear that democracy and the media landscape had both entered a new historical era. While there was no full innocence anywhere on the political spectrum, it has been the online onslaught on democratic values and tradition from the right wing that has most profoundly altered the political environment – not least with its embrace of 'post-truth' – and set in motion a destabilisation process against democracy. This has been adeptly furthered by actors from abroad, not least Russia. For many of us, our affect veered towards rage – where it seems to remain at present.

Parallel with these developments we have gradually been learning about the collection of private online activity data – and how this was being sold and used to shape the content offered to us. The algorithmic activities of Big Tech, making use of the big data they gather, open up not only a new chapter in media development but also usher in a new set of power relations that has major implications for the dynamics of democracy. That government agencies are also involved in extensive online surveillance of citizens that further underscores democracy's vulnerability.

After a few sensational scandals, it has become apparent that our private data were being used not just to shape our consumption habits but also to steer our political behaviour. Political messages are increasingly angled at us as groups and individuals, not as the general public. Public sphere(s) is not only being personalised and fragmented but also subjected to avatars, trolls, and robotised messages. And we have come to understand how various actors – local, national, foreign – can provide systematic and convincing material that is deceptive, misleading, and untrue – and how difficult it is to detect such disinformation.

The internet and social media have not lost their usefulness for civic purposes, but their democratic utility has been greatly conditioned and delimited by new power logics and dynamics. Just as with the often-unaccountable power within the corporate and banking sector, so too does power within the realm of the net and social media raise threatening problems for democracy. How democracy gets done (and undone) has been irrevocably altered by the new media landscape. Disinformation lies at the heart of the dilemma.

This landmark volume addresses this dilemma in very productive ways. The authors, Petros Iosifidis and Nicholas Nicoli, lead the reader through an illuminating analytic unfolding of not only what is going on in regard to social media and disinformation and why but also what might be done about it. There has in recent years emerged a discourse justifiably criticising the rampant disinformation of the new media environment. Yet, for the most part, this does not help us get beyond the expression of lament. In this book, the authors lucidly situate the problematic developments of disinformation in the context of democracy, citizenship, and functioning public spheres, offering clear conceptual points of departure that indicate how we as media users can better deal with such digital deception.

Disinformation is often portrayed in a common-sense way, which leaves it as an ominous, ever-present menace, one that may strike at any time. We must ever be alert, ever defensive, using critical scepticism as best as we can. This rendering, while true per se, remains ultimately nebulous and does not go far in equipping us in an efficacious manner. This volume instead provides us with an indispensable set of analytic tools for unpacking, classifying, and scrutinising the various dimensions of 'disinformation' – attributing very specific contours to the various manifestations of this phenomenon. It becomes a politically significant intervention that helps us better deal with the various forms of deception.

Yet Iosifidis and Nicoli go still further. They specify the many actors who, in various ways, can impact the character of social media. In particular, they review what major policy initiatives have achieved thus far – and also noting where they fall short. Recognising that voluntary or self-regulation is insufficient, the authors take us to a vista from where we can begin to see new policy potentials and new possible initiatives from an array of actors who shape social media. They are addressing a range of stakeholders in their presentation, not least us citizens, equipping them all to critically reflect from their respective horizons on the present state of digital disinformation and inviting them to collectively imagine new futures – for social media, for democracy.

With an array of actors involved, and given the hybrid character of social media platforms, the book takes a multi-perspective approach, underscoring that citizens, governments at various levels, regulatory bodies, researchers, think tanks, tech companies, telecoms operators, and journalist organisations all have roles to play in the struggle to reduce digital disinformation and thereby to protect and extend democracy. Iosifidis and Nicoli thus provide a launch pad for a much-needed debate aimed at a broad range of discussants. Media environments change; new technologies yield new possibilities – for use and misuse. Regulatory efforts must be updated if they are to be relevant and effective.

This is no easy task, and the authors are wise not to offer any glib remedies. Instead, they underscore that these issues have to be thrashed out – not least with an understanding of the massive and often competing interests that are at stake. Their focus is the West, but they acknowledge there is considerable diversity involved; despite the limited progress that the EU has made in this regard, national and local level regulation must be taken into consideration. As a further sober warning of what can happen if disinformation is not bought under control, the volume offers case studies of what Russia has been doing at home and abroad and how the fledgling democracy of Ukraine continues to reel under the impact of systematic deception in the media.

We grapple with disinformation in our everyday lives – while we seek to reduce the systemic level. For stakeholders generally, and for us citizens, in particular, this splendid contribution, through its clear conceptualisations, concrete empirical evidence, and insightful analytic trajectories, is ultimately an empowering text. It can help us move on to our next historical – and emotional – phase, one that is hopefully democratically enhanced. Let's put it to use!

Peter Dahlgren
Lund University

PREFACE

On July 7, 2020, the 170-year-old print medium *Harper's Magazine* published an open letter titled 'A Letter on Justice and Open Debate' (Harper's Magazine, 2020). It was signed by over 150 notable intellectuals from around the world, including, among others, Margaret Atwood, Noam Chomsky, Francis Fukuyama, Todd Gitlin, Khaled Khalifa, Steven Lukes, Steven Pinker, J.K. Rowling, Salman Rushdie and Gloria Steinem.

The letter states,

> *The forces of illiberalism are gaining strength throughout the world ... the free exchange of information and ideas, the lifeblood of a liberal society is daily becoming more constricted ... censoriousness is also spreading more widely in our culture: an intolerance of opposing views, a vogue for public shaming and ostracism, and the tendency to dissolve complex policy issues in a blinding moral certainty ... editors are fired for running controversial pieces; books are withdrawn for alleged inauthenticity; journalists are barred from writing on certain topics; professors are investigated for quoting works of literature in class; a researcher is fired for circulating a peer-reviewed academic study; and the heads of organizations are ousted for what are sometimes just clumsy mistakes.*

Rather than creating a spirit of unity, the letter caused an online outcry from liberals (for including transphobic signatories) and conservatives (who disagreed with the context), instigating a counter letter signed by over 160 *other* academics, journalists and cultural critics. The response embodies the internet's current belligerent state. Despite its inherent ability to construct a genuine public sphere, it has rather amplified individual and group convictions. So intense have these camps become that in order to preserve these convictions, an ethos of deceit and lies has transpired across the digital ecosystem, undermining much of the technology's affordances. Existing online threats have brought to the fore core principles of freedom of expression, citizen protection and cybersecurity. And it does not end there. Current internet structures have prompted agents – mainly from authoritarian regimes – to destabilise liberal democracies by means of computational propaganda and digital disinformation, further exacerbating the situation. As a result, trust is decaying across contemporary democratic societies, and previously intact portrayals of truth are becoming increasingly disputed.

The fickle nature of liberal democracies is incentivising authoritarian regimes around the world. Long-reigning autocratic leaders are taking actions on issues that in the West would be considered unthinkable. Ergogan's Turkey has converted Hagia Sophia into a mosque, causing internal rifts and a global outcry. Putin's Russia has recently announced a change in the country's law allowing him to remain in power until 2036, and Xi Jinping's China has just passed a draconian security decree against protestors, tightening its grip on Hong Kong.

The current state of affairs from around the world begs the question:

Can the internet's potential for creating a digital democracy truly be realised, or is it facilitating global societal rifts?

In order to meet the internet's potential for the setting up of an electronic agora, we may require a re-evaluation of its current setup. Social media in particular, such promising catalysts of digital democracy, need to be thought through again, as self-regulating models are failing, therefore inciting a complete platform regulation overhaul.

Digital Democracy, Social Media and Disinformation is an attempt to contribute to these issues.

Petros Iosifidis and Nicholas Nicoli,
July 2020

ACKNOWLEDGEMENTS

We would like to express our gratitude to the anonymous reviewers of the book proposal for their welcomed comments and suggestions at the beginning of this effort. We are indebted to Peter Dahlgren for providing the Guest foreword and to Leighton Andrews, Terry Flew and Robert Picard for writing the blurbs on the back cover. Many thanks are due to our research assistants Maria Larkin and Victoria Vitoslavskaya for their balanced and invaluable contributions in the two case studies. Mihaela Diana Ciobotea, editorial assistant at Sociology, Routledge has provided helpful advice throughout this project and we are grateful for her enthusiasm and support. The responsibility for any remaining errors, omissions and confusions is of course entirely ours. Every effort has been made to trace all copyright holders, but if any have been inadvertently overlooked, the publisher will be pleased to make the necessary arrangements at the first opportunity.

1

INTRODUCTION

Introduction

We must not underestimate the disintermediating, educational, emancipatory, entertainment and informative potential of digital technologies. However, we are beginning to realise the costs of reaching this potential as more people are connecting to these technologies. In order to comprehend these costs, Marshall McLuhan's *Understanding Media: The Extension of Man* (1964) and Walter J. Ong's *Orality and Literacy: The Technologizing of the World* (Ong, 1982) are useful points of reference. Applying historical and philosophical examinations, the two authors ascertain the impact of a medium upon culture and society. By the same token, Nicholas Carr's 2010 work *The Shallows: How the Internet is Changing the Way We Think, Read and Remember* (Carr, 2010) reasserts McLuhan's and Ong's theses vis-à-vis the digital realm. More recently, analysing the inner workings of the brain, evolutionary biologists, neuroscientists and psychologists have come to comparable conclusions on the impact of digital technologies (Landon-Murray and Anderson, 2013; Risko and Gilbert, 2016; Alter, 2017; Wolf, 2018).

The medium *is* the message, and with the possible exception of Gutenberg's printing press in the 1450s, the internet has instigated the most cultural and societal embodiment of mediation (van Loon, 2008). Examples of this include how, compared to non-digital societies, citizens of digitised societies are more likely to trigger their visual cortices, while merely skim through long-form essays (Carr, 2010). It is neither that the internet negates the written word nor that it does not value it, but as a consequence of the extensive time users spend online accessing visual content, they gradually find it harder to concentrate and think deeply about issues, preferring rather to engage with the mundane (ibid.). Nonetheless, the issue that networked citizens are more prone to engage with visually aesthetic content fails to provide a complete picture of the internet's accumulated impact.

With the advent of smartphones and social media platforms, online technologies are changing how and what we consume, how we feel, how we think, how we remember, how we see and, now, if, who and what to believe (O'Connor and Weatherall, 2018). Ultimately, the gradual rewiring of our brains has made our online and offline behaviours unpredictable at best, irrational at worst.

On a consumer level, lifestyle categories and self-objectifications of young adults looking to achieve more 'followers' and 'likes' raises serious concerns regarding the direction of digital media. As worrying as this is, internet intermediaries have focused on other issues rather than self-reform. In fact, their objectives are directly antithetical to these concerns since their overall purpose is to transform our brains' neuroplasticity and keep us 'hooked' in order to spend more hours within and across their ever-expanding platforms (Wu, 2016). In doing so, they can increase advertising expenditure while drawing users in, creating, as they do, highly impactful network effects. This mitigates shareholder pressure and keeps profits rising. As a result, most current online ecosystems are endemic to commodity fetishisms. Paradoxically, these were the same concerns of the early workings of the Frankfurt School, concerns that led to critically evaluating legacy media consumptions within capitalist systems. Marcuse's views of technology as a manifestation of a 'bourgeois ideology' (1968: 223) is pertinent, even today, in thinking critically about our consumptions of digital cultural texts. The same is true of the 'standardisation' witnessed across these platforms (Adorno and Leppert, 2002). Similarly, critical discussions on the cultural *production* of digital media remain imperative. For example, Fuchs' (2018) efforts in revisiting the critical cultural production theories of advertising in a digitalised environment is a welcome contribution. So too is Edwards (2018) on the political economy of public relations in the digital age and Nicoli (2012; Nicoli, 2013) on the erosion of public service television production values within a globalised digital context.

As relevant as consumer-level critical analysis is, it is on a citizenship level that our warnings need to be heeded. Encapsulating the logic of this volume is that, rather than attempting to stop a vessel's leaks, we should first be steering clear of the iceberg staring directly at us. Consequently, the caveats made in this volume render critical analyses of the system of production and consumption of culture a subordinated concern. The focus of this volume is toward a crisis in democracy rather than of the capitalist system, although the two, no doubt, interrelate on numerous levels. In fact, the association between capitalism and the liberal democratic order has vastly contributed to the neoliberal turn responsible for much of what is wrong today in our democracies (Srnicek and Williams, 2016). Nonetheless, it is the Frankfurt School's latter works that have been this volume's central conceptual framework. Described in detail in Chapter Two, Jürgen Habermas' normative model of democracy created a point of reference for how we should strive for liberal democracy. It gave us an understanding of the duties of civil society, the impact of universal systems of representation and the value of communicative action. Rather than moving in this direction, we have conversely seen the rise of other systems of government, most notably those of populist, autocratic-leaning regimes. As a result, scholarly focus has turned toward explorations concerning the expansion of populism (for example, Ingelhart and Norris, 2016; Eatwell and Goodwin, 2018) and examinations regarding the role of digital democracy and disinformation in its growth (Flew and Iosifidis, 2020; Iosifidis and Andrews, 2020).

Digital disinformation has indeed been a critical factor in democracy's decline, and we must again remind ourselves of the work of McLuhan and Ong concerning the repercussions a new medium can have upon societies, particularly one that had such high emancipatory potential. Lewandowsky, Ecker and Cook (2017) identify several reasons behind the growth of digital disinformation, including a decline in the social capital of citizens, the political and social polarisation of contemporary everyday life, rises in inequality, distrust in media and an overall cynicism toward government. All have played out over digital media and are therefore addressed in this volume. Rather than mediated citizens using the internet's vast potential to share thoughts across virtual spaces and open up to diverse viewpoints, they choose to selectively expose the aforementioned issues that matter to them individually rather than to society as a whole. In other words, in the current structure of digital media (for example, the way in which social media algorithms are applied), online-mediated citizens use these tools to confirm their own biases. In doing so, they create online 'camps' that amplify distrust and widen polarisation. As users generate content, they become more disposed to make up or use fake content to persuade others and make their own points more persuasive. Such a vicious cycle and ominous consequence will be familiar to social scientists studying group dynamics. In the 1970s, psychologist David G. Myers demonstrated that when situating two polarised groups together to discuss issues, they gradually become more hostile and polarised toward each other (Myers, 1975). The application of this phenomenon on a scale of billions is in fact how we have found ourselves steering toward the iceberg.

The new global order and the role of internet intermediaries

The trajectory of liberal democracy

Human progress over the past 300 years has been impressive (Pinker, 2018). Enlightenment ideals of reason have spread across the globe, creating more electoral democracies in more advanced, educated, healthy and, ultimately, happier societies. As Barack Obama famously pointed out (2016), 'if you had to choose a moment in history to be born … you'd choose now'. Within numerous liberal democracies created over this space of time, the growth in equal rights across the spectrum of race, religion, gender and sexual orientation has truly been remarkable. Despite these achievements, liberalism as we know it today, one of tolerance and universality, has had to fight off the assault of several regimes. As the liberal order spread in the twentieth century, it found itself having to fend off Communism, Nazism and, later on, Islamic fundamentalism. Nonetheless, its perseverance led to its most fundamental moment – the fall of the Berlin Wall and the dismantlement of the USSR. Liberal democracy has since spread across the globe at an extremely fast rate, offering hope of what a fair and tolerant world could look like. Freedom House noted (2019: 1),

> Between 1988 and 2005, the percentage of countries ranked Not Free in Freedom in the World dropped by almost 14 points (from 37 to 23 percent), while the share of Free countries grew (from 36 to 46 percent).

The 2008 global financial crisis and the rising inequality it has resulted in have allowed today's authoritarian, dogmatic regimes to rear their ugly heads and has brought democracies a step closer to resembling them. This is because as liberal democracies have become contaminated by neoliberal versions of itself, tolerance and universalism have ironically exposed their weaknesses. 'If liberalism is tolerant of divergences of opinion', asks Turner (2003: 6), 'how does it deal with opinions that abhor tolerance? To what extent can liberal regimes tolerate enemies from within, such as parties that reject the liberal rules of the game, the conventions of discussion that make persuasion possible?' Such a critical dilemma becomes a catalytically component of why polarisation and populism have grown, since the question asked by Turner is in fact embedded within the core of the liberal order. Neoliberal proceedings have exacerbated the conditions of the poorer classes and squeezed those in the middle.

As a result, social and political life is in a state of flux. Nations are turning inward to protect themselves from what they see as highly uncertain times. As populism continues to grow, it has given an opportunity to sovereign, inward-thinking leaders to strike a chord with many voters who feel let down by both the left and the right. Donald Trump's rise to political power in the US and the UK's Brexit vote took many by surprise. Yet for a few others (for example Fukuyama, 2018), the two events, and others like it, have been consequences rather than determinants of liberalism's breakdown, arguing that its demise has been grounded in the growth of identity politics that have shifted alliances away from bipartisan associations to socio-economic tribal ones (ibid.). This trajectory, warns Gessen (2020), is the first step towards autocracy.

Authoritarian regimes

The decline in liberal democracies in the West has prompted existing global authoritarian regimes to expand; the aforementioned Freedom House report notes (2019: 1) that,

> Between 2005 and 2018, the share of Not Free countries rose to 26 percent, while the share of Free countries declined to 44 percent.

The growth of these regimes has coincided with numerous jailing and killing of opposition leaders and journalists. The alleged murder of Saudi Arabian journalist Jamal Khashoggi in the Saudi consulate in Turkey is a case in point and was vastly covered in international news outlets as he wrote for *The Washington Post* and was a long-time critic of Saudi Arabia's prince, Mohammad bin Salman (Woolley, 2020: 9). Reports of journalist imprisonments in China, Iran, Russia, Syria, Turkey and Ukraine during this fickle period have no doubt contributed to the backsliding of global democracy. The control over media freedoms in authoritarian regimes has ominously resulted in the dispensing of the rules concerning government leadership terms. As a consequence, authoritarian rulers can remain in power for longer terms. It has been one of the main reasons as to why such leaders have managed to consolidate their power. Vladimir Putin, the president of the Russian Federation analysed in detail in Chapter Six, has secured his political leadership status until 2036 if he so wishes by holding a controversial referendum in 2020 that saw little media criticism and even less resistance from opposing leaders (Bodner, 2020). The same can be said for Xi Jinping in China, whose term limits of the presidency was abolished in 2018.

Internet intermediaries

At the centre of the shifting global order are the internet intermediaries. They become the subject of our analysis in Chapter Three. As political and social polarisation have widened across liberal democracies, discussions online happening on the platforms owned by internet intermediaries have become more hostile and partisan. In turn, this has further led to increased emotional narratives often disregarding reputable media outlets and the scientific community despite its painstaking methods of reaching consensus, a consensus borne from systematic debate, discussion, experimentation and peer-reviewed filtering. For many, experts have become the vilified elite (Turner, 2003; D'Ancona, 2017). Because of the ruptures across online ecosystems, different groups have sought to exploit the situation by identifying opportunities to trick gullible users who are more than eager to confirm their biases by consuming and sharing online content. They consist of disinformation agents and trolls working to either destabilise democracies or generate profits. We return to analyse disinformation agents in Chapter Five.

At the same time, we have seen a rise in computational communication professionals who data-mine the harvested social media data of users to then target them through ambiguous approaches. According to various studies and reports (notably the UK's *Department for Digital, Culture, Media & Sports report on Disinformation and Fake News* (DCMSC, 2019)), *Facebook* began harvesting personal information from its users unbeknownst to them – particularly after the company became a publicly traded entity. The harvested data could be used by application developers on *Facebook* (for a price), which in turn allowed companies such as *Cambridge Analytica/SCL* and their clients to send customised advertising messages based on profiling (Rosenberg et al., 2018). As described in the UK's

DCMSC report (2019: 41), Ashkan Soltani, former chief technologist to the US Federal Trade Commission, noted,

> it is either free – there is an exchange of information that is non-monetary – or it is an exchange of personal information that is given to the platform, mined, and then resold to or reused by third-party developers to develop apps, or resold to advertisers.

Computational communication professionals took advantage of tribal divisions spread across social media platforms by micro-targeting them and catering content that fit their belief systems. The effects have been devastatingly powerful. *Cambridge Analytica/SCL* analysed data (in breach of numerous terms of service that included those of *Facebook*), to accumulate and categorise between 50 and 80 million unsuspicious online users through psychographic profiling. Once grouped, the company was able to send specific political advertising messages customised to the desire of each user. If voters supported the US Second Amendment (the right to bear and hold arms), the advertising message could be tailored to them. Or, if a user continuously expressed their hostile views over migration on *Facebook*, they might then be profiled in a certain category and consequently shown advertisements by political parties on the threats of migrants stealing jobs or initiating crimes. Such questionable tactics helped the campaigns of Ted Cruz, the Republican Senator who defied the odds to end up the Republican Party runner up who faced Donald Trump in 2016. These same tactics also helped Donald Trump, who acquired the services of *Cambridge Analytica/SCL* during the presidential elections of 2016, as did the UK's Brexit campaigners. All three examples left many startled by their electoral success (see Rathi, 2018).

Across authoritarian regimes, social media platforms have been used somewhat differently. They have particularly come to the fore during attempted uprisings from around the world. The 2011 Arab Spring is remembered as a Twitter revolution, one that has led to genuine political change (Rosen, 2011; Wael Ghonim, 2012). So too the revolutions of 2004 and 2014 in Ukraine described in Chapter Seven of this volume. More recently, Russia in 2019 and China in 2019 and 2020 have sought to crack down on freedoms of expression and protests initiated or using social media. Yet while these regimes have censored and controlled social media platforms within their own borders, such as the examples analysed in Chapter Six on Russia, they have simultaneously used them to interfere in liberal democracies, attempting to destabilise the liberal order by identifying weaknesses and subtly manipulating narratives. When two-thirds of online users receive their information over social media platforms, it makes sense for foreign interference agents to use them to encourage conflict over heated topics (Summers, 2018). Therefore, the platforms have been used by foreign disinformation agents to organise activist campaigns, to portray legitimate news media outlets, to stage flash mobs and to stir racial tensions. Working alongside already existing tensions in liberal democracies, the fallouts from the above issues have led to an era of confusion, doubt, disorder and mistrust. The rise of mistrust is of growing concern in the business, political and social spheres. The 2019 World Economic Forum in Davos, Switzerland, identified 'trust deficit' as a barrier to economic growth, digital innovation and social cohesion. Trust, argues McDermott (2019), is 'the ultimate human currency'.

The response by the West has been to defend itself through numerous measures we unpack in Chapter Four. These include detection mechanisms such as fact-checking and news literacy to empower people to think critically about the content they consume. Response mechanisms also involve strategic communication efforts and technological advancements consisting of machine learning and blockchains. While the responses of the West have been promising, one wonders how deviant agents will counter. If, for example, innovations are applied to identify the linguistic cues of computational propaganda used by foreign agents (content created by artificial intelligence [AI]), they might respond with more advanced and untraceable AI. Such an outcome will ultimately lead to a social and technological arms race, fighting fire with fire and hence creating a zero-sum game. Possibly more dangerous, it can be asked how human-generated threats, such as those created by thousands of Chinese or Russian disinformation agents, are countered (King, Pan and Roberts, 2017).

Truth and lies in the digital age

In the 1996 James Halperin science-fiction novel *The Truth Machine* (Halperin, 1996), Randall Peterson, the genius protagonist of the book, invents a device that changes the world forever – this machine is an infallible lie detector that creates a world without lies. As the truth machine becomes more widespread, all facets of life gradually transform. Initially, divorce rates go up as couples are exposed to each other's adulteries and lies, tensions across nations surge and courtrooms are filled with cases of previously undetected deceit. But as people adapt to telling the truth, things begin to change for the better. There is a steady fall in break-ups, wars become extinct and judicial systems – courtrooms, lawyers and judges – are made redundant. While fictional, Halperin offers an insightful account of a world without lies. *The Truth Machine*, alas, is not real. Since the beginning of humanity, people have lied to each other, and will continue to do so, since to lie is very much a natural component of communication processes (Ricoeur, 2007). But as Sissela Bok's seminal work on the ethical considerations of truth and lies suggests, most people will tell the truth most of the time, and it is within this 'principle of veracity' that people feel they benefit from each other and therefore continue telling the truth (Bok, 1978). Yet as we have illustrated, the current digital landscape has created a world shrouded in contradiction, dispute and lies. Ominous rifts are now more apparent and dangerous because they are so easily amplified, manipulated and, worryingly, spread across the internet to millions of online users in a matter of moments. At the heart of this schism lies a networked ecosystem swaying opinions one way or another.

We have described how the priority of today's social media platforms is to keep users engaged for longer periods of time so as to be sold as commodities to advertisers. As a consequence, social media algorithms feed users with a personalised experience. Unless so marked, they do not distinguish good content from bad. Herein lies a deep concern in controlling digital disinformation, since the internet intermediaries are not willing to take responsibility for deciding what is true and what is not and are therefore reluctant to take action on censoring content. For example, by means of the company's formal announcements via its press room and through various senior employees, *Facebook* has pronounced its unwillingness to be seen as an *arbiter of truth* (Iosifidis and Nicoli, 2020). Clearly, the technology giant would rather avoid the responsibility of being identified as a content creator. In doing so, two overlapping assumptions can be underlined. First, *Facebook* is distancing itself from the rigorous censorship and regulatory measures associated with news media. Throughout its existence, the company has justified its proclamation to be seen as a technology platform on account of a US legislation implemented in 1996 known as Section 230 of the Communications Decency Act. Specifically, the legislation states: 'No provider or user of an interactive computer service shall be treated as the publisher or speaker of any information provided by another information content provider'. The law has effectively become a shield for *Facebook*, and other large internet intermediaries, by giving them immunity when it comes to political discourse on their platforms (Timmer, 2017). Second, social media are further asserting, in their reluctance to become embroiled in what is truthful and what is not, strong supporters of the *marketplace of ideas*. This concept has its origins in John Stuart Mill's On Liberty 'a philosophical essay originally published in 1859'. Mill used the metaphor of a market to discuss the spread of intellectual life, but the metaphor is used today mainly in the US as a strong complementary element to the First Amendment. It implies that there is no such thing as too much information, further supporting the notion that citizens are more than capable of distinguishing good information from bad (Napoli, 2019: 84). For *Facebook*, it rests on the notion of *buyer beware* – that its platforms can be used by whoever has a profile to disseminate ideas, and that networked citizens are more than capable of spotting deceitful information when they see it. We can conclude therefore that unlike non-technological communication, where telling the truth is at an advantage due to a 'principle of veracity', over the internet, truth and lies exist on a level playing field. For this reason, a growing group of internet activists are advocating the use of public interest algorithms as well as other open source technologies that are more capable of protecting citizens. These will allow for more control for users and greater transparency as to how data is used. These concerns and the policy mechanisms that revolve around them are the subjects of Chapter Three and Chapter Five, respectively.

Zuboff (2019) has labelled contemporary society 'surveillance capitalism' on account of the panoptic mechanisms of large technology companies. Taken as a whole, our everyday online behaviours are harvested, data mined and analysed by big data approaches in order to predict behaviours and trends. We are being watched without being able to see back. In that there is power that allows the technology companies to continue to grow. In highlighting her thesis, Zuboff reminds us of the free nature of online ecosystems. In order that online technology companies are endorsed to create such powerful systems of control, they must remain free. Free access of the internet over its burgeoning information platforms has allowed it to become a technological tool we often forget is there. As a result, we become inclined to let our guard down, forgetting the possible repercussions.

The illusion of free access and tacit technology use has, on the one hand, empowered citizens to actively take part in online public spheres, but on the other, it has devalued our online engagement. It is as though we are casually chatting in the street with an acquaintance or arguing with someone who cuts us off at an intersection. But in fact, online networks amplify issues and have therefore coincided with the erosion of news media (Picard and Pickard, 2017) as well as with the demise of liberal democracies throughout the world (Beaufort, 2018). Reflecting the negative turn in both democratic and information processes, Morozov coined the term 'net delusion' (2012) regarding earlier views technology optimists had of the internet's ability to liberate societies. As the internet has grown, its communication processes have become multifaceted. In describing these complexities, Marshall (2017: 17), echoing Morozov, suggests, 'it is in flux, like every other complex system, composed of other complex systems, which may not mesh well'. Disinformation, Marshall goes on, is endemic to information society and therefore contemporary society emerges into a 'disinformation society'.

In order to protect liberal democracy, it is becoming evident that some of its most cherished principles will need to be placed under examination. For some (for example, Napoli, 2018), the solution might be to tighten our freedom-of-expression policies since they are at the centre of the policy challenges facing regulators of digital disinformation. A functioning balance between governing the internet and safeguarding freedom of expression is not currently in place, Napoli argues. Others support the breakup of internet intermediaries as they have built powerful monopoly positions, therefore making it harder for new entrants to become established entities (Wu, 2018). In doing so, they can manipulate or lobby policies against them and consolidate their positions even further. Still others look at our current democratic crisis as a moral panic and therefore as an opportunity for news media to regain legitimacy and establish an equilibrium that can be used as a check on democracy that will once again strengthen it (Carlson, 2018). In the seven chapters that follow, we attempt to strike these issues at the root and conceptualise both the theoretical frameworks and policy initiatives in fighting digital disinformation.

Structure of the book

The book is divided into three sections. Section I consists of two chapters that review market trends, internet intermediaries and theories pertaining to digital democracy. Chapter Two specifically focuses on the public sphere and the growth of networked citizens expanding over social media. Chapter Three shifts its attention to populism within a digital democratic framework and introduces the concepts of post-truth, regulatory action and self-regulation.

Section II consists of two chapters and addresses the current state of the art of digital disinformation. Chapter Four analyses contemporary thoughts on digital disinformation. It breaks down the motives behind disinformation agents and examines what approaches are being used to combat the deviant behaviour. Chapter Five describes current policy measures on countering disinformation in the European Union, considered by many as the world's watchdog in digital technologies.

Section III sets the stage for deeper investigation by analysing two country cases, the Russian Federation and Ukraine. In each case, we explore the emergence, scale and scope of digital disinformation. Chapter Six deconstructs the Russian Federation's role in digital disinformation. In order to do so, it analyses its internal policy measures before turning attention to its interference strategies across the Western world. Chapter Seven examines Ukraine's facilitation of digital disinformation. Many consider the country the capital of computational propaganda and digital disinformation (Woolley, 2020). As such, the Ukrainian case concentrates on the Orange Revolution of 2004 and Euromaidan in 2014 to comprehend the state of the country and its associations with digital disinformation.

Finally, Chapter Eight brings together our insights from the previous seven chapters and offers our concluding thoughts. It asks readers to analyse regions separately but draw conclusions of digital disinformation holistically and globally. It further offers future directions for digital disinformation studies, freedom of expression and platform governance.

SECTION I

Market trends, internet intermediaries and theories

2

DEMOCRACY, PUBLIC SPHERE AND CITIZENSHIP IN A NETWORK SOCIETY

Introduction

This chapter covers lots of theoretical ground and provides working definitions of the terms *digital democracy*, *mediated citizenship*, *network society* and *online
public sphere* and takes a critical stance as to whether these have shifted social
dynamics. In the academic writing about democracy, especially in regard to the
media, a collective ambivalence emerges, with some writers expressing more
optimism and other commentators taking a dimmer view. The questions about
democracy become still more complex not least as modes of citizenship evolve;
the gradual shift to what is often dubbed 'mediated citizenship' raises various
issues, alongside with positive and negative forecasts (Iosifidis and Wheeler,
2016; Wahl-Jorgensen, 2008). This chapter explores the literature and academic
debates concerning the socio-politics of social media, with particular emphasis
on the political, social and democratic value of Web 2.0 technologies. These
technologies include websites and applications that allow anyone to create and
share online information, thereby engaging previously unconnected people and
enabling them to exchange opinions of relevance to the wider public.

In this context, the exercise and devolution of power is also analysed in regard
to the vertical communication between citizens and government. Academic
works on power especially in relation to media have been offered, among others, by Zukin (1991), who, three decades ago, contended that Disney World is
a landscape of power; and Corner (1997), who eloquently examined the power
within the television process. Today, the same can be said of a concentration of
symbolic power across online and social media landscapes. The term *social media*
refers to the sites and services that emerged during the early 2000s, including
social network sites, video sharing sites, blogging and microblogging platforms
and related tools that allow participants to create and share their own content

(Boyd, 2014: 6). The advancement of communication technologies and the rise of social media have created a space where social movements can accrue power. Bourdieu's concepts of habitus, capital and field point out the conditions under which this power can develop (Bourdieu, 1977). Indeed, social media networks have become part of people's habitus as a consequence of the socialisation and expansion of the space as well as the redirection of socio-cultural identity into the space.

But while the internet and social media platforms may have created a new space where power can be harnessed to increase citizens' social status and ideology, sceptics argue that the role of social media in the public sphere, democracy and civic engagement is not necessarily positive. For the so-called 'internet celebrants', the use of social media platforms has provided a means to spread democratic ideals, organise protests and demonstrations against authoritarian regimes and participate more directly in democratic polls and processes. But social media's positive effect on democracy is challenged by pessimists who contend that nowadays, the internet and social media networks have spread huge amounts of non-reliable information sources, 'fake news', misinformation and disinformation. Some scholars go even further to argue that tech giants such as *Facebook* and *Twitter* profit from users by selling their data to advertising companies (Fuchs, 2014). Coleman and Blumler (2009) claim that democracy fails to engender relationships of accountability and advocate an 'online media commons' as a policy direction to enhance the democratic character of cyberspace's role in the public sphere. Therefore, it is essential to design a suitable policy framework in order to enable democracy to flourish by building the skills and capacity necessary for both social media networks and citizens to form accountable communities of participation. In other words, policy makers are tasked to address the key question of how the use of technology in rulemaking can promote more collaborative and sustained forms of participation.

The public sphere

Public spheres, whether local, regional, national or issue-specific, are social constructions in the true sense of the word. This means that a community of communication can be constructed, deconstructed and reconstructed through interaction (Risse, 2010: 110). The term *public sphere* has been a nebulous and contested concept. It was first introduced in 1962 by German philosopher Habermas and defined 'as the realm of social and political life' (1974) which rests between the government and the society. The public sphere theory requires good communication between equal participants (informed, knowledgeable and sensible people) but also free guaranteed access for everyone to this procedure of political and social participation (Calhoun, 1966). Citizens must be active and must engage with the political and social situation (Dahlgren, 1991) and look for the public good instead of their private benefit. This concept of the public sphere was based on the roots of bourgeois society and the feudal pyramid and supported the principle that citizen participation in the public sphere is guaranteed and open to everyone. In Habermas' theory, the concept of 'consent' plays an integral role; according to his theory about the public sphere, the public discussion and resolution of public issues rests upon the agreement of citizens and members of the government to co-operate for the public good, resulting in a participatory democracy.

Habermas' public sphere ideally referred to a space in which democratic expression was allowed. For the German philosopher, the concept of the public sphere serves both as a historical tale and a normative ideal of public participation in politics in an informed and rational manner. Through this space for rational and universalist politics, one that is distinct from both the state and the economy, people were guaranteed the right to publicly express their opinions and interact with each other. It was a scene of activity in which people were addressed as citizens, as rational political beings, and not merely as consumers. Habermas conceived modern democracy as the only political ideology that could ensure interaction not only among people, but also between the state and the citizens. The space where such interactions would take place included face-to-face settings (for example, coffee houses, pubs, libraries and universities), but it also relied on print publications (for example, pamphlets, newsletters and newspapers), all of which facilitated a shared discussion among groups of people in society.

Thus the role of the media has been paramount in the spread of diverse opinions and the enhancement of the public sphere. During the nineteenth century in particular, the printed media provided a channel through which citizens could inform themselves about political matters, express their views and also communicate any concerns to the general public. The appearance of the first newspapers assumed an important role in the way the public sphere debated political and social matters. The launch of a number of newspapers provided the means through which private thoughts could become public. Habermas himself highlighted that the appearance of newspapers contributed to more freedom and the creation of public opinion, the very ingredients of the public sphere principle. Not only that; members of the newly formed bourgeois class organised themselves through discussion in public settings to criticise the government and hold it accountable for its actions.

Habermas describes an ideal – and some even say utopian – situation and has therefore received many critiques concerning his rational–critical public deliberation on matters of common concern that are often oriented towards consensus. At the risk of oversimplification, the criticisms have evolved around Habermas' account of history in relation to the press and the bourgeoisie, as well as relations of state and civil society; his political analysis, and specifically his ideal of civic participation in a type of direct democracy that contrasts sharply with the complexity of modern representative society; and his apparent neglect of exclusion from public discussions of non-mainstream groups based on gender, class and ethnicity (see, among others, Curran, 1991; Dahlgren, 2009). In particular, the apparent dismissal of the factor of power relations in society from Habermas' theory has led scholars such as Chantal Mouffe to characterise his approach as 'the dream of a fair society' (see Carpentier and Bart, 2006), basically contending that Habermas' neo-liberal model could not materialise since it dismisses societal power relations.

The German theorist himself, in a later work (Habermas, 1984), pronounced the decline of the public sphere. He pointed that during the twentieth century, the emergence of the public relations industry and the increased role of advertising and public relations, as well as the increased levels of concentration of media ownership and the appearance of press barons, exacerbated the processes of individualisation and commodification, leading to a loss of political consciousness, particularly class consciousness. As Habermas argued, large private organisations opted for political compromise with the state and with each other, excluding the public sphere, which gradually transformed under conditions of distorted communication and eventually disintegrated. The role of the media has been central to the replacement of the ideal speech situation – where all citizens have access to information and there is freedom of expression – to conditions of economic and political control. Whereas the development of the independent press at the beginning of the nineteenth century had opened up the possibility of rational public debate and public decision-making on political and judicial matters, it later came to function increasingly as a tool for managing and manipulating public opinion. Habermas mentioned that the rise of consumerist society led to political apathy, which distanced the public from politics, thus resulting in a weak public sphere. Since the public sphere ideally allows universal participation and democratic representation, the appearance of dominant corporate groups challenged these principles and, in essence, damaged the public sphere.

In sum, the notion of the public sphere celebrates a particular kind of publicness: one characterised by unfettered rational-critical public deliberation on matters of common concern, and oriented towards consensus, with the goal of holding policy-making authorities in the nation-state accountable for their actions (Wahl-Jorgensen, 2008). That public sphere was in principle open to all and was protected from the power of both the church and the state (Iosifidis and Wheeler, 2016). In the late eighteenth century, a new political class, the bourgeoisie, formed a public body which, in sharp contrast with the old authorities, notably the state and the church, provided the conditions for the development and dissemination of reason-based, public opinion. In his later work, Habermas acknowledged the sociological critiques relating to his original account of the public sphere and recognised the importance of inclusivity, the end of consensus government and the complexity of social systems and post-modern societies. Yet, he continued to support his normative approach that retains the public sphere as an ideal.

Despite its limitations, we believe that the concept of the public sphere is still relevant today as it provides a valuable set of theoretical resources with which to advance important issues relating to democratic society in the contemporary era. Further, Habermas' thinking offers a starting point for assessing the role of the media in a liberal, post-modern society, highlighting its influential position in shaping people's understanding of social and political issues, practices and identities. Not only that; as will be argued below, the debates surrounding the idea of the public sphere have taken on renewed interest with the emergence of the internet and social media networks, which can provide new communication spaces where public dialogue can be conducted. Concerning the question of media power, Castells (1996) analysed how digital media may affect power relations and lead to media's gradual dispersal and divergence in an ecology of interconnected consumer/producers ('prosumers'), or, as Miller and Slater (2000) put it, whether there might be even greater consolidation of power in the internet era.

Citizenship

By engaging critically with the idea of the public sphere, especially the notions of rational political dialogue and political engagement as well as citizen participation in policy-making, one should also refer to the contested concept of citizenship, that is, the position or status of being a citizen of a particular country or a community. The notion of citizenship can be found in the system of the ancient Greek city (*polis*), where rights were given and duties put upon citizens who were born in that polis and were treated as equals. Citizens had to be free (slaves were not citizens) and native-born males (females were excluded). In modern societies, the conceptualisation of citizenship was refined and became more inclusive. For Marshall (1950), citizenship status is bestowed upon those who are full members of a community and are equal in terms of the rights and responsibilities with which the status is endowed. Marshall's seminal work *Citizenship and Social Class* defined citizenship as incorporating civic rights (personal freedom) and political rights (the right to exercise political power as an elector), as well as social rights, that is, the right to live in a civilised society and enjoy security and economic welfare (Marshall, 1950: 10–11). According to Urry (1999: 318), citizenship entails symbolic resources distributed through various means of mass communication. Citizenship thus denotes the formation of civic, political and social rights and the forging of a societal consensus about the nature and extent of rights and obligations, as well as the balance between different often conflicting rights (Cammaerts, 2007).

There is certainly a place for reason and rationality in conceptions of citizenship, in the same way as there is a place for them in conceptions of the public sphere. In a liberal democracy, consensus can be reached in cases where a majority of individuals make the same or similar choices. While consensus in a democratic, pluralistic society is regarded as a key democratic value, at the same time, the personal autonomy of individuals is emphasised in determining which ideas prevail over others (Cammaerts, 2007). Not surprisingly, several scholars have taken a critical stance towards the idea of strictly rationalist constructions of citizenship, in the same way as others have been sceptical of the conceptual richness of the public sphere, as has been shown here. In an attempt to answer the question of what makes good citizens, some authors have argued that acts of citizenship do not arise from rational, detached observation but from a set of strong emotions, including anger, love, hate and a sense of injustice. In this context, the paradigm of the 'rational citizen' might be neither normatively desirable nor empirically possible (Wahl-Jorgensen, 2008). Marcus, Neuman and MacKuen (2000: 1) have contended that 'emotion and reason interact to produce a thoughtful and attentive citizenry'.

The articulation of citizenship rights, as described by Marshall, can be achieved through communication, which plays an important mediating role concerning the facilitation of dialogue. To understand fully how the citizenship engages politically with the media, Jones (1998, quoted in Wahl-Jorgensen, 2008) draws on a ritual view of media consumption, examining how 'acts of communication facilitate a sense of identification, community/sociability, security/control, expression, pleasure/entertainment, distraction, and even possession'. By paying more attention to how citizens actually engage with politics through media, we can better understand the strengths and limitations of existing opportunities for participation (Wahl-Jorgensen, 2008).

Networked public sphere and mediated citizenship

These days, the various media outlets, including traditional print and broadcast media but also social media networks, record the existence of citizens and make them reliant upon technology to circulate their views. The media have become a key contributor to the procedures and experiences of public sphere, citizenship and social identity constructions. *Mediatisation*, a current buzzword, refers to the colonisation of everyday life by the logic and the practices of the media (Couldry, 2008; Couldry and Hepp, 2017). Representations of space and place have been essential in the construction of contemporary public spheres and citizen communities.

In representative democracies, mass, social and personal media provide the key technological means through which publics are constituted and represented. Publics provide a space and a community for people to gather, connect and help construct society as we understand it (Boyd, 2014: 9). We understand a public (or publics) as an accessible space in which citizens can gather freely to discuss issues of common interest. The so-called 'networked publics' can be defined as publics that are being formed and restructured by networked technologies. People today can create their own publics through social media that allow them access to their friends and provide an opportunity to be a part of a broader public world. Through social media, people build networks of other people with common interests, so they create networked publics. These publics can take the form of meaningful political activities. Using the internet, social media and mobile phones to coordinate and communicate, activists in Hong Kong and the US, to take two recent examples, have banded together to, respectively, resist political regimes (Chinese rule, in this case), or form immigrant-rights protests demanding social justice (against oppression of the Mexican community) or form anti-racist protests following the George Floyd death by US police in July 2020'.

The very existence of these meaningful imagined communities is materialised through social media and other online technologies, which form the space (either in the spatial sense, or in the sense of an imagined community) in which the networked publics gather, connect and converse. Network publics are formed through a constructionist prism of an ever-changing online digital platform. Just as shared radio and/or television consumption once allowed people to connect through mass media, social media networks like *Facebook* and *Instagram* offer individuals additional means of exchanging ideas and taking part in public life.

But technology introduces new social possibilities that can challenge peoples' assumptions about everyday interactions. As Boyd (2014: 10–11) notes, the design and architecture of environments enable certain types of interaction to occur, and networked publics create new opportunities and challenges, such as a) persistence, which is the durability of online expressions and content; b) visibility, the potential audience who can bear witness; c) spreadability, the ease with which content can be shared; and d) searchability, the ability to find content. Indeed, through social media, we can easily spread information and share ideas with broad audiences (for example, through blogging and re-blogging), enhance the visibility of messages, access content from greater distances and make our communications searchable (because of the rise of search engines). The media have traditionally been used either as forums for economic domination, or as agents for acquiring political power, and/or for the dissemination of powerful interpretations. Social media networks have become an integral part of modern society by enabling new ways of being public and initiating meaningful activities, political or otherwise.

In a digitally mediated society, the online public sphere may allow us to identify a space for analysis. Drawing from Habermas's original conception, we can infer that a) public spheres are spaces of discourse, often mediated; b) public spheres often allow for new, previously excluded, discussants; c) issues discussed can be political in nature; and d) ideas are judged by their merit, not by the standing of the speaker (Poor, 2017). Most of these elements of the public sphere can certainly apply to the current era, for social media have created a fresh mediated discussion space that allows previously excluded people to have a voice, engage in rational–political debates and disseminate their ideas more easily and at a greater speed. In today's network society, power is multidimensional and is organised around digital, interactive and self-expanding networks whose participants have very diverse interests and values. In direct contrast to power relations that are embedded in the institutions of society, especially those of the state, social movements exercise counterpower by constructing themselves initially through a process of autonomous communication, free from the control of those holding institutional power (Iosifidis, 2020).

But the online forums and social spaces of the web differ substantially from the platforms for public debate constructed by traditional broadcast media in a number of ways. First, they attract many more people than traditional media (Iosifidis and Wheeler 2016). In January 2020, about 50 per cent of the world's population (or 3.8 billion people) were social media users (We Are Social, 2020). These numbers are out of reach for traditional media such as radio and television stations. But it is not only numbers or scale that matter; social networks allow much greater interactivity as well as the possibility of many-to-many communication on a global scale, rather than one-to-many, as is the case with broadcast media. Moreover, networked media is not constrained by national borders to the same extent as traditional media. The emergence of the internet and social media has thus led to the globalisation of the public sphere and public opinion. The space for public discourse has expanded, and the formation of public opinion increasingly takes place in a transnational context that crosses national boundaries. Whereas the traditional media in the form of the newspaper press and public television has been an integral part of the creation of a national public sphere, there is now a widespread assumption that new spheres of communication networks can provide the basis for shared concerns, common tastes and political and cultural debates at a global level.

In fact, the literature on the public sphere has expanded, and an important added element to public sphere theory is the concept of multiple publics, rather than one overarching public sphere (Dahlgren, 2001; Fraser, 1990). Instead of a unified public sphere, the internet era allows for the existence of workable multiple publics, with different, yet global, interests. There can also be different types of publics, organised according to various issues, for instance, issues of identity, race, religion and/or ethnicity. By using a multiple public sphere framework, one can also identify specific issue online publics, such as those in support of the environment, or various non-governmental organisations. The common denominator of such scholarly works is that there is a direct connection between the internet and the public sphere. Regardless of whether it is more appropriate to refer to a single or multiple public spheres, most scholars suggest that the online space (or spaces) should meet a number of criteria in order to be considered a public sphere: autonomy from state control and vested economic interests; discursive inclusion and equality; exchange of rational and critical opinions.

Most significantly, however, some commentators have sought to explore how the internet and online digital media shift the process of civic engagement. In her book *A Private Sphere*, Papacharissi (2010) suggests that online technologies reshape contemporary democracy by blurring and redefining the borders of public and private. Online technologies afford people both public and private spaces, rather than merely a public sphere. Indeed, Papacharissi suggests, the spaces presented by online technologies are hybrid spaces, simultaneously public and private; in this context, new technologies 'create a new civic vernacular for individuals, allowing an actualization of civic identity in tropes distinct from the deliberate model of the public sphere' (2010:130). Papacharissi contends that this new civic everyday language operates in the private sphere and claims that in post-modern democracy, civic identity can materialise outside the deliberative model of the public sphere. As the border between the public and private space has been blurred, she concludes that 'the private sphere describes and explains the mechanisms for civic connection in contemporary democracies' (ibid.:167).

Given that the performance and voice of citizens in contemporary mediated societies rely upon media (both social media and media of mass communication), the question is what kind of society we desire. Mansell (2012) asks how people imagine a digitally mediated society and whether alternative worlds or pathways are possible. Most people's ideas of a good society are aligned with the traditional concepts of equality, fairness and inclusivity. But given the growing technical ability to track, analyse and act on data and algorithms in the digital age, Mansell enquires what the consequences are for the public's right to access information, to the right of citizens to be free from surveillance and to their privacy. Have dominant trends in digitally mediated surveillance, power and practice congealed, or can they be better aligned with citizens' interests in social democracy and a good society?

Social media and democracy

A democratic social system can be defined as a model in which the supreme power is vested in the people and exercised by them directly or indirectly through a system of representation typically involving periodically held free elections. The origins of democracy can be traced back around 2,500 years to Athens, Greece. In the sixth century BC, the 'Ancient Agora' was the centre of public life in Athens, and this place can also be considered as the centre of democracy, as Athenian citizens were gathering to listen to speeches by philosophers such as Demosthenes, Plato and Socrates. The Ancient Agora was a place of direct democracy, as people were taking important political decisions and were voting by raising their hand. These political decisions were, however, made by male, property-owning citizens voting in public assemblies, meaning that the society was not entirely inclusive. Nowadays, most democracies around the world are representative ones, as people usually choose their leaders to represent them through general elections.

However, the internet seems to challenge this as it offers a powerful means for direct citizen involvement in public life and politics. It satisfies the need for a new form of democracy, a type of post-electoral democracy whose spirit and institutions were infused with a commitment to casting out the devils of arbitrary, publicly unaccountable power. In particular, the availability of information via social media such as *Facebook* and *Twitter* and the rise of user-generated content such as personal blogs have enhanced citizens' ability to communicate and self-organise. There has been an increasing amount of scholarship and grounded analysis on the emerging importance of social media in the public sphere, democracy and civic engagement. In a nutshell, there is a widespread assumption that social media applications such as *Facebook*, *Twitter* and *YouTube* are empowering people and making political processes more democratic. The internet's democratic potential has been highlighted in such works as Rheingold (1993) and Kellner (1997), whose central thesis is that cyberspace provides an ideal basis for transnational dialogical exchanges. De Sola Pool (1983) viewed computer-based communication networks like the internet as inherently democratic 'technologies of freedom'. Pippa Norris (2019) argued that democratic engagement has been reinvented for modern times.

The emerging citizen movements around the world thus serve as a check and balance on the prerogatives of government. Millions of citizens have taken to the streets of major cities around the world demanding fair governance and an end to corruption. Demonstrators temporarily swept away autocratic governments in many Arab countries such as Tunisia, Egypt and Libya in 2011, although most of them were later replaced by even more repressive regimes. Citizens in southern Europe have called for an end to austerity measures imposed by the European Commission that lead to economic exploitation and hopeless poverty. Anti-austerity movements such as 'Indignados' in Spain and 'Aganaktismenoi' in Greece have demanded an end to austerity and an increase in public expenditure. In Hong Kong, ongoing protests (at the time of writing) started in June 2019 against plans to allow extradition to mainland China. Around the world, tens of millions of bloggers have become a virtual citizens' lobby pushing for environmental change.

In October 2017, *The New York Times* published an article revealing the long history of sexual misconduct of, and allegations of sexual harassment against, Harvey Weinstein, one of the most powerful Hollywood producers. In the rapidly evolving scandal, just several days after it was first published, dozens of other women including well-known actresses and models as well as former Weinstein's employees also accused the mogul of sexual harassment of different kinds, resulting in Weinstein's resignation, a ban for life from the Producers Guild of America, and, eventually, a criminal conviction of rape after long legal proceedings (Tenbarge and Perrett, 2020). The exposed allegations of sexual abuse ignited the global social campaign known as the #MeToo movement against workplace harassment, which was mainly enhanced and spread by conversations on social media marked with the hashtag #MeToo, suggested on *Twitter* by the actress Alyssa Milano (Nicolaou and Smith, 2019). The #MeToo movement has become a powerful force in changing the overall discourse on the problem of workplace sexual misconduct, as more women (and men) were encouraged to reveal stories they had been afraid to share. In tandem, this case presents an example of how the social media movement and the affordances social media have granted to users undermined the spiral of silence and the domination of public opinion on the acceptability of sexual harassment at the workplace. The Weinstein scandal and the #MeToo social media movement reveal that social media undermine the established process of public opinion formation and the power it has over minority voices.

Undoubtedly then, Web 2.0 tools proved to be instrumental both in giving voice to minority groups and in mobilising popular movements, unrests and uprisings as has been described here. From this perspective, the network society is constituted from autonomous individuals who connect with one another in an ever-opening space within socio-cultural concerns, environmental issues, but also politics. Consequently, non-traditional political actors have affected new forms of consciousness through blogs, tweets, *Facebook* activities and online petitions (Iosifidis and Wheeler, 2016). The development of Web 2.0 tools has meant that advocates of open government have challenged closed information systems to become effective agenda-setters, as evidenced by the online activists entitled WikiLeaks, which made successful interventions into questions related to corporate malfeasance, as well as revelations over a former CIA operative Edward Snowden, who leaked intelligence information concerning the US National Security Agency's (NSA) surveillance of international internet and mobile phone traffic. Therefore, virtual technology can check on national governments and facilitate a more 'virtuous' citizenship to reconnect the public with the democratic process to allow for 'civic commons' to emerge (Putnam, 2000; Chadwick, 2006: 25).

The networked society makes it much easier to break down the obstacles which have previously prevented collective action (Shirky, 2009). Information, communication and technology (ICT) networks facilitate networked publics to construct their values, meaning and identity to affect new forms of solidarity, and the internet makes it easier to organise and agitate. Social media encourages the formation of self-directed open sources so groups of people can gather together and engage in their activities. Therefore, the old hierarchies of repression, corporate interest and hermetically sealed ideologies are removed to allow for an alternative expression of grassroots political behaviour. Such a dispersal of power means that cyberspace will create a public space which ultimately becomes a political space wherein 'sovereign assemblies to meet and ... recover their rights of representation, which have been captured in political institutions predominantly tailored for the convenience of the dominant interests' (Castells, 2012: 11).

Digital democracy: reality or illusion?

Yet the evidence is not always available to support such assertions, and a growing body of literature is calling for a more critical investigation of the complex interaction between social media and contemporary democratic politics. Sceptics such as Putnam (2000) and Morozov (2012) raised doubts about whether democracy has been enhanced. Putnam has expressed concerns that a democratic deficit has occurred with regard to a collapse in virtue and citizenship and this has led to a profound 'thinning' of the political community and the formation of the atomised citizen who is 'bowling alone'. He has argued that new forms of social capital are necessary to reconnect citizens with their societies. There is also consideration of the factors that are conducive to citizen engagement and an inclusive public sphere, and in this context the chapter refers to Evgeny Morozov's *Net Delusion*. In his volume, Morozov contends that the internet is a tool that both revolutionises and can be used by authoritarian governments, so in the latter cases, social media sites have been used to entrench dictators and threaten dissidents, making it harder to promote democracy. As Hoffman (2013) acknowledges, there are risks that these newly empowered citizens could become pawns for populist demagogues, but it could also be argued that this is far more likely to happen when the media are controlled by a few than when there are multiple and independent sources of information.

Many see today's roster of information-technology giants as an index of a bigger qualitative shift taking place to 'Platform Capitalism' (Srnicek 2017) or 'Surveillance Capitalism' (Zuboff 2019). US-based digital platform companies – *Google, Apple, Facebook, Amazon, Microsoft* and *Netflix* – have come under intense criticism in recent years for they have centralised control over the internet. Such concentrations of power pose a threat to democracy. While the digital giants have rewired the internet for surveillance and targeted messaging for commercial reasons, those capabilities have been hijacked in recent years by, for example, Russian-led disinformation operations designed to support the election of Donald Trump in the US and the Brexit referendum in the UK. They have further fanned the flames of political polarisation during elections in Brazil, Germany, the Netherlands and elsewhere, as well as sectarian violence in India and Myanmar, amongst other countries (Benkler, Faris and Roberts 2018; Bradshaw & Howard 2019; Ghosh and Scott 2018; Winseck, 2020). 'Big tech' firms have also come under fire for accelerating the circulation of hate speech, piracy, terrorist propaganda and misogynistic abuse. Public trust in social institutions has fallen as a result (Flew, Martin and Suzor 2019; Mckelvey 2018; Pickard 2020). Consequently, far from the internet being a 'technology of freedom', democracy has actually been in retreat worldwide for more than a decade (Freedom House 2019).

Conclusion

This chapter explored the concepts of the public sphere and citizenship and investigated how these have changed over the past three decades or so following shifts in society and technology. These shifts have forced us to revisit these theoretical concepts due to ongoing socio-cultural and technological advances. Specifically, the creation of the internet and the development of social networks impacted communication in both negative and positive ways. The work adopted a critical engagement with Habermas' idea of the public sphere, which also concerned the limitations of the strictly liberal, modernist and rationalist constructions of citizenship that characterise his stance. The chapter argued that both society and the public sphere should not be seen as a fractured space but understood through a constructionist prism of an ever-changing platform. The key question that was addressed here was whether social media contribute to democracy, revolution and the expansion of the public sphere and citizenship, or whether social media are first and foremost instruments of control and power. To answer this question, this chapter engaged both with social media advocates and sceptics and discussed various concerns that have arisen regarding the contribution of electronic networks to democracy. The next chapter focuses on media intermediaries and the regulatory action that may be required to make them more accountable to the public. It asks specifically: is a new generation of internet regulation needed to counter these trends and overturn a situation whereby platforms have amassed great power but have 'limited responsibility' for the illegal and harmful content available via their services?

3

SOCIAL MEDIA, POPULISM AND REGULATORY ACTION

Introduction

The political and economic potential of digital media and social media networks has recently come to public attention. Online media can contribute to changes in working and living practices, enhance democratic practices and improve the dialogue taking place in the public sphere. They therefore have the potential to intervene in civic cultures, citizen responsibility and participation. Specifically, Web 2.0 – the second generation of the World Wide Web that is focused on public collaboration and sharing of information online – has facilitated computer-mediated tools that allow for the creation and exchange of ideas across virtual communities. Social media or internet intermediaries can be defined as 'a group of Internet-based applications that build on the ideological and technological foundations of Web 2.0, and that allow the creation and exchange of User Generated Content' (Kaplan and Haenlein, 2010: 61). In terms of penetration, social media users have passed the 3.8 billion mark at the time of writing, with *Facebook* being the most popular social media platform at 2.6 billion active users monthly, followed by *YouTube* and *WhatsApp*, which reach 2 billion and 1.6 billion users respectively per month (Kemp, 2020; see also Statista, 2020).

These technological and market developments have been accompanied by the emergence of an era which has been described as 'attention economy', 'late modernity', 'platform capitalism', or 'post democracy'. Several scholars have defined this moment as being characterised by major transformations in democratic values (Beck 1992; Giddens 1991). The new platforms hold unprecedented structural market power due to the benefits of 'network effects'; their dominance and reach allows them to make unparalleled investments in new technologies in artificial intelligence, cloud computing and machine learning. They have empowered people to compete against the traditional political classes or media establishments, facilitating uprisings and political protests, and consequently regime change, particularly in totalitarian and despotic regimes. The most striking example is the 'Arab Spring', which was essentially a series of anti-establishment protests and uprisings that took place in the early 2010s in the Arab world, initiated by the social media, seeking increased social freedoms and greater participation in the political process.

Viewed this way, social media platforms provide the representational basis upon which citizens can participate in politics and define a wider sense of the common good (Iosifidis and Wheeler, 2016). In effect, the internet intermediaries contain the potential for the fuller realisation of a democratic set of public spheres in which a true level of engagement and fulfilment will occur (Habermas, 1962) and at the same time facilitate citizenship through the provision of free and accurate information. Yet, social media have been seen to provide the means for extremist and terrorist organisations to engage in the politics of fear at national, regional and global levels. Affairs which are now clearly on political agendas include the role of internet intermediaries in respect of addressing hate speech, violence and harassment, child pornography and their role in respect of piracy and abuse of copyright. Protection of minors has gained renewed interest in the online world with an attempt to define enhanced safeguards for user data and the vulnerability of minors to sexual predators, their exposure to hate speech, as well as online bullying.

Further, social media have become platforms for the spread of populism and the rapid circulation of what has become known as digital disinformation, misinformation and fake news (Wardle, 2017; see also Chapter Four). While false and fabricated news is not new to the journalistic and communications world, Carlson (2018) notes that digital media offer new capabilities and spaces for the spread of societal threats and deviances such as information of dubious quality. Once social media began to be adopted by politicians, political parties and voters themselves, especially after the 2010s, there was a seismic shift in how social media and politics could intertwine. There has been considerable focus in the context of both the 2016 US presidential election and the 2016 UK referendum on EU membership as to what extent disinformation had an influence on the outcomes (Carlson, 2020; House of Commons, 2017; Iosifidis and Wheeler, 2018). The Brexit campaign in the UK, whose repeated focus on xenophobic claims about Turkish citizens and their likely entitlement to enter the UK, coupled with the false pledge about Brexit leading to an additional £350 million per week for the NHS, were widely spread on digital media (Cummings, 2017). On the other side of the Atlantic, successful US presidential candidate Donald Trump relied heavily on Twitter output to get his messages through (Fuchs, 2017). It is clear that social media has provided additional tools for politicians to further their political campaigns. There has been considerable debate and contention in the area (see, for example, Napoli, 2019), but detailed analyses of digital disinformation, misinformation and fake news are only now emerging. What is certain is that disinformation pays.

As we shall illustrate in Chapter Four, there are clear economic incentives for agents of disinformation, and these relate to the level of engagement that social media users undertake (Tambini, 2017). Fake websites can raise money from advertising on their sites through, for example, *Google Adsense* or through *Facebook* advertising on their pages. There is an industrialisation of digital disinformation in certain quarters, with what are called 'troll factories' (Stahle, 2017), and also the use of propaganda bots on social media. More likes, more shares and more clicks lead to more money for advertisers and platforms (Tambini, 2017).

The focus on issues relating to the power of the internet intermediaries such as *Facebook*, *Google*, *Amazon*, *Apple* and *Netflix* over recent years has been valuable, but policy solutions have been scarce (Iosifidis and Andrews, 2020). Part of the purpose of this chapter is to address some of the political, policy and regulatory issues which arise from the increased power of internet intermediaries and the impact of the spread of digital disinformation. Are standard economic tools adequate for assessing the nature, behaviour and economic impact of these conglomerates? Are additional regulatory actions needed to analyse the social welfare effects of these organisations, including free speech? Given that these platforms have enabled the spread of populist and nationalist movements, can we argue that they enhance the public sphere? In effect, the chapter examines the evolving online ecology through the lens of political economy, public policy and democratic participatory values of social media.

Populist and nationalist political moves

Populist and associated nationalist movements are spreading fast. In Europe, most of the populist parties are on the political right. In Britain, for example, while right-wing populist parties failed to win seats at the 2019 general election, they nevertheless influenced domestic politics and played a key role to the Conservative victory. More specifically, UKIP (the UK Independence Party) and the Brexit Party maintained and even reinforced public debates on issues such as EU membership and mass immigration, which in turn divided the British political system and were ultimately exploited by the Conservative Party. In order to keep their voters, the Tories adopted most of the Eurosceptic and anti-immigration rhetoric of Nigel Farage–led Brexit Party and eventually appealed to the working and lower middle-class population by predicating on the idea that mass immigration has made their lives worse and that the free circulation of people from the EU must be slowed. In France, Marine Le Pen's Front National (FN) but also Jean-Luc Mélenchon's La France Insoumise (LFI) epitomise the typical radical right populist organisation, the former by primarily mobilising grievances over immigration, and the latter by showing a left-wing egalitarian and socially inclusive profile. Both LFI and the FN oppose EU membership and globalisation, and their populist attitudes have found support among the younger generation as well as lower social classes, who are typically more anti-immigrant, more authoritarian and motivated by economic concerns (Ivaldi, 2018).

The Party for Freedom (PVV) in the Netherlands, founded by Geert Wilders, is the Dutch version of an ideological family of nationalist parties linked by their opposition to immigration and to the political and cultural elites (Vossen 2016). PVV can also be conceived as a radical right-wing Dutch party in the secular, historically predominantly Protestant parts of North-western Europe, including Denmark, Sweden and Germany, where anti-Islam rhetoric is mostly based on appeals to progressive values. Since 2017, a new radical-right party, dubbed Forum for Democracy, or FvD, led by Thierry Baudet, has begun to diminish PVV and in its debut at the 2017 general election won two parliamentary seats. Similarly, in Sweden, a right-wing populist party called Sweden Democrats (*Sverigedemokraterna*), is at the time of writing the third largest party in the parliament (*Riksdag*) and has effectively developed a narrative linking the surge of predominantly Muslim immigrants to a perception of a rise in violent crimes and perceived strains on the prized Swedish welfare system. This is striking, as traditionally the country has been known for its generous asylum and immigration policies, but this changed with the refugee crisis of 2015, marking the end of so-called 'Swedish exceptionalism', when political parties shifted their rhetoric in reaction to fears of a 'system collapse' from the influx of migrants (Tomson, 2020).

The list of right-wing populist parties in Europe is endless, for one could include the Alternative for Germany (AfD), Austria's Freedom Party, Vox in Spain, Law and Justice Party (PiS) in Poland, Viktor Orbán's Fidesz in Hungary and others. According to Lewis, Clarke, Barr et al. (2018), the populist political parties now attract about 25 per cent of votes in elections in European countries, as compared to about 5–7 per cent in the 1990s. The rise of populism in the 2010s can be conceived as part of a resentment against the policies of the last 30 years in Western liberal democracies; the perceived bipartisanship of the established political parties and political, economic and media elites generally; and rising inequalities and a sense of being disconnected from governmental decision-making. This has been more acute when it comes to the decision-making at an EU level. The EU has faced many crises in recent years, including Brexit and the Euro crisis, but the current trends of democratic backsliding in countries such as Hungary and Poland, where populist governments have violated the values of democracy, rule of law and human rights, have challenged liberal democracy and called into question the very foundations of the European project. Inglehart and Norris (2016) attributed the rise of new populist parties in Europe primarily to cultural factors, such as a backlash against multiculturalism and cosmopolitanism, but others such as Judis (2016) and McKnight (2018) have associated populism with an economic response against rising inequalities and neoliberal globalisation.

Outside Europe, noticeable examples include Pauline Hanson's One Nation in Australia, Recep Tayyip Erdoğan's populist evolution in Turkey and Jair Bolsanaro's 2018 political campaign in Brazil. Echoing the rise of populist far-right parties emerging in force within Europe, the Hanson-led One Nation

Australian party can be viewed as the generic xenophobic populist move of an anti-establishment nature that speaks for the 'voiceless and the powerless', capable of making racist remarks which undermine human rights while still appearing as the most democratic voice. The leader often presents anti-Islamic arguments as forerunners in her political image and regularly blames a 'foreign' enemy for unemployment and loss of identity (De Angelis, 1998). At the other side of the spectrum, and during his 17-year reign as Turkey's leader (he took power in 2003), Erdoğan has deeply embraced an emerging brand of Islamic, nationalist and populist rhetoric. Erdoğan's speeches since he assumed the presidency (thanks to a constitutional change), particularly after an attempted coup in 2016, have been his most consistently populist of his career, sharpening his fury at perceived enemies at home and abroad (see Ahval, 2019). Meanwhile, Jair Bolsonaro, who came into power in Brazil in 2018, has expressed views that are widely considered as sexist, homophobic, racist, illiberal and, as witnessed in his handling of COVID-19, in opposition to scientific consensus. Furthermore, unlike right-wing populist movements in the US and Europe, whose rhetoric focuses mostly on immigration, a substantial amount of Bolsonaro's illiberal views concerned gender issues, often reflecting misogynous beliefs (Barros and Silva, 2020).

Jair Bolsanaro's 2018 political campaign in Brazil echoed US President Trump's nationalist focus on Making America Great Again – MAGA (Flew and Iosifidis, 2020). Trump epitomises the association of contemporary populism with nationalism, often counterposed to an ideology of globalism. When populist leaders speak of the legitimate authority of 'the people', in opposition to 'the elites' (Mudde and Kaltwasser, 2017), they are referring to a national people with its own defining history, culture and identity that is largely coextensive with the territorial boundaries of the nation-state. The US president has repeatedly highlighted the extent to which he saw his presidency as being about serving national interests rather than advancing global priorities. Trump's third United Nations speech of his presidency was largely used to deliver a nationalist manifesto, denouncing globalism and illegal immigration and promoting patriotism as a cure for the world's ills (Borger, 2019).

However, there are populisms of the political left too (SYRIZA in Greece, Podemos in Spain, the Jeremy Corbyn movement in the UK). SYRIZA is the Coalition of the Radical Left that ruled Greece from 2015 to 2019 with a pledge to go against neoliberal reform and put an end to austerity measures imposed by the European Union and IMF (International Monetary Fund). In July 2019, the party lost the general election to conservatives, having largely abandoned its radical left programme by failing to undertake sufficient battle with the neoliberal forces and also 'betraying' the results of a referendum in which the Greek people rejected austerity. The left-wing party finally signed up to acceptance of the EU and IMF-led bailout conditions, and during the last years of its rule, it hardly voiced its earlier populist rhetoric and eventually failed to turn promises into policy.

Transporting the Greek populist experience to Spain yields some clear insights. Podemos, a left-wing populist party with a similar rhetoric rooted in anti-austerity and anti-establishment views, shook Spain's political order by protesting against inequality and corruption. Podemos can be conceived as a thoughtful venture by a group of young radical thinkers and intellectuals testing out their ideas in the 'real world', but as it attempted to forge a new consensus, it inevitably drifted away from its radical roots. It appears that populist experiments often identify and capitalise on some real social concerns, but are mainly unable to offer workable alternatives and in effect face the choice between demise or mainstreaming.

Meanwhile, it is striking how the former UK Labour party leader Jeremy Corbyn, with his 'un-celebrity' celebrity performance and unlikely ascendancy from Parliamentary backbencher to political leadership, has shown how an 'outsider' politician could effect a political reversal by galvanising his 'affective capacities' into the mainstream of politics. The construction of a social movement via Momentum, a left-wing British political organisation, has been instrumental to Corbyn's organisational success and political legitimacy. The Corbyn phenomenon demonstrates the blurring of the lines between political insiders and outsiders in the social media age. The ways in which politicians present themselves to the public, together with developments in digital technologies, provided new avenues for politicians to boost their popularity.

Populism and social media

An interesting point is the way in which both right-wing and left-wing populist movements took advantage of social media in order to establish a political platform to represent themselves and mobilise their supporters. Indeed, as the internet rapidly expanded, the new communications formats offered politicians of various political spectrums greater opportunities to reconfigure their campaign strategies and secure high levels of visibility (Iosifidis and Wheeler, 2018). New-media tools play a key role in spreading nationalistic as opposed to cosmopolitan views. Alongside opening up opportunities for dialogue and difference (see Iosifidis and Wheeler, 2016), new communication tools such as Twitter and Facebook can bypass the mainstream media's frequently liberal-cosmopolitan stance and allow people to talk to each other directly, organise in groups and rallies and accelerate the spread of nationalism. The populist approach has served well a number of political leaders that have defied the establishment, with the most noticeable achievements being Brexiteers and the rise of Donald Trump, but this can also be seen in the appearance of populist underpinnings that defy liberal democracies in countries such as Poland, Hungary and Turkey. Politicians like then UKIP leader Nigel Farage in the UK took advantage of these new media to disemminate their nationalistic, anti-immigrant messages and capture popular fears that the nation may not survive an influx of foreigners (Iosifidis and Wheeler, 2018).

Social media platforms offer fertile online spaces to populist groups to circulate their views. Every person today with online access and a device can communicate personal opinions that typically reinforce subjective aspects of social and political issues, reject or accept what already exists online and, as such, differentiate 'us' from 'others'. Viewed this way, social media do not encourage the formation of a rational, informed deliberation, for they inflect and magnify an irrational public mood where 'chaotic enterprises are trapped in a daily staging where ethos, pathos and logos are all mixed up' (Paparachissi, 2015: 26). These virtual spaces, populated by publics whose actions are motivated by shared feelings, contrast sharply with the traditional Habermasian public sphere, a space where informed public dialogue is supposed to take place. While not ignoring that the mainstream media have been criticised for their failure to realise the 'ideal' public sphere, social networks, blogs and websites go a step further by serving to interact in isolation with those who already think what we think (Sunstein, 2008). Rationality is thus weakened, as the political messages that are circulated online are highly emotional and covered with a symbolic meaning. It is striking to observe the way in which populism functions and spreads with the help of social media networks in order to mobilise political emotions, exploit the public sphere and disrupt individual realities. Populist leaders take advantage of the digitisation of the public sphere and present themselves as 'allies' to people.

It can be said that the rise of populist leaders in many parts of the world has been seen as symptomatic of a rise of distrust in institutional elites and established models of governance, as well as arising out of concerns about growing social inequality and a perceived decline in economic opportunities. The literature generally points to a mix of socio-economic and cultural factors that can explain the rise of populism, and note that it can take a variety of political forms, from right-wing nativism and 'illiberal democracy' to the 'left-populism' proposed by Mouffe (2018), Eatwell and Goodwin (2018), Moffitt (2020), and Norris and Ingelhart (2019). In order to understand the link between social media and the rise of populism, Postill (2018, 2019) argues that we need a global, comparative approach that can scrutinise claims about the direct effects of new media technologies on political change. It is suggested that six issues should be examined in the context of a collective search for a global theory of the link between social media and populism: the origins of populism; ideology and populism; the rise of theocratic populism; non-populist politicians' use of social media; the embedding of social media in larger communication systems; and the vexed question of how to ascertain (social) media effects. This section has contributed to the discussion by attempting to assess the connection between social media and the rise of populism in various national contexts, both Western and the rest of the world. We fully understand the limitations of our approach, including the small geographical coverage and the lack of field research. Future thinking on social media and populism should consider a larger set of cultural contexts as well as primary research to fully understand the impact of social media on populist successes.

Post-truth politics and social media

It is concerning that the increased regularity of the influence of social media networks in politics has been associated with the spread of so-called 'post-truth politics' and digital disinformation. As social media has moved from the periphery to the centre of political campaigning, it is hardly surprising that there is growing interest in the issue of online platforms' accuracy and trust in news and politics. The types of engagement with social media are highly questionable in preserving political consensus and have exposed the deficiencies in modern democracies (Iosifidis and Wheeler, 2018). Therefore, at least from the selective examples we have presented here, a mixed picture has occurred with regard to the usage of online techniques in representative democracies, and there are still many questions about whether they actually encourage a greater form of public efficacy. Most observers today concur that especially in regard to social media, modern communication technologies have impacted profoundly on politics and participation. But the problem is that there is still no overarching agreement in terms of how and to what extent this impact takes place, and what significance it has for democratic politics. In the cases of Trump's Twitter strategy (both in his campaign and within the early period of his presidency) and the use of social media by Brexiteers, it is clear that social media engagement has been highly controversial in relation to democratic deficits and that the usage of online techniques has left open questions as to whether democratic consensus can be achieved (ibid.).

Tech giants such as *Facebook*, *Twitter* and *Google* are major sources of news and information and have provided additional tools for politicians to further their political campaigns. The internet and social media, as the exemplary global technologies of openness, were once seen as being at the forefront of the dismantling of the barriers to cultural modernity presented by traditional institutions, such as oligopolistic mass media (Flew and Iosifidis, 2020). But it is a matter of concern that they are also associated with the spread of disinformation. Not only that; *Facebook* and *Google*'s vast range makes their platforms particularly attractive to advertisers, along with their ability to micro-target audiences based on the data they have accumulated about users. As Damian Tambini has argued, fake news is sustained by advertising revenues derived from online platforms. More likes, more shares and more clicks lead to more money for advertisers and platforms (Tambini, 2017).

Facebook, *Google* and their likes have significant, and strategic, market power, and their dominance of the online advertising market is growing. In order to curtail the erosion of information policy, reform will no doubt be essential (Freedman, 2018). But are national and regional regulators in a position to address the issues which are raised? The UK's *Disinformation and 'Fake News' Report* (DCMSC of the House of Commons, 2019) and *Cairncross Review* (Cairncross, 2019) and the *European Commission's Report on Disinformation* (EC, 2018b) are three recent examples seeking to investigate how precisely such a reform policy might be implemented. In the UK, Ofcom should have the power to intervene. Other regulators, such as the Competition and Markets Authority, can also interfere in respect of overall competition and anti-trust issues. The dominant position held by *Google* and *Facebook* in respect of mobile advertising is key, and we should take responsibility for regulating it.

Academics have, for some time now, attempted to identify potential solutions to these concerns, but despite some existing noticeable research work, more research needs to be conducted with regards to overseeing social media. Wu (2016) argued that social media like *Facebook* should serve the public (rather than their own interests) by becoming 'public benefit corporations'. Napoli and Caplan (2017) favoured the articulation of new or modified frameworks that reflect the hybrid nature of social media platforms – content producers, but also investors in platforms for connectivity (Iosifidis and Andrews (2020), called for a new category of 'information utilities' which would encompass truly dominant internet intermediaries such as *Facebook* and *Google*. Picard and Pickard (2017) recommend transparency and that platforms make public and concealed choices regarding filtered, targeted and personalised content so that users not knowingly influenced. But the authors warn that the same policies cannot apply universally, as objectives and methods vary in different national, political and social settings.

Winseck (2020) agrees that a more forceful response to the platforms is overdue but argues that too often the case for doing so is based on misguided conceptualisations of 'big tech' and poor evidence. In his work, he strived to illuminate those weaknesses and help lay the groundwork for a new generation of internet regulation by proposing four principles drawn from telecoms and public utility regulation: structural separation, line of business restrictions (firewalls), public obligations and public alternatives. Winseck claims that these ideas take us back to the genesis of regulated capitalism and offer a richer intellectual and political taproot for thinking about internet regulation based on bright line *ex ante rules* versus media policy, self-regulation, voluntary codes or the *ex post* tools of anti-trust law. He goes on to argue that, where IT firms are engaged in media-like activities, existing frameworks for audiovisual media services can be selectively used to address public interest concerns, while governments, not private corporate actors, should regulate *illegal* content (hate speech, disinformation, insider trading, fraud and piracy) based on the rule-of-law and norms of a democratic society, either using laws that are already on the books or creating new ones when needed. Winseck's position is not to diminish the need for a new generation of internet regulation, but he expresses strong reservations about the tendency in recent years to make internet content regulation the first tool in the toolbox to be used. He rather prefers that content regulation be used as a tool of last resort after the potentials of structural and behavioural regulatory approaches have been tested. But as mentioned here, more ideas are needed.

Self-regulation

Just as important is how social media organisations take on more responsibility and apply self-regulating mechanisms that stifle disinformation across their platforms. It would obviously be preferable if social media platforms were able to address the fake news issues themselves. As mentioned above, they have taken some actions in respect of fake news sites, but as journalists like Carole Cadwalladr have pointed out, problems remain. *Facebook* is working with fact-checking sites to point up disinformation. Some have suggested that there could be technological solutions to identify disinformation, but others have suggested that there are too many examples of the algorithms failing to uncover disinformation   (https://www.city.ac.uk/people/academics/petros-iosifidis#profile =publications) or that this may give *Facebook* or *Google* too much censorship power.[2] In Chapter Five, we shall illustrate how the EU has attempted a self-regulatory process but has ultimately failed in achieving favourable outcomes on account of a non-audited ethos. That is, in order to make a self-regulating approach a feasible option, it would need to offer more audited options via civil society institutions. Ultimately, employing an executive editor and other editors for different segments, as well as internal human fact-checkers, would help. *Facebook* needs to recognise its responsibilities and invest some of its profits in employing a strong editorial team or teams headed by an executive editor, supported by fact-checkers. *Facebook* itself should dedicate itself to being a champion of the truth, more actively support its users in taking action on disinformation and collaborate with genuine media organisations on ensuring recognition for their content (Iosifidis and Nicoli, 2020).

Deepfakes

The appearance of deepfakes poses a more serious threat to democracy and presents another challenge for social media and regulators alike in controlling them. A deepfake, also called *synthetic media*, is any video that uses a programme to replace one face with another. Some are highly complex and can imitate voices in which a person in an existing image or video is replaced with someone else's likeness. For instance, during the 2016 US election, many accounts were set up to initially act in a trustworthy manner and build support before being used for manipulation (Pomerantsev, 2019). Even sources, given enough time, can be faked. There is a back-and-forth arms race between deepfakes and the algorithms that can detect them. *Partnership in Artificial Intelligence*, in collaboration with AWS (a service offering multiple options for federating one's identity), *Facebook* and *Microsoft*, recently established a deepfake detection challenge (Schroepfer, 2019).

When it comes to politics, deepfakes can be present at a high level (for example, general elections), though most of the problems lie in smaller-scale issues, like local elections (Ascott, 2020). This is because national elections fall under much higher levels of scrutiny, and content put out by campaigns, as well as that which could potentially be deepfaked, will be analysed. With the need for smaller civic leaders and local politicians to promote themselves constantly on social media to build their platforms, less high-profile targets now also have far more video content of themselves. This means there is ample footage for deepfake creation, and it emphasises the fact that local and civic elections are a potential weak point for democracies. Unlike deepfakes of heads of state and other high-profile individuals, the method of distribution for small-scale use is easier. Such hyper-localised fakes present problems at the lowest and smallest levels of civic accountability and could have a tangible impact on voting patterns. In terms of addressing the problem, the Centre for Data Ethics and Innovation has made several recommendations to the UK Department for Culture, Media and Sport. The best policy solution to help those who will be most vulnerable to legislative changes is for 'technology companies, particularly those running social media platforms, [to] include audio and visual manipulation within their anti-disinformation strategies' (Centre for Data Ethics and Innovation 2019: 18). We return to the dangers of such digital manipulation in Chapter Four.

Misinformation and coronavirus (COVID-19)

The problem regarding fake news has taken a new dimension in the current uncertain era of the coronavirus outbreak. In fact, *Facebook, Google, LinkedIn, Microsoft, Reddit, Twitter* and *YouTube* are said to join forces to fight disinformation related to the coronavirus outbreak. The companies claim that they are working closely together on response efforts to COVID-19 (the disease caused by the new coronavirus) and, while helping self-isolated people to stay connected, they are also jointly combating fraud and misinformation about the virus, elevating authoritative content on their platforms and sharing critical updates in coordination with government healthcare agencies around the world (https://about.fb .com/news/2020/03/coronavirus/#joint-statement).

It appears that in the fight against the novel coronavirus, social media platforms were quick to take steps to help limit the dissemination of life-threatening disinformation that could worsen the pandemic. *Facebook, Twitter* and *YouTube* have each moved swiftly to remove coronavirus disinformation that encourages people to take actions that could put them at risk. *Google* is privileging information from official health agencies, such as the World Health Organization (WHO), and has set up a 24-hour incident-response team that removes disinformation from search results. *Facebook*-owned *WhatsApp* has joined forces with the WHO to provide a messaging service that offers real-time updates (Kreps and Nyhan, 2020). In addition, and in a bid to stop the spread of false information, *WhatsApp* has imposed a limit on the number of friends-users that forward these messages. If a message, labelled on the app with a double arrow icon, has already been forwarded more than five times, users will be limited to sending it to one more contact at a time. The move does not completely prevent the message spreading, as users can still manually send it to multiple contacts, but it prevents this occurring in a single click (Field, 2020).

To help people identify accurate information about COVID-19, *Facebook* has added a new version of their COVID-19 Information Centre, dubbed 'Get the Facts'. It includes fact-checked articles from their partners that debunk disinformation about the coronavirus. The fact-checked articles are selected by the organisation's news curation team and are updated weekly (Rosen, 2020). *Alphabet* (*Google*'s parent company) also provides coronavirus updates in line with the World Health Organisation's *WhatsApp* Health Alert. Sundar Pichai, CEO of *Alphabet*, stated on 6 March 2020,

> we weigh a number of factors grounded in science, including guidance from local health departments, community transmission assessments, and our ability to continue essential work and deliver the products and services people rely on.
>
> *(Li, 2020)*

YouTube, a *Google*-owned service, has banned all conspiracy-theory videos falsely linking coronavirus symptoms to 5G networks and has pledged to delete videos violating this policy, including an interview with renowned conspiracy theorist David Icke claiming that 'there is a link between 5G and this health crisis' (Kelion, 2020).

At the time of writing, we cannot evaluate the effectiveness of these measures. However, social media platforms should be praised for making a concerted effort to limit disinformation and harmful content about the virus and thus stifle conspiracy theories on the pandemic. Social media platforms may not be the most trusted sources when it comes to news about coronavirus, but their appeal is still significant. As a response to the COVID-19 outbreak, the UK's communications regulator Ofcom has commissioned an ongoing weekly online survey of c.2,000 respondents to monitor how people are getting news and information about the crisis. Official sources, such as the NHS and the government as well as traditional broadcasters, remain the most trusted sources for information on the pandemic, with social media and closed groups being less trusted. During the third week of the 'lockdown', BBC services were the most-used source by a significant margin, with 78% of the respondents, or four in five, saying they used the public service broadcaster as a source of news and information; 54% used non-BBC broadcasters, followed by officials (43%), social media (39%), newspapers, either online or printed (38%), and family, friends or local people (28%). A mere 10% said they used closed groups such as *WhatsApp* groups and *Facebook* messenger (Ofcom, 2020). This is, of course, an online survey with a limited sample (2,000 adult respondents aged 16+), but it still reveals that social media usage as a news source is trusted by a significant segment of the UK population (just below 40%).

Having briefly explained above the strategies adopted by social media platforms to limit disinformation and harmful content about the virus, the question is whether they can (or should) adopt a similar approach to political speech and political disinformation. Can tactics that work against dangerous health disinformation be equally effective when applied to politics? For a start, false stories about the novel coronavirus are relatively easy to detect compared with political disinformation. The platforms themselves acknowledge that standards are far easier to establish and enforce in health and medicine, and therefore false claims can be quickly identified and removed, as *Facebook* has done in partnership with national and global health organisations. By contrast, standards of truth and accuracy in politics are more subjective and likely to provoke controversy, not least because it is difficult to strike a balance between free speech and public harm. In a democratic and free society, there is an acute need to protect freedom of expression. Identifying false claims about politics is a laborious affair that requires difficult judgments about the nature of truth. The pandemic, on the other hand, has generated a strong consensus in favour of limiting harmful content. In short, as most social media platforms argue,

> the domain of medical information differs enormously from that of politics, where free speech must be protected and where exposure to false information does not threaten people's health. The best a liberal democracy can do is limit the influence of misinformation, not try to eradicate it like a virus.
>
> *(Kreps and Nyhan, 2020)*

Conclusion

So, what needs to be done to oversee social media and ban misleading content on issues not necessarily related to health? If voluntary and/or self-regulation is not enough, what other avenues are available to police social media and prohibit the spread of digital disinformation? These are some of the questions that are addressed in the following chapters. Suffice to say here, tackling digital disinformation requires more than voluntary action by the major online platforms, as there is substantial evidence that there are financial disincentives for them to do so. Digital disinformation needs to be identified as a multifaceted problem, one that requires multiple approaches to resolve. Governments, regulators, think tanks, the academy and technology providers need to take more steps to better shape the next internet with as little digital disinformation as possible. While some level of self-regulation is applied upon social media platforms, it is also clear that digital literacy programmes have an important role to play, not least to ensure that young people are aware of the dangers of disinformation on social media that they use. Now is the time to commence a full debate on the future of news and the best means to protect it, and regulators themselves should be challenged as to whether they believe that a regulatory regime put in place before *Facebook* was founded, and before the smartphone existed, is still relevant in every aspect to the challenges society now faces. Chapter Four investigates various approaches towards countering digital disinformation, ranging from fact-checking, to news literacy, to public awareness.

Notes

1 http://www.huffingtonpost.com/entry/facebook-fake-news_us_5852c248e4b0
2edd41160c78

2 http://www.bbc.co.uk/news/technology-38181158; https://www.theguardian.com/
technology/2016/nov/29/facebook-fake-news-problem-experts-pitch-ideas-algorit
hms; https://www.bloomberg.com/news/articles/2016-11-23/facebook-s-quest-to
-stop-fake-news-risks-becoming-slippery-slope

SECTION II

The current state of the art of digital disinformation

4

DIGITAL DISINFORMATION AND WAYS OF ADDRESSING IT

Introduction

We are on the cusp of a digital epoch driven by artificial intelligence and machine-learning algorithms (Tegmark, 2017). In this omnipresent digital milieu, an increasing number of people are choosing to lead their lives online within environments that are increasingly mimicking offline settings (Woolley, 2020). The 2018 Steven Spielberg film *Ready Player One* captures the essence of this near future where the main characters experience more significant digital lives than their irrelevant 'real' ones. With digitalisation and mediatisation upheld to such societal heights (Couldry, 2008), it would be foolish to believe that deceit and lies – such powerful human communication undertakings – would be absent from digital communication processes. Deviant behaviours are already abound across online technologies albeit we are still at the dawn of a digital era (Zuboff, 2019). On an interpersonal level, but more prominently on a societal level, where the battle to gain our attention is *strategically* thought-out by unethical entrepreneurs, leaders, governments and enemies alike, online deceit and lies are considered opportunities and weapons. As we have described in Chapter Two, the weaponisation of deviant online behaviour has exacerbated both political and social polarisation across liberal democracies and has facilitated systemic crises across the globe (see also Beaufort, 2018).

One of the most threatening deviant digital behaviours is a phenomenon termed *digital disinformation*. Hidden in the overabundance of online content is a plethora of disinformation used for economic gain or political and ideological goals. Examples include swaying voters during an election process (Bennett and Livingston, 2018), or obscuring decisions for parents in vaccinating their children (Ecker, 2018). The whiplash speed in which this phenomenon has spread across digital platforms has made it a catalyst of a 'post-truth' era that D'Ancona

(2017: 7) calls 'a phase of political and intellectual combat, in which democratic orthodoxies and institutions are being shaken to their foundations by a wave of ugly populism'. *Post-truth*, selected as the Oxford Dictionary word of the year in 2016, has become ubiquitous to the point that governments and international bodies across the globe are searching for concrete solutions to stifle the threats associated with it (see Chapter Five). Mitigating digital disinformation has thus taken on added significance in the current global context.

The purpose of this chapter is to offer definitions of the term *disinformation* before exploring viable and effective approaches towards countering the deviant phenomenon. We divide these approaches in two broad categories: *detection* and *response*. We consider in our definitions the taxonomies of the phenomenon as they currently stand. These revolve around three elements: the *agents* (or creators of the disinformation content), the *message* (content and its characteristics) and the *interpreter* (the victim and the impact the message had on him/her) (Wardle and Derakshan, 2017: 22).

Defining disinformation

Disinformation is 'false, incomplete or misleading information that is passed, fed, or confirmed to a targeted individual, group, or country' (Shultz and Godson: 1984: 41). Bennett and Livingston (2018: 124) define disinformation as 'intentional falsehoods spread as new stories or simulated documentary formats to advance political goals'. Humprecht (2018: 1975) offers a similar definition only with an added profit variable. He conceives disinformation as information that is intentionally created and uploaded on various websites, and thereafter disseminated via social media either for profit or for social influence.

Communication historians Garth Jowett and Victoria O'Donnell (2019) posit that the term *disinformation* dates back to the Cold War era. During this time, a division of the KGB (the main security agency for the former Soviet Union from 1954 to 1991) known as *dezinformatsia*, from another Russian word, *dezinformatsiya*, was established in order to apply covert techniques for influencing foreign countries (Shultz and Godson, 1984). Due to its concealed nature and use of false information, Jowett and O'Donnell link the term to their own definition of *black* propaganda (2019: 21–23), a communications process intended to identify the sender of the message as the one it actually means to discredit.

Such techniques are part of a collection of methods used as malicious conventional and non-conventional forms of threats. These are known as *hybrid threats* and can include military and non-military activities (Hoffman, 2010). Examples of these activities range from cyberattacks on critical information systems to the disruption of energy supplies or financial services. They can also include chemical and biological threats. In terms of disinformation, hybrid threats are designed to be difficult to detect and comprise content that can exacerbate political distrust or identify weaknesses in open democracies and cause confusion or disapprobation (Pawlak, 2015). The most significant aspect of hybrid threats is that they 'intentionally blur the distinction between times of peace and war making it hard for the targeted countries to devise policy responses in a proper and timely manner' (Cederberg and Erosen, 2015: 2). Bradshaw and Howard (2017) refer to a specific category of disinformation agents as 'cyber troops' (or government and political actors that manipulate public opinion online). In a comparative analysis from around the world, the researchers noticed increased use of cyber troops and computational propaganda for political purposes (Bradshaw and Howard, 2019).

During the twentieth century, disinformation agents were inhibited on account of the limited potential of analogue, linear media technologies. Examples of this included the spread of disinformation via print media, 'to weaken adversaries … planted in newspapers by journalists who are actually secret agents of a foreign country' (Jowett and O'Donnell, 2019: 24). Disinformation in the digital era is notably easier to adopt. The phenomenon is therefore undeniably more threatening. The European Commission (EC, 2018b: 3–4) outlines that disinformation is much like the aforementioned definitions; that is,

> verifiably false or misleading information created, presented and disseminated for economic gain or to intentionally deceive the public and may cause public harm. Public harm comprises threats to democratic political and policy-making processes as well as public goods such as the protection of EU citizens' health, the environment or security.

Yet it also recognises the extreme manner in which the internet exacerbates disinformation. Specifically,

> on a scale and with speed and precision of targeting that is unprecedented, creating personalised information spheres and becoming powerful echo chambers for disinformation campaigns.
>
> *(2018b: 1)*

Misinformation

The precision and speed of online technologies combined with the capacity to make content seemingly authentic is at the heart of the problem (Heinrich, 2019). This is because the effectiveness of digital disinformation lies in the ability of digital technologies to be used by citizens to inadvertently share content across their own networks as soon as it reaches them. When disinformation is unintentionally and unsuspiciously shared, the process is known as *misinformation* (Fetzer, 2014). Put another way, misinformation is the spread of false information, but it is sent or shared without harmful intent. Since many of us share deviant content unknowingly to recipients who are also unaware of the disinformation, the impact is greater. This is because when people's persuasion knowledge is not activated, they are more prone to accept messages, making electronic word of mouth such a powerful communications model (Friestad and Wright, 1984; Nicoli and Papadopoulou, 2017).

Deviant agents of disinformation therefore depend on misinformation in order to achieve their objectives. Moreover, because of its gruesome effects, democracy and its underlying institutions have come under enormous threat. Journalism, for example, is under pressure to function within a 24-hour news cycle and therefore frequently falls prey to misinformation. The same can be said of information regarding health (for example, vaccination doubts), global warming, political communication, immigration policies and numerous other findings backed by the scientific method (O'Connor and Weatherall, 2018). Ultimately, through misinformation, the phenomenon of digital disinformation has created an information crisis, leading to a series of moral panics that in turn has accelerated a new world order. Distrust in information has forced people inward, giving rise to new forms of nationalism and populism (Iosifidis and Wheeler, 2018). Consequently, public trust in social institutions has fallen (Flew, Martin and Suzor 2019; Pickard 2020). Digital democracy, a once sanguine ideal with aspirations to transcend normative components of the public sphere into a reality, now drifts farther apart from Habermasian principles than ever before (see Chapter Two). The erosion of digital democracy has been identified as an 'epistemic' crisis of public spheres (Dahlgren 2018: 20).

Disinformation content types

Social media are designed to take hold of our attention and not let go (Wu, 2016). They are where so many of us gather to share content and to consume news, rapidly overtaking legacy news media as our preferred destinations for knowing what is happening in the world (McNair, 2018; Hågvar, 2019). *Facebook*, for example, 'has become the largest and most influential entity in the news business, commanding an audience greater than that of any American or European television news network, any newspaper or magazine in the Western world and any online news outlet' (Manjoo, 2017). In fact, at the time of writing, most media groups rely on social media to drive traffic to their own websites by sharing on them clickable news stories several times a day (Ju, Jeong and Chyi, 2014; D'Ancona, 2017). As such, social media are ideal for agents to disseminate deviant content, consequently becoming the most prominent harbingers of our current epistemic crisis (Napoli, 2019). Deviant agents build websites that mimic trusted news media publishers in order to drive unsuspicious users there via social media posts. The approach is an effective means for disinformation agents to generate profits or to influence perceptions and attitudes of unsuspecting users – or both. It is also the reason why policy reform recommendations address the issue of disrupting the revenue sources of deviant agents head on (see Chapter Five).

Digital disinformation mimicking news media content, what we refer to as 'fake news', is dangerous, widespread and comes in numerous forms. Fake news can be audio-based or text-based, can use still images or – as we illustrated in

Chapter Three in our definition of deepfakes – can be audiovisual. Deepfakes – video or audio that is artificially synthesised through deep learning techniques to look or sound like real people through media manipulation (Iosifidis and Nicoli, 2020) – is concerning because the algorithms continuously learn and improve. So troubling is the technology that even the platforms are heeding their warnings. *Facebook* announced its intentions to collaborate with partners in order to stifle the deviant behaviour (Bickert, 2020). Nonetheless, the increasing sophistication of artificial intelligent forms of deep learning will mean that certain deepfake content will trickle down to unsuspicious citizens. One can imagine during times of political unrest (for example, the protests triggered by the death of African American George Floyd in June 2020), a deepfake portraying a political leader and tipping the scales towards a civil war or worse still.

Other disinformation types come in the form of infographics, while some are sent as sources from fake think tanks (*fake tanks*) or fake academia (for example, fake conferences and journals) (Elis, 2017). One of the most effective disinformation types is the meme. Memes can be textual, visual or audiovisual concepts that interpreters have a frame of reference for, and they are represented, more often than not, in a humorous manner; disinformation memes have been manipulated in order to go viral, to stir emotions and to set a narrative within a certain framework (Ong and Cabañes, 2019). Some of these message types are created as originals while others are digitally manipulated. On account of the emotionally motivated design of the message, disinformation memes are more likely to be shared than other forms of information (Vosoughi, Roy and Aral, 2018). This is because emotional content is easier to comprehend (than content that appeals to logic) and therefore engages more effectively with recipients (D'Anconda, 2017). Recent examples include those of the Leave.EU ('Vote Leave') campaign during the 2016 EU referendum in the UK, where Brexit supporters had a more powerful and emotional message that was conveyed effectively via social media (Iosifidis and Wheeler, 2018). One widely shared meme during the campaign offensively stated, 'we didn't win two world wars to be pushed around by a Kraut' (referring and showing the image of Angela Merkel) (O'Grady, 2019). The originality and often shocking content of the message is designed to generate more than normal engagement and clicks, rousing users to share the message across their own network. All these content approaches have one defining element: to stir an emotion from an interpreter that will in turn disrupt social cohesion by sharing the content further (Ross and Rivers, 2018).

Digital disinformation is compounded by bots, or automated robot codes that disseminate information over social media on an unpresented level (Ferrara et al., 2016). Bots are dangerous because, through the use of algorithms, automation and human curation, they can distribute disinformation much faster than any human and can continuously regenerate, shuffle around content and redistribute it (Luceri et al., 2019). If *Twitter*, for example, tries to control bots by not allowing any profile to send more than 1,000 tweets a day (something which many bots do), bots are simply modified through human curation to send out 999 tweets.

Bradshaw and Howard (2019: 4) refer to these actions as part of the phenomenon of computational propaganda. In their study of social media manipulation, they refer to the way in which cyber troops use political bots to amplify hate speech, illegally harvest data, micro-target unsuspicious users or 'deploy an army of trolls to bully or harass political dissidents or journalists online'. The more sophisticated chatbots become, mimicking emotions and carrying on conversations and arguments with real people, the more the threat to democracy. This is because, as with deepfakes, it will become harder to distinguish chatbots from humans.

Disinformation agent types

Two of the most pressing questions in disinformation studies involve who the agents are and what motivations lie behind their actions (Ong and Cabañes, 2019). The European Commission divides these motivations into economic, political and ideological causes (EC, 2018b). Similarly, Benkler, Faris and Roberts (2018) have identified five parties that circulate digital disinformation in their study of the U.S. digital landscape reflecting the above motivations in North America. These are

1. Bodies close to Russian government;
2. Right-wing groups;
3. Groups that make money such as those based in Macedonia;
4. Formal campaigns using marketing tools (i.e. *Cambridge Analytica;*)
5. Peer-to-peer distribution networks.

Based on these motivations, agents have been categorised as either official or unofficial (Wardle and Derakshan, 2017: 29). Official actors have been the most sophisticated and well-funded. Most often, they are a part of an ongoing information warfare effort on the part of one state trying to manipulate users in another. For example, in their study of *Facebook* announcements on disinformation, Iosifidis and Nicoli (2020) noticed that the technology giant identifies Russia and Iran (among others) as official state actors practicing disinformation on the platform – what *Facebook* calls 'coordinated inauthentic behaviour'[1]. In one seminal *Facebook* announcement, the company identified that the motivations of these actors were to 'distort domestic or foreign political sentiment, most frequently to achieve a strategic and/or geopolitical outcome' (Weedon, Nuland and Stamos, 2017: 4). Bradshaw and Howard (2019), citing a *New York Times* article by Myers and Mozur (2019), have included China in their list of governments using disinformation upon foreign states. According to the article (2019: 5), China is using these techniques 'to paint Hong Kong's democracy advocates as violent radicals with no popular appeal'.

Political and ideological motivations also come from internal agents. In such cases we might see unofficial actors attempting to manipulate perceptions either through disinformation or trolling. Online trolls often attempt to provoke by arguing or insulting while also undermining and intimidating users. In his book *Antisocial: Online Extremists, Techno-Utopians and the Hijacking of the American Conversation* (2019), journalist Andrew Marantz describes how he spent several years studying alt-right trolls wanting to spread their ideology (and hate speech) online. He describes the way in which right-wing activists would get together on social media and send out coordinated disinformation messages until they were picked up by thousands of other users and often were even picked up as stories by right-wing mainstream media such as *Fox News*. In such instances they would succeed in increasing the virality of the message and by doing so would therefore succeed in 'hijacking democracy' (Marantz, 2019).

Apart from political and ideological motivations, many agents create and spread digital disinformation purely for financial reasons. It is mainly in such cases where the fabrication of digital news publishing – 'fake news' – occurs. Working much like news publishers, these deviant agents attempt to drive traffic to their sites often through novel clickbait where they receive advertising and earn money. Such agents can work alone in remote corners of the world (including within liberal democracies) or increasingly, in troll farms. Troll farms are usually unofficial in nature and create fabricated content and share it on social media to manipulate the perceptions of users (Walker, 2017). The small town of Veles in Macedonia has been well-documented as a hub where young digital disinformation agents work to generate traffic to sites for the purpose of attracting advertising funds (Wardle and Derakshan, 2017). Other well-documented troll farms are found in Iran, Mexico, Saudi Arabia and Turkey (Titcomb, 2017). Cyber troops working in troll factories, according to *The Guardian*'s Shaun Walker (2017), have even gone as far as to get in touch with activists in the US to pay them to organise protests and events.

Approaches toward combating digital disinformation

Given the complexity and threats associated with digital disinformation, most entities involved in tackling the phenomenon agree on battling back through multiple, overlapping approaches rather than through one single method. These entities include civil society, governments, the media, non-profit organisations, policy-makers, research institutions and social media themselves. To do so they place the phenomenon within a communications process consisting of an understanding of the senders, the messages and the receivers involved. We have already seen how this helps in grounding definitions and causes of digital disinformation (agents/messages/interpreters). To combat disinformation, we divide the disinformation process in two significant parts – *detection* and *response*. In Chapter Five, we illustrate how these two fighting-back mechanisms are applied within the EU by academicians and researchers, journalists, technology platforms, task forces, regulatory bodies and various other entities of the European Union. In this section, we describe the approaches used. We identify fact-checking and news literacy as the main detection mechanisms involved in combating digital disinformation. If information is detected, a response can be used to combat the phenomenon. Responses to digital disinformation involve communication strategies consisting mainly of debunking, rebuttals and myth-busting but also of various technologies that can be applied to the cause. The two technologies discussed below involve artificial intelligence (the algorithmic processes, or codes allowing machine learning) and the blockchain (a technology allowing for a cryptographed and decentralised piece of data that is timestamped and cannot be manipulated).

Detection

Fact-checking

One of the most significant ways of detecting digital disinformation involves the process of fact-checking (Guarino et al., 2020). Fact-checking determines the correctness of factual statements and can be divided into human-based and automated systems of artificial intelligence and machine learning (Nguyen and Kyumin, 2019). Fact-checking can be internally set up by a media organisation and applied before a message is sent out to large audiences, or it can be done after it is disseminated. Fact-checking after the content has gone public across social media platforms or on search engine results is often done by external, third-party, independent fact-checkers. The rise in independent fact-checking organisations has been facilitated by the growth of digital disinformation over social media platforms. Most of the content detected by independent fact-checkers is attained after the messages are sent out.

Internal news media fact-checking consists of a significant yet arduous journalist process that controls the veracity of the content before it gets disseminated, consequently allowing the content shared to be as accurate as possible. In turn, citizens can be informed in a truthful manner and make more rational decisions. Indeed, journalistic fact-checking, particularly throughout the twentieth century, has allowed news outlets to become trusted sources of information. German media outlet *Der Spiegel*, for instance, in its Hamburg headquarters, employs 60–80 full-time fact-checkers (and also frequently outsources numerous freelancers) (Silverman, 2010). Its investment in fact-checking has contributed toward it becoming one of the most prestigious news media organisations in Europe (Zarofsky, 2019). In spite of criticism of the media sector,[2] internal news media fact-checking has undeniably enabled news media to become one of the most important institutions of liberal democracies. As a consequence, the news media have time and again managed to expose the wrongdoings of liberal society and keep citizens objectively informed. A citizenry that trusts the information it consumes no doubt leads to a healthier democratic process. Ultimately, in-house news media fact-checkers have been used both in the past and today to identify errors and amend them before they reach an audience. On the rare occasions on which erroneous or questionable journalistic content is broadcast or published (often by mistake or because of an individual error), it is quickly retracted and corrected.

As news media have become more intertwined with digital tools and social media platforms, fact-checking processes have shifted toward a detection rather than prevention mechanism. By the end of the noughties, most of the main technology platforms added a function to their services known as the *share* option, which eternally shifted the dynamics of fact-checking. We have illustrated in the previous section how and why deviant agents have grown accustomed to spreading disinformation on social media platforms. It is the *share* option, introduced by *Facebook* two years after its launch (and of course the retweet option on *Twitter*), that allowed agents to take digital disinformation to the next level since users could now unintentionally (and sometimes intentionally) spread deceitful news. By all accounts, the misinformation age we are currently witnessing emerged in 2006 with the inception of the *share* option; it merely took another ten years to apprehend the dangers associated with that option (via the meddling of the US elections and the Brexit referendum in 2016) and to become the impetus for the democratic threats discussed in this volume. By the end of 2016, the US presidential elections and the UK's decision to leave the European Union through a voting referendum, left many observers perplexed with the outcomes. It is in fact mainly the shockwaves of 2016 that finally prompted *Facebook* to increase its post-published, digital fact-checking detection process. This is something we shall return to in Chapter Five.

Following these events and the subsequent *Cambridge Analytica/SCL* scandal in 2018, pressure mounted on *Facebook* to take notice of how it was being used for digital deviant behaviour. On account of the way and speed in which deceit and falsehoods were spreading, *Facebook* was forced to announce the launch of its third-party fact-checker project. The company began outsourcing the services of independent fact-checkers to flag and analyse disinformation. Prior to the announcement, various fact-checking organisations began collaborating with each other, creating partnerships to strengthen their position to take responsibility of the daunting task of checking what is true and what is not on social media (Ananny, 2018). Now, several years after the start of the project, there are more than 60 fact-checking organisations working with *Facebook*. Today, fact-checking has become somewhat of a cottage industry, as more organisations are being created to fact-check the internet's content (You, Vo, and Lee, 2019). In the next chapter, we shall look closer at the various global but mainly European initiatives created to do so.

In closing this section, it is necessary to add that fact-checking is very much a direct defence mechanism that naturally comes with numerous difficulties. Putting aside the sheer scale of fact-checking the whole digital ecosystem, when a story is detected and debunked, it is still not likely to be enough to undo the damage done to democracy. Say, for example, a *Facebook* post is flagged by a user as potentially fake; it then gets analysed and categorised either as true or false or something in between. However, the speed with which it has spread and gone viral might have made the damage irreversible (see Lewandowsky, Ecker and Cook, 2017). And rebuttals – a response mechanism we address below – are often not effective in changing pre-shaped perceptions. Even when a rebuttal does manage to change the mind of certain recipients, it might not be shared back to all interpreters of the initial disinformation.

News literacy

An underlying theme of this book is that whilst it has taken a relatively short amount of time for digital technologies to become a threat to democracy, there are no quick-fix solutions. The thesis of our work falls in line with most other comparable studies in that it contends that a consorted and continuous effort is required to stifle disinformation and facilitate a digital democracy that supports the public interest. Included in these studies is the widespread advocacy and development of information and news literacy across all ages and demographic standings. News literacy is currently the most significant subcategory of media literacy (Richter, 2019). It comprises three dimensions: access and use; critical understanding; and participation and production processes (ibid: 319). Similarly, the *National Association of Media Literacy Education* defines media literacy as 'the ability to access, analyze, evaluate, create, and act using all forms of communication' (2019, para. 1).

It is worth noting that media literacy has not always garnered this recognition. During the very early years of the digital era, media literacy researchers were banging the drum regarding the importance of learning media skills, but this mainly fell on deaf ears. Livingstone (2011: 13) identified a gap between aims and implementation that perhaps given more emphasis to the 'many researchers … advocating a turn to the normative', and digital democracy would not have reached its current distressing state. Nonetheless, news literacy is today recognised as arguably even more significant than fact-checking in combating deviant online behaviour; it is further considered an encompassing approach vital to holistic and deliberative democracies (Buckingham, 2019). If we are to design democracies where citizens play a central role in how they are shaped, it is crucial that channels of information – not necessarily all, but most – can be trusted. As citizens become more news literate, they will no doubt become better at evaluating which of these channels function properly and which do not. A general feeling is that by increasing news literacy, trustworthy news and information channels will rise to the surface of the information landscape, curtailing even citizen endorsements of conspiracies (Craft, Ashley and Maksl, 2017).

Accessing, evaluating, creating and acting upon news are, by and large, individual acts. The starting point for better comprehending these themes is to therefore attain a lifelong learning mindset. This entails self-reflecting and acquiring a general understanding of the inner workings of journalism, news drivers and news production more generally. In terms of self-reflection, very much *how* we understand news is based on our own beliefs, biases and ideologies.

Apart from cultivating our own mindsets, news literacy as a field of study can use other similar fields to establish itself. Communication studies, albeit more recently established than many social science disciplines, has almost 100 years of practice and understanding for news literacy to draw from. Cultural studies, political economy of communication, film studies – all significant subcategories of communications studies – have allowed us to acquire an acute understanding of the way in which ideologies drive content, how production and distribution mechanisms work and how we understand visual storytelling. Grounding news literacy within a critical understanding of communications and media can be beneficial to this new area of study, a study so crucial to digital democracy. Similarly, the field of journalism studies – a sister field to communication studies – has acquired years of actionable, applied and knowledgeable research. The field has consequently adapted to the cultural, economic, political, social and technological turns of our time and is therefore a key component in the creation of an efficient field of news literacy (see Greenwood, 2018 and Steensen and Ahva, 2017).

The intersection of digital disinformation and news literacy concerns identifying, detecting and understanding dubious information. It involves a pedagogy of how digital technologies work, which elements are used to fuel disinformation (for example, personality quizzes and clickbaits), and which to counter disinformation (for example, *Facebook*'s disputed tags). A combination of these fundamentals will help establish our resilience toward suspect news and disinformation. As we demonstrate in Chapter Five, there are a plethora of projects seeking to further our understanding of news literature and digital disinformation. The technologies available to disinformation agents and cyber troops continue to grow. It is therefore important that digital literacy curricula remain up to date. One effort in this is the construction of digital intelligence, referred to also as the 'digital quotient' (DQ Institute, 2019). It is based upon the assumption that digital literacy is a key component of the twenty-first century and will enable citizens not only to enter the workforce more effectively but also to comprehend information in a better manner, allowing them to be more active and informed (Stiakakis, Liapis and Vlachopoulou, 2019). The DQ Institute identifies eight digital competencies that are gradually being used to build a standard ranking approach, with points three and four particularly important in defending oneself against digital disinformation. These are (DQ Institute, 20019):

1. *digital identity:* the ability to build and manage a 'healthy' online and offline identity
2. *digital use:* the ability to use technology in a balanced, healthy and civic way
3. *digital safety:* the ability to understand, mitigate and manage various cyber risks through safe, responsible, and ethical use of technology
4. *digital security:* the ability to detect, avoid and manage different levels of cyber threats to protect data, devices, networks and systems

5. *digital emotional intelligence:* the ability to recognize, navigate and express emotions in one's digital intra and interpersonal interactions
6. *digital communication:* the ability to communicate and collaborate with others using digital technology
7. *digital literacy:* the ability to find, read, evaluate, synthesize, create, adapt and share information, media and technology
8. *digital rights:* the ability to understand and uphold human rights and legal rights when using technology.

Response

Awareness and communication strategies

Methodologies and techniques accumulated over the years, particularly since the beginning of the 1950s, have allowed the disciplines of marketing and public relations to flourish. Much of our knowledge in communicating strategically to mass audiences was in fact realised during the Second World War, and it is not a coincidence that advertising and public relations (PR) grew soon after (Edwards, 2018). From the 1970s onwards the growth of multinational organisations and franchises catering to a burgeoning homogeneous global audience resulted in the consolidation of the advertising and PR sectors. Strategic communication has further benefited from scientific grounding and the establishment of university degrees in these fields around the world (Falkheimer and Heide, 2018). As a result, entities are in a better position to apply strategic communication approaches. Identifying publics through effective stakeholder mapping, and the creation of applicable content strategies to engage with them, are crucial in the success of any strategic communications campaign (Gregory, 2013; Smith, 2013). Once identified, tactics involve advertising and brand storytelling (Lambert, 2009; Walter and Gioglio, 2015), media relations (Carrol, 2011) and transmedia communication (Jenkins and Green, 2013). Parallel to the expansion of these sectors, interdisciplinary academic research on behavioural economics (Thaler and Sunstein, 2009), decision-making (Kahneman, 2011), neuroscience (Sapolsky, 2017), and persuasion (Cialdini, 2006) have further shed light on our understanding of human behaviour, public opinion and perception. The work of Cass R. Sunstein and Richard Thaler on nudge theory, and Daniel Kahneman on human biases and decision-making, earned Thaler and Kahneman respective Nobel Prizes in Economics and have contributed vastly to the ways in which societies can be better organised around human behaviour.

The application of strategically communicating to the masses is the privilege not only of large corporations but also of entities such as citizen groups and civil society, activist movements, non-profit/non-governmental organisations, international bodies and other similar entities working for the public interest (Zerfass et al., 2018). Consequently, the aforementioned approaches can be used to combat disinformation in ways that bear no relation to for-profit corporate campaigns. International bodies can be more proactive in designing and implementing awareness campaigns on the dangers of digital disinformation. Decision makers, educators and youth groups can be made more conscious of the importance of news literacy (it is also relevant to note that many of these strategic approaches are actually embedded within news literacy programs). And strategic communication for combating disinformation can be applied to more seemingly unconventional approaches. For example, applying pressure on large corporations to do more in countering disinformation can be hugely beneficial on account of the resources available to such entities. One way of doing so is to motivate large organisations to support education and news literacy through corporate social responsibility programmes (Nicoli and Komodromos, 2019).

Strategic communication is consequently being considered as a discipline to combat digital disinformation once the content has been detected. This approach is therefore a defence mechanism that counters the damage of the original deviant message. Examples of this approach involve debunking, rebuttals or myth-busting. These mechanisms are used to expose falsehood and communicate truthful alternatives in a swift, strategic manner (Lewandowsky, Ecker and Cook, 2017). We should note, however, that debunking, rebuttals and myth-busting do not always work and might even backfire, as they often do not fit with people's worldviews. According to Gordon, Ecker and Lewandowsky (2019), research suggests that misinformation continues to influence people's cognition despite rebuttals and myth-busting. This phenomenon is known as 'continued-influence effect'.

Despite the continued-influence effect, giving people the factual alternative remains important, as doing so can help plant the seeds of doubt required in those who believe the fake information (Ecker, Hogan and Lewandowsky, 2017). As such, there are a growing number of debunking organisations from around the world (some fact-checkers also attempt to rebut false stories) who strive to stifle digital disinformation stories. In the following chapter, we shall address the policy measures used by the EU in using strategic communication to counter misinformation. These policies centre around the *StratCom* task forces and the newly established *Rapid Alert System*. But it remains important, precisely because of the continued-influence effect, to further our understanding of best practices in debunking, myth-busting and refuting stories. Ecker (2017: 82), for example, warns that by repeating the false story in an attempt to refute it, there is a chance that people will then forget the retraction and remember the falsehood. In one example, Ecker notes that *Politifact*, a well-known fact-checker, debunked a Trump tweet, stating, 'Of the white homicide victims in the U.S., 81% are killed by black people' (ibid: 83). The debunked *Politifact* retraction might have backfired since thousands of people would have reread the original tweet. According to the researcher, a better way might have been to state, 'Trump spreads fake statistic from Nazi source. Myth that Blacks kill 81% of white murders victims. Fact: it is only 15% (FBI statistic)'.

Finally, it is important to consider frequent perpetrators of digital disinformation. When those communicating the falsehoods are known to be serial disinformation agents, or official agents and cyber troops (for example, the numerous accusations of Russian and Iranian disinformation agents identified by *Facebook*, Iosifidis and Nicoli, 2020 and analysed in Chapter Six), then the strategy might need to be changed and made more proactive than just refuting a falsehood. Put another way, shifting strategic attention to discrediting the *source* of the disinformation campaign might be more of a priority or required simultaneously with responding to detected deviant messages. This is a more aggressive communication strategy that places the discourse of disinformation very much in an 'information warfare' climate and is a large reason why resilience to hybrid threats is important.

Technological advancements

Artificial intelligence (AI)

According to the European Parliamentary Research Service study on AI (EPRS, 2019: 12), 'Artificial Intelligence refers to advanced forms of machine learning, generally classified as algorithmic processes powered by advanced computing techniques such as neural networks and including in particular Deep Learning'. Machine learning, on the other hand, is a subset of AI 'in which a programme is built to alter itself, without explicit human intervention or further human coding' (Woolley, 2020: 86).

Facebook and *Twitter* have for several years now begun to adopt AI and machine learning to combat disinformation. *Facebook*, for instance, although hiring over 5,000 staff to identify hatred or offensive content (which seems to be the most effective way of identifying bad content), has also invested heavily in AI and machine learning to identify disinformation – particularly the kind derived from computational propaganda (Iosifidis and Nicoli, 2020; Woolley, 2020). In the 2018 US congressional hearings over *Facebook*'s involvement in the US presidential elections, Mark Zuckerberg apparently mentioned the words AI over 30 times (Harwell, 2018) within the context of how to solve digital disinformation – again showing the company's commitment to using such technology. Tools that have been used by social media to detect bad content include *Deeptext*. According to *Facebook*, this software is 'a deep learning-based text understanding engine that can understand with near-human accuracy the textual content of several thousand posts per second, spanning more than 20 languages' (Abdulkader, Lakshmiratan and Zhang, 2016).

Other companies such as *Google* have used similar technologies (Woolley, 2020:100). The logic in the use of such AI tools is that disinformation might follow specific lexical structures that the software can pick up (Choy and Chong, 2018). It derives from the semantics of the lexical field of research that involves the analysis of words and how they are structured together. Put another way, words acquire a meaning by being compared to other words in the sentence (Trier, 1931). In this manner, defence AI can comprehend which sentences use a natural language manner of processing (NLP) (see Ibrahim and Safieddine, 2020). A recent paper with over 30 co-authors from an artificial intelligence company based in San Francisco called *OpenAI* described how they modelled a deep learning NLP system with over 175 billion parameters known as GPT – 3 (Brown et al., 2020). According to the paper, it can complete linguistic tasks just like a human. Although the paper recognises weaknesses in connecting sentences, the research could be extremely dangerous in the hands of disinformation agents. In fact, the *OpenAI* researchers have been reluctant to share the source code (of even the earlier GPT – 2 model) precisely for this reason (Tiernan, 2020). One can therefore imagine what it would mean if such technology did indeed fall into the wrong hands, especially when combined with other audio-visual deepfake technologies.

Weaponisation of computationally automated content used to confuse, polarise and provoke deviant behaviour cannot be countered easily, regardless of what the social media platforms do. But in the same manner in which these technologies are adopted by disinformation agents, they can also be used as a defence mechanism to identify the content, flag it and categorise it. This has thus far worked because existing computational propaganda is not hitherto intelligent, requiring only basic level coding to put such technologies into practice (Woolley, 2020). The fear is that the technology will gradually become smarter and harder to identify. Unless a more stringent policy is devised, AI as a countermechanism will be harder to apply. Although it is beyond the scope of this book to dissect these issues, it might always be the case that more offensively oriented AI (that is, the agents designing disinformation and spreading it) will always have an advantage over defensively oriented AI (detection algorithms used to identify bad content or fact-check it one way or another). If we add that social media companies – driven by profits and shareholder pressures – will want to patent and protect their innovations rather than share them with others, the advantage of disinformation agents seems destined to endure. This has also been the conclusive result of a large-scale European Parliament study on the use of AI in combating disinformation (EPRS, 2019).

Blockchain

Another promising technology in the fight against digital disinformation (one that essentially overlaps with AI) is the blockchain. The decentralised modus of the technology is undoubtedly playing a major role in disrupting significant industries, firms, institutions and individuals. Tapscott and Tapscott (2016) posit that despite the promise of flatter organisations in the twenty-first century, most firms are still hierarchical in nature. According to the authors, the blockchain will disrupt organisational structures to the extent that many will surely become vastly flatter. Yet the blockchain is destined to disrupt more than just organisational configurations. Its affordances are already beginning to alter numerous societal structures, in particular those that require a certain level of trust to function. For example, blockchains have inherent attributes that favour the information ecosystem. They are completely transparent, they are immutable so the original data cannot be altered, they work on an open network and they are completely secure. If we consider that disinformation serves the interests of centralised bodies that are hard to trace, one begins to realise the impact such a technology will have. The decentralised nature of the blockchain is therefore destined to disrupt the information ecosystem. A decentralised approach toward news dissemination means that priority can be placed on the content. The blockchain news story travelling from one user to another will serve everyone's interest as no single party can control it. The blockchain in news media therefore has the potential to be a game changer, since the content on the information ecosystem that works on a decentralised blockchain network can be officially verified (Dickson, 2017). Again, this holds true whether the content is advertising or editorial based. Furthermore, access to archived content will also be secure to store and retrieve safely. According to Ivancsics (2019),

> blockchains can serve as secure registries for important metadata, such as a story's time of publication, bylines, tags, and so forth. As a tool for sales teams, blockchain-based registries can rank and filter trusted advertisers and ad content, and become an alternative to the often inscrutable auction-mechanism of digital ad exchanges.

There are caveats nonetheless that have nothing to do with the technological advancements of each breakthrough innovation. If, for example, users are aware of the source of their content and of how it got to them on account of the blockchain, they will be in a better position to decide as to whether to redistribute it. This is particularly the case when the majority of the public are in agreement. This might happen with a health crisis such as the COVID-19 pandemic, for example. In such a case, politicians, public opinion and the scientific consensus are more likely to be in agreement with each other and, when identifying the source of the content, will not disseminate it to their own network. Yet as illustrated in Chapter Three, when the content is vague, divisive or personal, for example, with political opinion pieces, the affordances of the blockchain might not be enough to keep people from sharing content as their motivations might be a priori deceitful. If a supporter of a serving government wants to gather more support for that government, they might be more inclined to share a fake story despite knowing it is fake. And it is precisely on such occurrences that social media platforms can take more decisive action; once the disinformation is identified from the source, they should be more inclined to take it down before it spreads.

Conclusion

Disinformation over digital networks has not been resolved as of yet (there are of course no guarantees that they ever will be). In fact, liberal democracies are only now beginning to establish typologies of definitions and understandings of the scope and motivations of disinformation agents. These understandings are first and foremost required in order to counter the deviant phenomenon. For many, digital disinformation is instigated by profit motives; agents of this type have found ways to emotionally stimulate the curiosity of unsuspected online users who, by consuming the content, generate incomes for the agents. Others do so to instil their own ideological beliefs. They often work silently on online bulletin board, recruiting like-minded agents before attempting to increase the virality of content through disinformation. The most ominous kind are those that are part of hybrid threats. These consist of operations from foreign countries searching for weaknesses in open democracies in order to take advantage of them.

As liberal democracies become more familiar with digital disinformation typologies, they will become better equipped to find solutions to combat the phenomenon. A predominant understanding entails that efforts and resources to combat disinformation must come from numerous stakeholders with different backgrounds. Borne out of these backgrounds, the four approaches identified in this chapter to combat digital disinformation consist of fact-checking, news literacy, strategic communication and technology. To put these in practice requires systemic efforts as well as large investments in both knowledge and resources. This becomes even more pertinent since liberal democracies often find themselves fighting with the same tools as deviant disinformation agents but on the defence instead of the offence. Whether a deviant agent spreads digital disinformation or an entity is countering, the tools used are ultimately similar, creating, as we have mentioned in the introductory chapter, a cultural, political, social and, importantly, a technological arms race between deviant agents, liberal democracies and unsuspicious digital users.

As social media gain popularity, it is becoming more difficult for them to oversee and control disinformation content strategies used by agents. This is despite a study by Allcott, Gentkow and Yu (2019) positing that misinformation on *Facebook* declined during the period between December 2016 and July 2018. In another study on how *Facebook* responds to disinformation, Iosifidis and Nicoli (2020: 6) noticed that 'deviant initiators ... adapt to online changes' very quickly, making it difficult for the platforms to self-regulate. Regardless of how many fact-checkers *Facebook* uses and how highly sophisticated its machine-learning processes are, it has itself admitted that more policy reform frameworks are required across the sector (Zuckerberg, 2019; see also Chapter Five). In a similar vein, Samuel Woolley (2020), a growing authority on automation and AI persuasion, gives a damning account of how these technologies can easily be crafted and manipulated by quasi-skilled coders. Worryingly, Woolley argues that we are only at the start of a disinformation age that will intensify as technologies continue to advance.

Notes

1 It should be noted here that *Twitter* has also begun to identify and categorise foreign manipulation operations.
2 The media industry has been heavily criticised throughout the latter 'deregulation' period of the twentieth century (see Bagdikian, 1983; Herman and Chosmky, 1988; Garnham, 1990). Criticism came in the form of the rise of soft news content; the consolidation of the sector; heavy reliance on advertising; and stakeholder pressures to earn higher profits that ultimately affected editorial content. All these concerns have been facilitated by a neoliberal wave sweeping through the last three decades of the previous century. Apart from criticism derived from an economically determined turn, the media have also been condemned for ideological biases, with journalism often denounced for the practice of selective exposure (Iyengar and Hahn, 2009).

5

EUROPEAN POLICY STRATEGIES IN COMBATING DIGITAL DISINFORMATION

Introduction

In this chapter, we turn our attention to policy efforts in combating digital disinformation within the European Union (EU). The EU has earned a reputation through its various rulemaking bodies as the world's principal digital watchdog (Harris, 2020). However, contrary to its tighter approach towards digital privacy, EU digital disinformation policies, that culminated in 2018, have thus far been of a light touch, with legislators cautious of intervening in areas concerning freedom of expression (Iosifidis and Andrews, 2020). Since 2018, a series of global events, comprised of an unprecedented global health pandemic and increased unrest around the world, have exposed the weaknesses of a light-touch approach and have facilitated further turbulence across liberal democracies. As a consequence, we have seen an amplification of digital disinformation content[1] that will potentially induce policy-makers to adopt tighter interventionist policies.

On the surface, it seems that social media are willing to take part in the efforts of policy-makers and civil society in fighting back against digital disinformation. This has not always been the case, but the platforms are now genuinely doing more to advance technologies and invest in more resources. Such examples can be seen in their support and use of more independent fact-checkers, in hiring more staff, through various global programs, in research to increase the use of AI and machine learning, in supporting the news media sector (for example, the *Facebook* Journalism Project and *Google* DNI [Digital News Innovation]), and in helping improve digital literacy rates around the world (*Google's* Be Internet Awesome and *Twitter*'s partnership with UNESCO's Global Media and Information Literacy Week). Indeed, the platforms are publicly announcing their support of a more regulated sector. 'I believe good regulation may hurt *Facebook*'s business in the near term but it will be better for everyone, including us, over the long term', stated Mark Zuckerberg in a *Financial Times* op-ed (Zuckerberg, 2020). He was at the time echoing similar sentiments he had expressed at a European conference only a few days earlier in Munich (BBC, 2020), as well as those of a *Washington Post* (and *New York Times)* piece a year before (Zuckerberg, 2019). The fact that Zuckerberg's latest support for tighter regulation came during a US presidential election year and shortly before the outbreak of the COVID-19 pandemic is of critical importance because, as we have mentioned, social media disinformation content has since been amplified. *Facebook*, it seems, wants to avoid a repeat of the criticism that came its way following the 2016 Russian interventions of the previous presidential elections (see Chapter Six).

Yet as we shall illustrate in this chapter, social media are not doing enough. They have, overall, not been transparent in how their algorithms function in designing user news feeds and timelines, and despite its call for more regulation, *Facebook* still permits unrestricted political advertising on its platforms. On this topic, other platforms are doing better. *Twitter* has eliminated political advertising altogether, whereas *Google* has tightened its own policies on political advertising, particularly those concerning micro-targeting. In previous chapters, we described how advertising on social media has been a thorny point in the digital landscape. Napoli (2019: 39) has called it the 'advertising challenge' in which the provider of audience attention also ominously provides audience data in a vertically integrated manner. It is an example of how technology in this space is advancing at a faster rate than policy reform, and it is our hope therefore that policy measures will continue to investigate ways to regulate and scrutinise technological advancements, even if these measures are restricted to playing catch up. The methodologies used by Cambridge Analytica to give its clients competitive advantages over their rivals is a case in point because those same methods violated the privacy rights of millions of users (see Chapters One and Four). Technological progress too often exceeds our comprehension regarding the threats involved when implementing them; this is true even of those designing the technology. In this chapter, we demonstrate how EU policy recommendations concerning digital advertising have sought to offer the platforms self-regulation options, but here again, we could argue that disinformation roaming the digital information ecosystem has grown at an even faster rate, particularly with the added threats of misinformation associated with the COVID-19 pandemic.

Reforming social media's political advertising polices is of the utmost importance, but it is not the only area of concern. Another that requires persistent policy reform as a way of combating digital disinformation involves support of the news media. It is essential that the sector remains trustworthy and reliable. If users can distinguish and trust the source of the information they consume, it weakens the efforts of disinformation agents who promote content in an ambiguous manner (Woolley, 2020). Allowing users to be more involved in the journalistic process is a burgeoning requirement of the digital age. One cannot be involved with the journalistic process of content created by a bot, for example, because there is no process involved other than computational automation. In being more involved, therefore, trust can be re-established between citizens and news media. It is the ultimate bond in liberal democracies. News media, and research on improving audiences' engagement with news content, consequently needs to be supported in a more deliberate manner. And here too, the platforms are directly involved as we have portrayed in previous chapters. As long as news media continue to be consumed on social media, the sector will need to work closer with them, particularly since this is where younger audiences are consuming news.

Using the exploratory backdrop of the previous chapter, policy strategies highlighted in the chapter involve fact-checking procedures (while improving, they need more standardised, global efforts), digital and news literacy programmes, empowering consumers that use social media, empowering the research community to work closer with these platforms and strategic communication efforts, especially for hybrid threats. We should mention from the outset that we concentrate our analyses mainly on regional efforts of the European Council, the European Parliament and, importantly, the European Commission. While we are aware of how EU Member States, the UK and of course US states individually take policy measures on digital issues such as disinformation into their own hands, and in most cases are even encouraged to do so, we take a more macro-level view. It is our belief that in most cases, macro-level recommendations such as the ones described below usually trickle down to micro-level application and deliberation.

Europe's digital disinformation policies

The European Union has gone to great lengths to mitigate the risks of digital technologies. The right to be forgotten in the mid-noughties (the legal right of citizens to delete personal information online) and the General Data Protection Regulation (GDPR) (a regulation that protects citizens from how their data is used online) instituted in 2016 reflect the European Union's commitment in regulating the digital ecosystem. It has further opened anti-trust investigations into numerous large technology companies in an effort to create a level playing field. In doing so, by extension, it hopes to create a window of opportunities for European startups that allow them to flourish, scale up and become significant global players (Chee, 2019). The EU has further announced plans via a White Paper to amend digital policies in order to create a single European data space (EC, 2020a). The objective of these policies is to offer further incentives to EU companies so as to remain competitive in the digital data sector, particularly in the race for artificial intelligence (AI) tech and Green transition. However, while the EU's interventionist policies over digital privacy have been palpable, and rightly so (Flew and Suzor, 2019), its digital disinformation policies have been slower to develop. The EU has hitherto instead chosen a self-regulatory policy framework route. However, with the outbreak of the COVID-19 pandemic, escalating fears of further polarisation, increased hate speech, intensifying racism and violent protests that have also led to looting (triggered by the US George Floyd incident in mid-2020), as well as continuing hybrid threats from around the world, a more concerted effort to intervene, through direct policy, seems to be growing.

The EU's macro-level fight against digital disinformation dates back to early 2015. Since then, several policies and recommendations have become established, and we can consider them as signpost indicators not just in the EU but also around the world. These stem from various EU bodies, and in the table below, we identify the main milestones that have made the most impact. The StratCom task forces, although below are bundled into one section, focus on the East StratCom task force since this is where the European External Action Service is concentrating its efforts. Chapter Six will illustrate the reasons as to why Russia is considered a continuous threat for open democratic processes around the world and hence why the East StratCom is the most heavily supported. We then examine the work done in bolstering the region's capabilities and resilience to external threats. The most significant policy of this milestone has been the establishment of the Hybrid Threats Cell. The next milestone concerns our most relevant analysis. It involves the *Multi-Dimensional Approach to Disinformation: Report of the Independent High Level Group on Fake News and Online Disinformation* (EC, 2018a). The recommendations made in the report have become the blueprint for the Commission's own policy reform on *Tackling Online Disinformation* (EC, 2018b) as well as the actual output, the self-regulating propositions of the code of practice (EC, 2018c) and the action plan adopted shortly after (EC, 2018f). Table 5.1 illustrates these milestones, and in the sections below, we analyse each one in detail.

StratCom Task Forces

The East StratCom (strategic communication) Task Force was created following a European Council meeting in 2015. In that March 20 convention, it was concluded that in order to counter Russia's ongoing disinformation campaign against the EU and Ukraine, proactive actions focusing on communication strategies were required to safeguard the region and its Eastern neighbouring areas (European Council, 2015). The resulting action plan drafted three months later stressed the importance of establishing a communication team that implemented strategic communication approaches that would, in turn, 'maintain an overall coordinating and monitoring role in relation to its implementation' (European Sources Online, 2015: 1). *The Action Plan on Strategic Communication*, as it was titled, outlined a series of measures in which the communications task force would be responsible in executing. These included the support of media freedoms from Russian digital interference and the communication of EU policies in eastern EU regions. The communications team, headquartered in Brussels, was established in September 2015 as part of the European External Action Service (EEAS). The task force and its overall efforts have been criticised as inadequate

TABLE 5.1 Important European initiatives on countering disinformation

ACTION	DATE	EU BODY
StratCom Task Force(s)	September 2015	European External Action Service
Joint Framework on countering hybrid threats – a European Union response/joint communication on increasing resilience and bolstering capabilities to address hybrid threats	April 2016/ June 2018	High Representative of the Union for Foreign Affairs and Security Policy/European Commission/ European Defence Agency/EU Member States
A Multi-Dimensional Approach to Disinformation: Report of the Independent High Level Group on Fake News and Online Disinformation	March 2018	European Commission/High Level Expert Group
Tackling Online Disinformation: A European Approach	April 2018	European Commission
The Code of Practice	October 2018	European Commission
Action Plan Against Disinformation	December 2018	European Commission

and insufficient (for example, Rettman, 2017). Eastern bloc countries, in particular, are seeking more persuasive measures in the form of the establishment of a Russian-speaking television channel (Panichi, 2015), and this is possibly the reason why the *Tackling Online Disinformation* report (EC, 2018b) further addresses the issue of adopting a more thorough strategic communications approach to tackling disinformation.

East StratCom is made up of strategic communication professionals who seek to monitor and identity media from various regions, mainly across the Eastern European bloc. It has thus far archived over 7,000 pro-Kremlin disinformation examples (see Chapter Six). The task force has concentrated its efforts on myth-busting and rebuttals across the EU and in the Eastern Partnership Countries. To do so, it has created an open access subscription-based newsletter, a website and a relatively strong presence on social media platforms known as *EU vs. Disinformation (EUvsDISINFO.eu)*. The task force also organises training for EU institutions and briefings for Member State governments, journalists and researchers. Arguably, its strongest tool is its website, which archives much of the above information in one location. Its tone is easy to follow, presumably to attract younger as well as older generations, and it has up-to-date information on digital disinformation. In addition to the East StratCom task force, the EU has created two more task forces to defend digital disinformation from other regions. These are the Western Balkans StratCom task force, which covers those areas, and the South StratCom task force, covering the Arab-speaking world and focusing on Islamist radicalisation (Rettman, 2017). Judging from the lack of information on the Western Balkans and South task forces (no online presence), the EEAS's investment in them is at an early stage and it is choosing to concentrate efforts on the East StratCom task force.

Joint Framework on Countering Hybrid Threats/ Joint Communication on Increasing Resilience and Bolstering Capabilities to Address Hybrid Threats

The EU's High Representative for Foreign Affairs and Security Policy represents and coordinates the Common Foreign and Security Policy of the European Union. This entity brings together several bodies that together deal with foreign affairs and security policies and work closely with the European External Action Service. The *Joint Framework on Countering Hybrid Threats* (EC, 2016) and the *Joint Communication on Increasing Resilience and Bolstering Capabilities to Address Hybrid Threats* (EC, 2018d) are significant because they conceptualise and classify the dangers involved in hybrid threats as highly destabilising to the democratic process. As such, for these reports, the High Representative has worked together not only with the Commission services and the European Defence Agency but also in consultation with the EU Member States in order to meet several key objectives in combating hybrid threats. These are:

- Recognising hybrid threats (identifying key vulnerabilities);
- Improving awareness (through information exchange and strategic communication);
- Building resilience (that is, the capacity to withstand stress and recover from the challenges);
- Increasing cooperation on hybrid threats (with third countries and with NATO);
- Responding to crisis and recovering.

Based on these objectives, the reports outlined 22 specific actions detailing the manner in which it will meet its goals. As a result, the EU Hybrid Fusion Cell was established in 2016 and is considered of vital importance in fighting digital disinformation. Set up within the EU Intelligence and Situation Centre, its purpose is to monitor information threats by foreign actors (EC, 2018b). The report also helped establish the European Centre of Excellence for Countering Hybrid Threats in order to exchange information and best practices with the North Atlantic Treaty Organisation (EC, 2018b). The EU has on numerous occasions stressed the importance of all Member States agreeing on strategies on the application of the above actions. Yet coordinating and harmonising such high-level strategies across the Member States is no easy task as each Member State comes with their own needs and desires when it comes to hybrid threats.

The 2018 *Joint Communication on Increasing Resilience and Bolstering Capabilities to Address Hybrid Threats* (EC, 2018d) further bolsters these goals, particularly following the nerve-agent attack in Salisbury in the UK. The two communications complement the work done not only by the East StratCom task force in fighting digital disinformation but also by the two task forces created to cover the Western Balkans and the Arab-speaking world.

A multidimensional approach to disinformation: Report of the Independent High Level Group on Fake News and Online Disinformation

The European initiatives and policy actions analysed thus far have sought to curtail *foreign* digital disinformation agents. As such they have been the responsibility of the Common Foreign and Security Policy and the European External Action Service. *The High Level Group Multi-Dimensional Report* published in March 2018 (EC, 2018a) and the resulting European Commission's *The European Approach for Tackling Online Disinformation*, released in April 2018 (EC, 2018b), are attempts to confront *all* forms of digital disinformation and were catalysts for the creation of a vital, albeit non-binding, code of practice later that same year (also analysed below) (EC, 2018c). The High-Level Expert Group report dates back to late 2016, shortly following the US elections. Concerns regarding digital disinformation were continuing to develop despite the aforementioned policy efforts. In December 2016, then-president of the European Parliament, Martin Schulz, called for a European solution to tackle disinformation (euinfocenter, 2017). This was followed by a resolution on 'Online Platforms and the Digital Single Market' in June 2017 (Shattock, 2020). Reflecting exactly how high on the agenda the fight against disinformation had become, the European Commission brought forward a series of consultations with a wide range of stakeholders and surveys that were conducted across the Union. The Commission also launched a public consultation, receiving 2,986 replies, and a Eurobarometer opinion poll covering the 28 Member States (EC, 2018b). The research explored EU citizens' attitudes to fake news and digital disinformation. It specifically covered issues concerning trust in news, and confidence in identifying news (and disinformation). The study further sought to deconstruct how EU citizens perceive the dangers and threats of disinformation for democracy. The data gathered and analysed by the EU showed high levels of concern across the region. As a result, in November 2017, the European Commission set up a High-Level Expert Group (HLEG). The group consisted of academics, news media, civil society organisations and online platforms, and by April 2018, it had drafted the report on how it would tackle the phenomenon (EC, 2018b).

The report set the tone for the EU's response on fighting back against digital disinformation, and has since become one of the most significant global policy recommendation reports concerning the phenomenon. The conclusions made in the report are based on five intervention area pillars: to enhance transparency of the digital information ecosystem, to promote and sharpen the use of media and information literacy, to develop tools for empowering users and journalists, to safeguard the diversity and sustainability of European news media and to calibrate the effectiveness of the responses through continuous research on the impact of disinformation (EC, 2018a: 35).

1. *Transparency of the information ecosystem*

Transparency across the information ecosystem is paramount in combating digital disinformation. The key objective in increasing transparency is to make it easier for online users who are consuming information to trust the content more. Once this is achieved, then media and information literacy (the next pillar) can be more effective in the fight against digital disinformation. A starting point for this to succeed is for the content's source to be easily identified. Ultimately, even digitally illiterate users should be able to better comprehend the digital content they are consuming (see Chapter Four). If citizens have an understanding of how to access the sources of digital media value chains, it will be harder for disinformation agents to achieve their goals. Of course, it would make more sense if such mechanisms were automated through technological advancements such as those touched on in the previous chapter, but based on the speed with which disinformation agents adapt to technological change (Woolley, 2020), the ability of users to individually identify devious sources will always be relevant. Against this backdrop, the HLEG report specifically identifies three areas of cooperation whereby stakeholders can ensure high transparency standards (EC, 2018a: 22–24). These are to increase the transparency of funding sources so that all sponsored content is clearly identifiable, to increase the transparency of online news sources and journalistic processes and, finally, to increase the transparency and efficiency of fact-checking practices.

During the period leading up to the HLEG report, social media platforms provided little information on sponsored content and advertising expenditure on their respective platforms. Yet addressing this issue in an effective manner, for example by disrupting the advertising revenue streams of disinformation agents, can significantly diminish disinformation content. Especially problematic is when targeted political advertising is practiced on social media (Tambini, 2017) since the platforms are not under the same legal obligations of transparency as news media outlets. They have therefore self-regulated at different speeds, which has resulted in them having different impacts on digital democracy. This was pointed out by the code of practice sounding group as a serious roadblock. Had there been quantifiable key performance indicators on how the platforms would be regulated, political advertising transparency would not be a persisting problem. *Twitter* has banned political advertising, but *Google*, and particularly *Facebook*, have been reluctant to do so (*The Guardian*, 2020). 'Political message reach should be earned' noted *Twitter* CEO Jack Dorsey in October 2019 (Friedersdorf, 2019). The implication made by Dorsey is that unless a politician announces something newsworthy, something making people follow or retweet their content, then it should not be paid for in order to be consumed. Conversely, *Facebook*'s policy allows political ads to run on its platform even if the content is misleading. The technology giant supports its decision on the basis of freedom of speech and a lack of regulation.

> We're updating our Ad library to increase the level of transparency … ultimately, we don't think decisions about political ads should be made by private companies, which is why we are arguing for regulation that would apply across the industry. The Honest Ads Act is a good example – legislation that we endorse and many parts of which we've already implemented – and we are engaging with policy makers in the European Union and elsewhere to press the case for regulation too. Frankly, we believe the sooner Facebook and other companies are subject to democratically accountable rules on this the better. In the absence of regulation, Facebook and other companies are left to design their own policies.

These were the words of *Facebook*'s director of product management, Rob Leathern (2020), announced in a *Facebook* blog post. In the same post, Leathren describes several updates of its political ads policies. These include more control from users to choose how they are reached and a mechanism allowing users to see fewer political and social issue ads. Nothing nonetheless was mentioned on censoring political ads that contain misleading or untrue content. *Google*, on the other hand, has political content policies that comply with local legal requirements (for example, silence periods several days/hours before an election). In its own announcements platform on its blog, the company VP of product management, Scott Spencer, wrote, 'We provide a publicly accessible, searchable, and downloadable transparency report of election ad content and spending on our platforms, going beyond what's offered by most other advertising media' (Spencer, 2019). *Google* has also set itself restrictions that would otherwise allow advertisers to micro-target users who fit specific profiles. These tools in the past included 'Custom Affinity', 'Custom In-Market', 'Remarketing', 'Customer Match', 'Similar Audiences', 'onboarded DMP lists', '1P data' and '3P data'.

The second area of collaboration identified in the report involves online news media outlets becoming more reliable and trustworthy. Trust can be defined as an individual's perception of the reliability of another entity. It is vital that news media are protected and supported to assuage the burgeoning tendencies of social and political polarisation around the world particularly with identified correlations between trust in news and political polarisation and unrest (EBU, 2018a: 4). News media trust has steadily been in decline as the digitalisation of communications has expanded (Peters and Broersma, 2012). This is despite a recent rise in news media trust reported by various studies (e.g. Jones, 2018; Matsa et al., 2018). One reason could be that news-media trust reached a low point in 2016 and has gradually risen since then. Europeans long value the role of journalism in liberal democracies, and recent trends show certain edifying results. For example, younger Europeans trust digital news outlets less than linear news media such as print and broadcast, albeit they do not use these channels as much (Matsa et al., 2018). There are also regional differences in trust as the European north seems more trusting of news sources than the south. The 2018 Eurobarometer's trust in media report also confirms a widening gap between broadcast and new media whereas social networks are trusted the least (EBUa, 2018: 4). Since younger cohorts are consuming digital media more than linear media, policy recommendations are needed to support journalist reliability and trustworthiness on online networks and on social media in particular.

News media becoming more reliable and trustworthy requires journalistic transparency, mainly achieved by making content more visible through source indicators, regardless of which platform users are consuming from. Much of this was discussed in Chapter Four. Technological advancements such as blockchains in journalism and artificial intelligence (AI) and machine learning support can offer clear indicators of sources. Social media are also contributing solutions that verify news organisation sources (see below). However, knowing the source of the content is not the only parameter required to increase trust. More efforts are needed to develop professional journalistic codes of conduct, regardless of the political leanings of the outlet. The aforementioned studies by EBU (2018a) and Matsa et al. (2018) highlighted the need of citizens to know more about *how* the stories are researched. Citizens further feel the need to understand the journalistic process more, while also desiring to know how journalists and news media outlets can be held accountable for their work (Heyamoto and Milbourn, 2018).

One vital point to consider is the relationship between social media platforms and digital news publishers. It would make sense if the two most significant stakeholder groups of the information ecosystem collaborate more closely in identifying policies that safeguard quality news in liberal democracies. In a similar manner in which sponsored content over social media platforms requires continuous reforming, mechanisms supporting quality journalism need to be constantly improving too. Certain changes over the past several years have been made by social media platforms (Iosifidis and Nicoli, 2020) that allow users to identify trustworthy news media. *Facebook*, for example, has a 'news feed preferences' option in its settings that empowers users to design their own news feed. Both *Twitter* and *Facebook* also have a blue verification badge authenticating pages and accounts. One of the most important elements of social media is to allow pages to be deemed trustworthy or not. While *Facebook*, in particular, has made efforts in rating trust, more needs to be done in collaboration with publishers and with *Facebook* users to better 'rank' content. Doing so will further allow these outlets to build stronger foundations of quality and trust required in the digital era (see the analysis below on empowering users and journalists).

One collaborative initiative mentioned in the EU report is that of the *Trust Project*. This is a consortium of news companies from around the world searching for transparency standards. Within the consortium, social media and search engines are included as external partners. On the website's (thetrustproject.org) description section, it states,

> Over two years, Trust Project researchers interviewed people in the U.S. and Europe to find out what's important to them when it comes to news. It turns out they don't just want to weed out imposters. They want to know who wrote or produced a story, what expertise they have, and whether the publisher has an agenda. Transparency matters. Lehrman took the research and invited top news leaders around the world to build a digital standard that meets people's needs: The Trust Indicators.

Global standards and collaborative efforts between all news media stakeholders is indeed helpful in combatting digital disinformation. Examples such as the *Trust Project* and the efforts made to create tools that empower users allow for easier news literacy curricula to be designed so that students can acquire the skills to identify quality news media outlets on channels other than their own. Nonetheless, more still needs to be done to protect quality news media and the vital role they have in protecting democracies around the world. The UK's *Cairncross Review* on sustainable journalism (Cairncross, 2019) highlights some noteworthy new models for how policies might help support news media. One significant recommendation is that governments should explore direct funding options for local news and that more significance should be placed on public interest news. Exploring such policy options might indeed allow users to regain trust in news media as we become more accustomed to identifying quality journalism.

The third point of the EC report supporting transparency involves actions to increase the transparency and efficiency of fact-checking practices, predominately by supporting 'the creation of European Centres for interdisciplinary and independently evidence-based research' (EC, 2018a: 24). By 2016, over 60 per cent of fact-checking organisations in the EU were independent ventures and were not tied to specific media groups. During that same year, 'at least 34 permanent sources of political fact-checking sites are active in 20 different European countries from Ireland to Turkey' (Graves and Cherubini, 2016: 8). In 2019, ahead of the May EU Parliamentary Elections, 19 news organisations collaborated to create *FactCheckEU* in order to fact-check political rhetoric and misinformation (Funke and Benkelman, 2019). One example of a European centre for fact-checking is the Social Observatory for Disinformation and Social Media Analysis (SOMA). At the time of writing, the observatory had grown to 65 organisations from 23 countries. SOMA is also highly collaborative amongst its members with a high output of publications. The initiative falls under the European Union's Horizon 2020 research funding scheme. SOMA's members include researchers, fact-checkers and news media from across the EU, and it uses several tools to fight disinformation through verification software created by the *Athens Technology Center* (ATC) and *Deutsche Welle*. These tools, according to the researchers (Guarino et al., 2020: 445), are able to monitor disinformation through python-based software used for text and graph mining. Put another way, possible disinformation identified by SOMA can be tracked over both time and space in order to verify the content (ibid., 437). The software can detect disinformation from datasets on technology platforms and relate them to sentiment, polarisation and network analyses. From a policy analysis perspective however, little is mentioned on how the platforms respond to the detection once flagged. This is of course of no fault of the platform, but more nonetheless needs to be done to understand the actual process of debunking and the way citizens respond to it. This relevant point, that fact-checking and debunking are two separate tools, was analysed in the previous chapter.

On a global level, the standout institution on fact-checking is the *International Fact-Checking Network* (IFCN), which runs as a unit of the *Poynter Institute*. Its role is to bring together fact-checkers worldwide in order to collaborate on best practices in the field. Importantly, the IFCN has struck up partnerships with *Facebook* and *Google*. Both use fact-checkers that are members of the network. *Google's* search engine results and *Facebook* content on news feeds are now fact-checked via an internationally agreed code of practices. These are, a commitment to non-partisanship and to being honest in regard to corrections, and to the transparency of sources, funding and methodologies used (IFCN, 2020).

2. *Media and information literacy*

Chapter Four demonstrated the significance of acquiring digital skills in contemporary societies. Echoing this notion, the EU regards digital literacy as one of the most crucial skills of the twenty-first century and in fighting back against digital disinformation. Policy recommendations and support of digital literacy programmes are therefore in abundance and are reflected in numerous citing's in EU policy reports, consultations and directives. The HLEG report (2018a: 25) states that 'media and information literacy is acquiring a strategic importance for digital citizenship as basic educational competences were for citizens of the industrial age'. Yet the report also highlights several obstacles, notably, a need to include media literacy in the OECD PISA rankings and to develop a more comprehensive EU and Member State approach to adding such curricula within courses. It recommends integrating media literacies within national schools, training teachers and engaging with libraries and fact-checkers. It further supports such programmes for all ages, which again is imperative in covering ground on the digital divide. Within this context, the Audiovisual Media Services Directive (AVMSD) reiterates the value of acquiring knowledge to use and create media content responsibly and safely. Furthermore, the directive has established a legal framework prompting more efforts from the EU and the Member States but also more efforts from platforms such as *Facebook* and *YouTube* (EP, 2018).

The European Union's Media Literacy Week, an initiative similar to other Media Literacy Week Events organised around the world, was launched in 2019 with the objective of promoting media literacy projects across the EU.[2] The initiative allows entities and efforts from all Member States to showcase the work done on promoting media literacy. These are further enriched by panel discussions, workshops and stimulating political dialogue with institutional leaders (Media4Democracy, 2020). It is worth mentioning here that EU standards on media literacy vary. In Sweden and Italy, for example, information literacy is part of the curricula in schools. While there are initiatives across other EU states to follow in these footsteps, the speed in which they are being implemented differs considerably.

While educational bodies continue to add media literacy in school curricula catered for younger cohorts, a plethora of workshops, training and tools continue to expand across the EU for various other ages. According to Media4Democracy (2020), one such example is the Better Internet for Kids platform curated by the Safer Internet Centres. This programme is inspired by another global effort in media literacy known as Safer Internet Day (saferinternetday.org). In the EU, the initiative is organised with the support of the European Commission and concentrates mainly on digital issues concerning the safety of children online, addressing issues such as cyberbullying and the recognition of harmful content. The value of these events involves the participation of schools and governments, but also in activating other players vis-à-vis the support of sponsors (mainly telecommunication companies) in enriching them and in mobilising children to participate. To summarise, the EU has followed a similar path to UNESCO in its recognition of the importance of citizens acquiring digital skills and media literacy. This is witnessed in the EU's literature and support of many such projects. An overview of the media literacy projects appearing in the EU repository of events that are on show at the EU's Media Literacy Week illustrates a palpable growth in training and workshops on media literacy but also specifically in those dealing with methods on how to use social media platforms to combat disinformation (EC, 2020b). The next section of the HLEG report overlays this point with an added emphasis on training for media professionals.

3. *Empowerment of users and journalists*

It is imperative that social media's tools to combat digital disinformation are functional enough for users and media professionals to use and understand. This argument is highlighted in the report in this third point, whereby these tools are described predominantly as 'aggregate quality signals' (EC, 2018a: 27) and consist of identity labels, source transparency indicators and verified content labels. Doing so will improve the way in which users personally comprehend and evaluate content they receive through social media. Although this point does not imply a direct link with media literacy, by empowering users with an understanding of how platform tools function, curricula can be designed in an easier way for students to learn and understand the functions. As aforementioned, the blue verification flags used by *Twitter* and *Facebook* consist of such examples. Blue flag verification allows the entity to be identified with a sort of built-in reputation badge. In order to receive blue flag verifications, users requesting them are required to provide certain documents that prove they are who they say they are.

In previous chapters, we described how social media platforms avoid the notion of being seen as arbiters of truth, preferring rather to be seen as technology companies offering blank canvases for users to generate content. They are therefore reluctant to remove any content from their platforms. *Facebook*, for example, rarely removes content unless it is seen as harmful or suspicious; most content, even fake content that is flagged as such, is rather penalised by lowering its rank on users' news feeds. This is because users do not infinitely scroll and engage with *all* of the content of their news feeds. The same is true of *Google*. The algorithms that are used in ranking the search results of users are not well understood or shared by the company. Its original algorithm, *PageRank* (named after *Google* founder Larry Page), is now used along with other algorithms. The search engine uses algorithmic methods that evaluate hundreds of factors in order to rank the order of what it sees as useful to the user. According to *Google*, if it identifies suspicious websites that have sought to manipulate its algorithms, or if they classify content as bad, then the result is pushed down the ranking order, making it more unlikely that users will view it. Social media consumption, like all media consumption, is limited by time and space. *Facebook* and *Google*'s down-ranking logic is that content which is ranked low will potentially not be consumed since users will not scroll down for so long (Iosifidis and Nicoli, 2020). Examples of such content include clickbaits, ad farms, sensationalism and misinformation that is flagged and fact-checked. Another example of *an aggregate quality signal* is the *Facebook* function 'related articles'. In 2017, the platform announced it would be using the function instead of 'disputed flags' for posts that were detected as false. Such content is often shared more, so the 'related articles' function will allow users to track the source of the story without the false one potentially doing more damage.

In *Twitter*'s case, until 2015, the platform's algorithms prioritised reverse-chronological order of tweets, but since then it has sought to gradually change its user experience. The platform's sensitivity toward time remains important since it is seen as a 'live' (real-time) first platform. It now allows the user to choose between 'reverse-chronological order' and 'show the best tweets first'. Like the other platforms, the algorithms are continuously changing. At the time of writing, *Twitter* uses three options – 'ranked tweets', 'in case you missed it' and 'remaining tweets in reverse-chronological order' (Lua, 2020). The platform also uses an Advertising Transparency Center, allowing users to preview the ads running on the platform, specifically those targeted toward each user. It has also begun labelling 'potentially misleading' tweets, affecting tweets from all users, including influential people such as US presidents (Kelly, 2020).

Apart from aggregate quality signals, point three of the report refers to an overall understanding of elements required for users and journalists to be aware of how these platforms function. Examples of what this might refer to is an understanding of how the various platforms design news feeds and timelines and use algorithms for varying user experiences. The way in which *Facebook* ranks its users' news feed is highly complex and has not been explained by the organisation in much detail. Its previous algorithm, called *EdgeRank*, offered a little more clarity since the components were far less – these were 'time of post', 'relevance' or 'affinity to user', and 'weight of post' (the level of its engagement). *EdgeRank* was used by the platform until 2011. Since then, the new approach to ranking a user's news feed uses close to 100,000 parameters (McGee, 2013). The platform's complex news-feed ranking algorithm tries to balance the demands of brands and entities that sponsor content with those of making users' time spent on the platforms valuable and meaningful. It should be noted that certain functions are offered that increase users' control over what they consume. One example of such a function includes a tool on knowing why users are consuming the content on their news feeds. *Facebook* calls this 'why am I seeing this post?' introduced in 2019. The function, offered as a link in the post itself, when pressed, will open a separate window that *describes* to the user the following: 'we've heard people want to learn more about how their news feed works. That's why we've added more ways to help you better understand and manage what you see'. The platform also has other functions allowing users to choose which content to watch first. Effectively one can choose the pages (specific news media, for example) one wishes to view. At the same time, users can also prioritise which friends' posts show up first, ultimately tailoring the news feed to one's own preferences. It is imperative that such tools are taught in media literacy programmes and work in parallel with curricula on identifying harmful content and misinformation.

The empowerment of journalists offers similar concerns to those of user empowerment. The pressures of the profession are now escalated due to a highly competitive environment that includes bloggers, celebrities, citizen journalists, influencers and podcasters all vying for the eyes and ears of citizens and consumers alike. The COVID-19 pandemic has kept billions of people in their homes around the world, consequently prompting even more amateur content from creators who also want to grab a piece of the digital landscape. While more people generating content online is ultimately seen as a positive outcome, journalists need to be given access to digital tools to stay ahead of the curve. As things now stand, news media will need to find tools to stay relevant by offering more engaging content than is offered elsewhere. In this manner, they will remain relevant parts of the democratic process of liberal democracies. Such tools might involve journalistic innovations and methods such as infographics, drones, interactive mechanisms and transmedia journalism that will enrich, entertain and inform citizens.

The algorithmic approaches to which content is presented and when, can become quite complex. The platforms have not hitherto been willing to share precise details of how content is ranked, continuously making advancements in how they apply them. With machine learning and AI technologies further advancing the sector, the obfuscation of the process for the layperson will only grow. It is therefore important that users and journalists are aware of the tools offered by social media platforms, continue to create more open source tools themselves and, in this way, become more empowered to control their own news feeds, profile pages and publishing sites. They can in this way bypass a platform's default news-feed algorithms.

4. *Diversity and sustainability of the news media ecosystem*

As mentioned in the previous section, it is imperative that the news media ecosystem is active, financially stable, offers a wide range of media plurality and remains innovative and technologically up to date. Considering that they must do so while managing to stay engaged with younger and older audiences, and one begins to realise the enormous challenges the sector faces. These are the trials and tribulations of a sector with declining news audiences and press readership. To overcome these challenges, the HLEG identifies diversity and sustainability as crucial factors. The logic of the report is that a strong news media sector can help an under-attack democracy on many levels. And as we have mentioned, a healthy news media sector results in audiences consuming trustworthy content that truly matters rather than content that deceives and misleads.

The report identifies specific actions for this to be achieved. All positions of the political spectrum need representation without interference. Yet editorial independence needs financial support. The report specifically notes, 'careful consideration should be given to the use of public funding for well-defined activities aimed at increasing the long-term economic substantiality of a pluralistic news media landscape' (EC, 2018a: 30). Many scholars have identified the role of a stronger public service media environment (Nicoli, 2014a; Nicoli, 2014b; Horowitz, 2018) to help sustain a news media environment. Others, for example the UK's aforementioned *Cairncross Review* (2019), have argued for more government intervention across the whole industry, highlighting the need to do more to support community and local media. Ultimately, the report notes that solutions facing a disempowered news media landscape might be better dealt with through further research on a European level. Little has been done so far. A multidisciplinary perspective including the social sciences and humanities in specific EU calls could be a good starting point. *Horizon Europe*, which takes over from *Horizon 2020* until 2027, will need to identify calls supporting research on media management, news media, the journalistic process, issues of polarisation and the media's role in mitigating democratic threats. Importantly, more research will need to be done on how news media can become engaging and relevant to younger audiences that are finding the news less essential in their lives.

Like so many of the issues presented in this chapter, media literacy will offer solutions. But rather than deal with applied and practical workshops that teach the use of social media platforms or identify sources of news and good and bad content, the curricula in this circumstance will need to inspire students to be active, informed and more critical thinkers. It particularly needs younger cohorts to be curious and interested in journalistic processes. To achieve this is noticeably difficult. Within the *National Association of Media Literacy Education* definition of media literacy, it covers 'the ability to analyze and evaluate' (2019, para. 1 – see Chapter Four). Younger audiences are technologically savvy and engage with content on many levels. Entertainment media such as over-the-top video services and social media platforms are winning the battle for the eyeballs of younger audiences. News content consumed over social media platforms is not relevant enough for healthy functioning democracies. We reiterate that journalism will need to innovative and offer alternative storytelling solutions to how news stories are consumed, ideally on their own platforms. Indeed, storytelling is the principle manner in which humans make sense of the world around them (Snowden 2005; Couldry, 2008). Harari (2015) posits that it is the notion of storytelling that separates us from other creatures, while Papacharissi's concept of 'sensemaking' through storytelling (2019: 2) can offer solutions to a sector in dire need or an overhaul (Beaufort, 2018).

5. *Process and evaluation*

The last point of the HLEG report sets the scene for the next significant milestone of EU policies regarding the fight against digital disinformation. Specifically, the process and evaluation section states (EC, 2018a: 31):

> The HLEG invites therefore the European Commission to consider how it can promote a general, European-wide code of practises reflecting the respective roles and responsibilities of relevant stakeholders, especially online platforms, media organisations, fact-checking and research organisations.

But the report does not finish there. It further stresses the importance of ensuring not only the implementation of the recommendations made in the report through the code of practices, but also that the code to be continuously reviewed through a 'progress report' that further ensures its effectiveness (EC, 2018a: 34). In this section, the report has devised ten principles borne out of its five pillars as a guideline to how the EC should implement the code. These principles are important because they have helped create the foundation of the EC report *Tackling Online Disinformation: A European Approach*. They are (32–33):

1. Platforms should adapt their advertising policies, including adhering to "follow-the-money" principle, whilst preventing incentives that leads to disinformation, such as to discourage the dissemination and amplification of disinformation for profit. These policies must be based on clear, transparent, and non-discriminatory criteria;

2. Platforms should ensure transparency and public accountability with regard to the processing of users' data for advertisement placements, with due respect to privacy, freedom of expression and media pluralism;
3. Platforms should ensure that sponsored content, including political advertising, is appropriately distinguished from other content;
4. Platforms should take the necessary measures to enable privacy-compliant access to data for fact-checking and research activities;
5. Platforms should make available to their users advanced settings and controls to empower them to customise their online experience;
6. Platforms should, in cooperation with public and private European news outlets, where appropriate take effective measures to improve the visibility of reliable, trustworthy news and facilitate users' access to it;
7. Where appropriate, trending news items should, if technically feasible, be accompanied by related news suggestions;
8. Platforms should, where appropriate, provide user-friendly tools to enable users to link up with trusted fact-checking sources and allow users to exercise their right to reply;
9. Platforms that apply flagging and trust systems that rely on users should design safeguards against their abuse by users;
10. Platforms should cooperate by i.a. providing relevant data on the functioning of their services including data for independent investigation by academic researchers and general information on algorithms in order to find a common approach to address the dissemination and amplification of disinformation.

Tackling Online Disinformation: A European Approach/ Code of Practice/Action Plan against Disinformation

Building on the recommendations of the HLEG report, the European Commission composed the report *Tackling Online Disinformation: A European Approach* (EC, 2018b), which facilitated the formation of the code of practice on disinformation. The report reemphasised the significance of the ten principles laid out in the HLEG recommendations (turning them into nine defined objectives), and further added details on the processes, the scope, the motivations of deviant agents and the definitions of the term *disinformation* (see Chapter Four). Furthermore, the range of efforts identified in the report highlighted the persisting threats of digital disinformation to core EU values. The report has consequently become established across the EU, and around the world, as a leading example of how to combat disinformation through self-regulation, placing at its centre the code of practice.

One addition to the report by the EC that had evaded the HLEG recommendations involves the importance of strategic communication in countering internal and external disinformation threats (EC, 2018b: 15–16). A possible reason behind this inclusion is that strategic communication, although recognised

as an important function in the fight against digital disinformation, has hitherto not been sufficiently put into practice. Exceptions include the *Disinformation
Review Newsletter* (see section on StratCom task forces) and the efforts of the
East StratCom task force in cataloguing and raising awareness of pro-Kremlin disinformation. Despite the addition of the Hybrid Fusion Cell created in
2017 (whose mission is not to directly apply strategic communication), we have
only witnessed a measured and gradual application of strategic communication
to counter disinformation. One could argue that a more supportive approach
toward its application might have mitigated Russia's exertions to destabilise the
EU's open democracy ethos through a series of disinformation campaigns concerning the COVID-19 pandemic (see Chapter Six).

Possibly on account of a strong European ethos on freedom of expression,
Tackling Online Disinformation: A European Approach stopped short of recommend-
ing direct regulatory intervention as the EU has done with digital privacy issues
(for example, GDPR). Yet manifested in the code of practice, the report's relevance is to have set in motion a process bringing together numerous stakeholders while creating a significant piece of policy reform grounded within a
self-regulatory framework. In fact, the code of practice on disinformation (EC,
2018c) 'is the first worldwide self-regulatory set of standards to fight disinformation voluntarily signed by platforms, leading social networks, advertisers and the
advertising industry' (EC, 2019). These organisations refer to *Facebook*, *Twitter*,
YouTube/Google, and *Mozilla* but also include other significant European stakeholders such as the *European Brands Association*, the *European Advertising Standards
Alliance*, the *European Newspaper Publishers Association*, the *European Broadcasting
Union*, the *Interactive Advertising Bureau Europe*, the *World Federation of Advertisers*
and academics and civil society entities (EC, 2018e); the code was signed off in
October 2018 while others continue to follow suit by signing up (for example,
Microsoft signed in May 2019) (EC, 2020c).

Despite these achievements, the multi-stakeholder meetings of the aforementioned entities had difficulties in coming to an agreement. The working groups
that would have to adhere to the self-regulations, and the sounding board that
oversaw the implementation of the HLEG recommendations and the EU report
on tackling disinformation within the codes, were at odds on numerous aspects of
the policy reform. As shown in the minutes of the third of the four forums organised to formulate the code, the sounding board highlighted their concerns, with
some even leaving the meetings and forcing the commission to respond (ibid):

> failure to adopt a credible Code of Practice could lead to regulatory action;
> further, in the absence of an action at European level, Member States may
> take their own actions, which could lead to a very fragmented regulatory
> landscape.

Upon signing of the Code of Practice, the sounding board issued several warning signs that included a lack of quantifiable objectives and key performance

indicators allowing the platforms more room to self-regulate in a manner that better suits them. It further noted that no enforcement tool was implemented, leading to the sounding board's unanimous announcement, 'it is by no means self-regulation, and therefore the platforms, despite their efforts, have not delivered a Code of Practice' (EBU, 2018b). The Code nonetheless was agreed upon in September by the European Commission. It was based on five commitments of the working group (EC, 2018c):

1. Scrutiny of ad placements, disrupting ad revenues of disinformation agents and their websites (e.g. Google's Annual Bad Ads Report)
2. Political advertising and issue-based advertising, making political advertisements more transparent (e.g. Facebook's View Ads and Pages Transparency services)
3. Integrity of services, addressing fake accounts and online bots (e.g. Youtube's spam policy)
4. Empowering consumers and improving visibility (e.g. Reporting Twitter Ads, Mozilla Information and trust Initiative (MITI))
5. Empowering the research community to be provided with data on the functioning of the platforms' services (e.g. Facebook Social Science One Partnership, Twitter's "do more with data" initiative).

As part of the efforts to monitor the effectiveness of the Code of Practice, the European Commission devised an action plan in December 2018 that included commitments not only to coordinate the milestones on combating digital disinformation mentioned in this chapter, but also to monitor the effectiveness of the Code of Practice with the assistance of the European Regulators Group for Audio-Visual Media Services (ERGA) (EC, 2018f: 10). A strong component of the plan is to reinforce cooperation between Member States and the EU in four key areas: improve detection; coordinate responses; work with online platforms and industry; and raise awareness and empower citizens to respond to disinformation online (EC, 2020d).

Achieving this action plan has led to two important outputs that are only indirectly connected with the Code of Practice. These are the creations of a Rapid Alert System and a European Digital Media Observatory (EDMO). The Rapid Alert System is a dedicated digital platform that works directly with delegations from each Member State. Its task is to mitigate disinformation campaigns in real time and share information and insights between the European members (EEAS, 2019). EDMO is tasked with establishing a hub in four pillars that serve to tackle disinformation. These are fact-checking, research, media literacy and policy.

Conclusion

The European Union has gone to great lengths to combat disinformation, arguably more so than any other region in the world. Although one might argue that too many EU entities are involved in the procedure, the 2018 Action Plan (2018f) is an attempt to harmonise efforts and lessen the bureaucracy. The plan's rapid alert system is an example of how through one digital platform, the whole of the continent can streamline efforts, regardless of the varying needs of each Member State. But the policy recommendations and enactments of the Code of Practice seem unlikely to be sufficient. Occurrences following the application of the Code of Practice support a case for more direct regulation. The EU Parliamentary elections in 2019, *Facebook*'s reluctance to offer more transparency on its political advertisement policies and the COVID-19 pandemic demonstrate the need for further efforts in fighting digital disinformation. These incidences have added to the sustained levels of digital disinformation around the world that will leave legislators, not just in the EU but around the world, with no other option but to directly regulate digital platforms.

Yet the EU report on tackling disinformation (EC, 2018b) and the subsequent Code of Practice are reminders of macro-level policymakers' reluctance to regulate the sector, despite the caveats from the sounding board of the multi-stakeholder meetings in the summer of 2018 and the incidents mentioned here. Their hesitancy stems from the fact that a heavy-handed regulatory approach might not solve the threats of digital democracy and might in fact threaten the EU's ethos of freedom of expression. Nonetheless, certain Member States have taken matters into their own hands. A 2019 study by the European Parliament's Committee on Civil Liberties, Justice and Home Affairs (the LIBE Committee) identifies several examples of Member States fighting back against not just disinformation, but also other detrimental digital content such as hate speech (EP, 2019a). There is now a hate-speech law in Germany known as the Network Enforcement Act (NetzDG) (or the *Facebook* act), under which platforms could be fined 50 million euros; the French National Digital Council has held a consultation on the regulation of platforms, and the French National Assembly has been discussing a law on 'false information', while in Italy, a law has been adopted on fake news that gives Italian authorities the right to fine up to 5,000 euro (ibid., 100–104). Other EU Member States are destined to following suit. The actions taken by separate constitutions around the world accentuate the dangers of the foreseeable future.

While one can argue that some improvements have been made since 2016, the complexity of the algorithms used by social media – algorithms that have such an impact on today's digitally dependent societies – are, by and large, opaque and secretive. The reasons behind such concealment are surely motivated by profits and shareholder pressures. Despite their unwillingness to offer more transparency, the platforms will sooner or later have to share information and collaborate more. These organisations continue to hide behind an identity of offering technology solutions for others to create content with. In doing so, they have effectively the same status as internet service providers (ISPs) under the US Communications Decency Act, 1996 and EU law (the E-COMMERCE Directive 2000/31/EC of 8 June 2000). Under UK Communications law, the Office of Communications (Ofcom) is unable to regulate the technology platforms for similar reasons. A solution might therefore be in offering new definitions within communications legislation to address the role of the information intermediaries and distinguish them from ISPs. The manner in which users are rendered to information bits, or units that add up to big data, highlighted in Shoshana Zuboff's *The Age of Surveillance Capitalism* (2019), is destined for tighter reform. As technologies such as deepfakes continue to offer disinformation agents more opportunities to threaten open societies, regulators will need to ramp up their efforts. The EU has started to look more closely at alternative measures of regulation. In a study on the use of AI, the European Parliamentary Research Service (EP, 2019b) identifies six possible options for regulation, with the first being the current status quo, which they highlight as an example that cannot persist. Other options include an audited self-regulator that the EU and its various public interest institutions can agree upon, and the last is a statutory regulation that involves the licensing of social media in a similar way as media entities are licensed and regulated.

Notes

1 In a comparative analysis in 2019, Bradshaw and Howard (2019) found evidence of social media manipulation in 70 countries (up from 48 in 2018 and 28 in 2017). This trend does not seem to be slowing down, particularly when factoring in the global pandemic.
2 Unfortunately, EU Media Literacy Week 2020 was cancelled on account of COVID-19.

SECTION III

Country cases and digital disinformation

6

RUSSIA AND DIGITAL DISINFORMATION

Introduction

In October 2019, *The Economist* covered a story of a bogus report that '22 German soldiers had desecrated a Jewish cemetery in Kaunas, a city 100km from Vilnius' (*The Economist*, 2019: 76). The article cited the concerns of the Baltic State of Lithuania through one of the country's foreign ministry diplomats. According to the article, the apparent desecration of the cemetery is one of many examples of disinformation spread into Lithuania via Russian sources. The diplomat goes on to warn that were such a story to succeed in its objectives, 'support in Germany for keeping troops in Lithuania could falter' (ibid.). Such is the nature of Russian disinformation planted throughout the world – particularly the Western world – that it has made the Russian Federation a target of immense criticism in Europe and the US over the past two decades. The focus of this case study is to conceptualise Russian digital disinformation interference toward liberal democracies around the world.

In this chapter, we address the scope and techniques of the country's digital disinformation interference tactics. We then turn our attention to various examples from around the world regarding how Russia has implemented its digital disinformation campaigns. Before we do so, we believe it is also necessary to address specific internal communication policies of the Russian Federation as the two are directly and indirectly connected. While the Russian Constitution guarantees freedom of expression and of assembly, since the turn of the century its regulatory bodies have sought to put a stranglehold on anything and anyone criticising the Russian Federation. Russia's control over its internal communication landscape means it can protect itself from negative portrayals abroad as it continues to pursue its information warfare in the West. For example, it is not in Russia's interest to show how the Baltic States have successfully integrated into European liberal democracy. Nor does it wish to idly sit back and watch while sections of its population and its media advocate for a deeper relationship between Russia and the West's egalitarian global order. Conversely, Russia's aim is to undermine the West and its economic and political achievements both in Russia and through its disinformation campaigns across the Western countries themselves.

Freedom of expression, social media use and digital democracy policies within Russia

The Russian Federation's 1993 constitution states, 'Freedom of the media is guaranteed. Censorship is prohibited'[1] (Gaydareva, Eshev and Markov, 2020). However, since the turn of the twenty-first century, the actual practice of freedom of expression combined with the potential of digital democracy have triggered a regulatory process within Russia that demonstrably contradicts the country's constitutional assertions. As a consequence, digital tools conducive to democratic processes have been applied in Russia with mixed results. On the one hand, they have prompted the mobilisation of demonstrations and have helped change perceptions and empower citizens, particularly younger, connected cohorts. On the other, they have exacerbated the suspicions of the government and its controlled media outlets[2] toward the West. This has led to a direct impact on the manner in which Russians perceive the internet, with only 23 per cent considering online media reliable, while 70 per cent consider television a more reliable media source (Krasnoboka, 2017).

Numerous protests have taken place since the formation of the Russian Federation, but it is notably those over the last decade that have stipulated the most draconian measures and regulatory action. It is not a coincidence that the Russian Federation's response to these rallies is on account of the digital tools used to mobilise protestors. 'Wired, sophisticated urbanites ... many of whom have decided, quite suddenly, that a political system they have long tolerated is intolerable' noted Ellen Barry of *The New York Times* in 2011 (Barry, 2011). Similarly, social media platforms with live-streaming affordances have empowered citizens to propagate events as seen during a 2019 rally in Moscow to protest the exclusion of government opposition from the city council board (BBC, 2019a). These tools have initiated discussions about national tribulations that federal television channels have been reluctant to cover.

During the 2019 summer protests, Russian authorities expressed concerns over foreign interference in the political situation in Russia. The chairman of the Federation Council's temporary commission for the protection of state sovereignty and prevention of interference in Russian internal affairs, Andrei Klimov, said in an open statement that foreign forces used *YouTube* videos during the August 10 authorised rally on Moscow's Sakharov Avenue in order to manipulate Russian citizens, encouraging them to violate the law (TASS, 2019a). Citizens started receiving information on their digital devices from sources for which they had never signed up. According to the Russian telecom watchdog, the *Federal Service for Supervision of Communications, Information Technology and Mass Media* (*Roskomnadzor*), 'some structures' were buying *YouTube* advertising tools (push notifications) to disseminate information regarding unauthorised events aimed at disrupting elections at various levels across Russia. These notifications were also sent to users who had not signed up for *YouTube* channels on these structures (TASS, 2019b). When this happened, *Roskomnadzor* noted that if *Google* did not take retaliatory measures, Russia would consider this as interference in its sovereign affairs and obstructing the organisation of democratic elections in the country. According to RT[3], violations by *Google*, *Facebook* and *YouTube* were committed not only on Election Day on Sunday, but also on Silence Day, a media moratorium preceding Election Day (RT, 2019). Thus, Russia concluded that it was subjected to digital interference through social networks. This served as a threat to the stability of the political situation in the country and the provocation of citizens to participate in unauthorised rallies. Participation in uncoordinated rallies is illegal, as is the call to participate in them through notifications on social networks because, according to the Russian Federation, it could lead to harming the state and its citizens.

In addition to popular social networks from around the world (*Facebook*, *YouTube*, *Instagram*), Russia has its own social network platforms. Two notable examples are *Vkontakte* (meaning 'in touch') and the messenger platform *Telegram*, both created by Pavel Durov. It is worth noting that only 35 per cent of the population use the internet in Russia; that figure declines to just 12 per cent in rural areas (Krasnoboka, 2017). Nonetheless, *Vkontakte*, or *VK*, remains very popular and is available in numerous languages, albeit oriented mainly to Russian speakers. Founded in 2006, *VK* is the largest European social network, with more than 100 million active users (Baran and Stock, 2015). In 2019, it was the twelfth most visited website in the world (Similar Web, 2019a; Website Ranking, 2019). The platform is easy to use, featuring personal messaging as well as a database with numerous video and audio files and other web-technology tools. Like other platforms, *VK* allows users to message each other publicly or privately. Also, it helps users to share and tag images, audio and video; to create public pages, groups and events; and to play browser-based games (Baran and Stock, 2015). *Vkontakte* is considered extremely influential and occupies a significant place across the digital landscape of Russia. Before becoming a part of the *Mail.ru group*,[4] use of the platform was widespread among Russian speakers from around the world. According to Bennetts (2019), *Vkontakte's* founder, Durov, was forced to give up control of the company after he had backed anti-Kremlin protests in 2011–12, essentially not allowing Russian authorities access to the identity of pro-Ukraine activists. During that time, the platform had been active in the Baltic States and particularly in Ukraine. As we shall illustrate in the following case study (Chapter Seven), in a significant intervention in May 2017, the president of Ukraine at the time, Petro Poroshenko, as part of ongoing sanctions against Russia for the annexation of

Crimea and participation in the war in the Donbass, signed a decree imposing a ban on *Mail.ru* and its social networks, including *Vkontakte* (BBC, 2017a). *Telegram*, the Russian popular messaging platform, recently came under threat by Russian regulators. In April 2018, a court decision was implemented blocking the messenger platform within Russia. A 'freedom of internet' rally shortly transpired, with protestors continuing to use the platform via VPN[5]. The platform has since reopened, with Durov apparently agreeing to hand over encryption keys to *Roskomnadzor.*

As we have illustrated, the mobilisation of citizens through digital tools has been the main cause of tighter policy approaches, since the Russian Federation fears that protests are often triggered from abroad through digital media. For example, anti-Kremlin protests in Russia are often blamed by the Russian Federation on the US State Department[6] (Arutunyan, 2020). As a result, regulatory action has generally been designed to provide security on the internet and social networks across the country. Internet regulation laws in Russia are seemingly aimed at protecting citizens from disinformation, foreign influence and threats of terrorist acts, as well as from inter-religious conflicts. It is worth noting that special attention in the regulation of the internet is also paid to protecting children from harmful information. Along with several other agencies, such as the Federal Drug Control Service, the Federal Consumer Protection Service and the Prosecutor General's Office, *Roskomnadzor* has authority to block certain types of content without a court order, for example, content that violates copyrights, information about juvenile victims of crime, images of child abuse, calls for unauthorised public actions (which serves the federation with protection against anti-Kremlin rallies) content that is considered extremist and information that encourages drug use.

A significant component vis-a-vis the regulation of the internet in Russia is the internet blacklist that the Russian State Duma passed in 2012. The blacklist is administered by *Roskomnadzor* and the Federal Drug Control Service of Russia. The list was described as a means to protect children from harmful internet content by allowing the government to take sites offline (BBC, 2012). Also, legislative amendments allowed the blocking of content suspected in 'extremism', 'inciting hatred', 'calling for illegal meetings' and any other actions violating the established order. This content can be blocked without a court order by the office of the Prosecutor General (BBC Russian Service, 2013).

One significant law regarding online regulation involves the foreign agents' and undesirable organisations law. Officially, the law is called 'On Amending the Legislative Acts of the Russian Federation Regarding the Regulation of the Activities of Non-Profit Organizations Performing the Functions of a Foreign Agent'. This law requires non-profit organisations who receive foreign donations and participate in political activities, register and declare themselves as foreign agents. Foreign agent law required groups covered by the legislation to submit regular reports on their funding, objectives, spending and the identity of their managers. The bill was signed by Putin on July 20, 2012 (Marrow, 2019).

Another significant legislation includes a law on insulting the feelings of religious believers.[7] In June 2013, amendments were introduced to legislation to tighten the responsibility 'for insulting the feelings of religious believers', including criminalising imprisonment for 'public actions expressing clear disrespect for society and committed to insult the religious feelings of believers'. The law allows prosecutors to penalise citizens for public actions expressing clear disrespect for society and insult toward the religious feelings of believers, as well as for such actions committed in places specially designed for worship, other religious rites and ceremonies. This law serves as a defence against inciting religious hatred and conflict and calls on citizens to respect the feelings of believers. In 2014, the first sentence was passed under the article: a 24-year-old resident of Izhevsk, who published an insulting picture of Muslims on the internet, received 200 hours of compulsory labour as a punishment (TASS, 2019c).

Internet service providers are lawfully responsible for identifying illegal content available to their subscribers; according to Maréchal (2017), this is on account of their intermediary liability. Moreover, *Roskomnadzor* can issue warnings to the editorial board of mass media and websites registered as mass media concerning 'abuse of mass media freedom'. According to the decree, 'Law on Mass Media', such abuse can include 'extremist' content, information on recreational drug use and the propagation of cruelty and violence, as well as obscene language. In 2016, a legislation called the 'Yarovaya Law' (or Yarovaya package/bag)[8] amended pre-existing counter-terrorism laws and separate laws regulating additional counter-terror and public safety measures (TASS, 2018). *The Moscow Times* (2018) noted that the law, known to its critics as the 'Big Brother law', requires telecommunication entities and internet service providers to store users' communications for up to six months and provide them to security services in case of a court order.

In 2017, President Putin signed a law allowing the Russian government to define media organisations that receive funding from abroad as foreign agents. The law gives Russia the authority to block online content, including social networking sites with extreme content (Polyakova, 2017). In extension to the law, in November 2019, Russia's lower house of parliament passed legislation that would allow journalists to be classed as foreign agents. All materials published by a person receiving money from abroad will be marked as distributed by a foreign agent. In addition, any person who distributes foreign media can be flagged as a foreign agent (Marrow, 2019). Accordingly, the law helps to detect possible foreign influence in media and the internet and protect citizens from such influences.

Arguably the most significant law within the context of digital disinformation and digital democracy is the anti-extremism law. This law is consistent with Russia's anti-extremist legislation strategy designed by Russia's Ministry of the Interior. According to the decree, the internet is considered as the main channel for disseminating dangerous information and therefore there is a need to counter threats through intensive monitoring of the internet and the imposition of traditional values for youth to follow (RT, 2014). People found guilty of financing extremist activities via digital channels face up to six years in prison. A crime is defined as 'the provision or collection of funds, knowing that these funds will be used to finance the organization, prepare or commit at least one extremist act or to support an extremist organization'. Public calls for extremism or attempts to humiliate people will be punished by imprisonment for up to five years. This applies to publications on the internet as well as publications across other media. The organisation and maintenance of political or religious communities spreading extremist ideology are currently punishable by up to eight years in prison, correctional labour or heavy fines.

In July 2017, Putin signed a bill that bans all software and websites related to circumventing internet filtering in Russia, including anonymisers and virtual private network (VPN) services which do not implement the blacklist, and instructional material on how to do so (BBC, 2017b; Idisova, 2017). There is, furthermore, a law protecting citizens from misinformation. This law on blocking false news was adopted in 2019. The law, which provides for the blocking of false and distorting (fake) news, supplements the list of information to which access may be limited at the request of the Attorney General or his deputies. Specifically, a ban is introduced on the

> dissemination in information and telecommunication networks of inaccurate socially significant information disseminated under the guise of reliable messages, which poses a threat to the life and/or health of citizens, property, the threat of mass disruption of public order and (or) public safety, or the threat of creating interference with the functioning or termination of the functioning of life support facilities, transport or social infrastructure, credit organizations, energy facilities, industry or communications.
>
> *(TASS, 2019d)*

If such information is identified over the internet via registered online publications, the Attorney General or his deputies, implementing the Russian Law 'On Mass Media', can contact *Roskomnadzor* with a request to take measures to restrict access to the relevant sites. *Roskomnadzor* will have to immediately notify the editors of any network publication that violates the law of the need to delete inaccurate information, and the publication will be obligated to immediately remove such material. If the editorial office does not take necessary actions, *Roskomnadzor* will send communication providers, 'a requirement to take measures to restrict access to the network publication'. If the site owner then deletes the false information distributed, he/she will be able to notify *Roskomnadzor* about this, which, 'after checking the reliability of this notification' will immediately notify the telecom operator of the resumption of access to the information resource. In addition, a law was adopted to combat insulting state symbols and state institutions. This law prohibits information 'expressing indecently, which offends human dignity and public morality, obvious disrespect for society, the state, official state symbols of the Russian Federation, the Constitution of the Russian Federation or bodies exercising state power in the Russian Federation' (TASS, 2019b).

Russian digital disinformation

Objectives, scope and techniques

Russia's authoritarian president, Vladimir Putin, has fundamentally different views on how societies should function and be governed compared to those of liberal democracies. On the eve of the 2019 G20 summit in Osaka, he proclaimed, 'the liberal idea' had 'outlived its purpose', citing the public's turn against immigration and multiculturalism as prominent factors leading to its disempowerment (Barber, Foy and Barker, 2019). As such, the main objective of the Russian Federation's foreign policy is to undermine liberal democracies in the West. In the early noughties, when President Putin consolidated his powers, he set in motion what one might have considered an ambitious plan at the time to disrupt the West. Less than two decades later, and we can safely assert that to a large extent, he has succeeded. In fact, so potent and effective has Russia's assault been on the West that Taylor (2019) argues, with a few exceptions (for example, France's response to Russia's interference in the 2017 elections), the West has only been able to *react* to Russia's campaigns. While this might be the case, we must also add a caveat that Russian digital disinformation and its hybrid threat strategies are still not completely understood and therefore not all can be identified. For instance, the Russian troll factory the *Internet Research Agency* (described below) is a well-known entity that has been assessed and monitored for several years. Yet others are only now being discovered. A report conducted by *Graphika* in 2020 identified a troll factory known as *secondary infektion* that began operations in 2014 and has posted over 2,500 pieces of content online (Nimmo et al., 2020), most of which did not manage to gain significant online traction (although the entity did obviously succeed in covering its tracks). In addition, the Russian military intelligence arm, the General Staff Main Intelligence Directorate (GRU) has also been identified as a major disinformation hub. Numerous other platforms are only now been categorised as potential threats (ibid.).[9]

Apart from employing digital disinformation tactics, Russia's arsenal in disrupting liberal democracies includes hybrid threats such as those described in previous chapters; these can include cyberattacks, chemical warfare and support of political groups in the West (mainly by giving exposure and support to obscure alt-right factions). Nonetheless, digital disinformation has been the country's most potent and used approach. Contemporary Russian digital disinformation strategies are thoroughly different from those of its Cold War prototypes. Rather than being limited to strategically planting stories in obscure corners of the world via legacy media (Jowett and O'Donnell, 2019), they have used a plethora of new methods available to them via online platforms. These methods, illustrated throughout this volume, involve technologies that can depict up-to-date information on what the world is going through at any particular moment. The content strategies applied to online platforms have the purpose of rousing concerns that are delicate and divisive in open democracies (a natural consequence of societies that uphold freedoms of expression). Such provocation leaves liberal democracies easily exposed to external threats. Somewhat ironically, since the breakdown of the Soviet Union, Russia and the West have built closer relationships, further exacerbating the exposure of contentious issues for Western democracies (Giles, 2019).

A significant component in Russia's disinformation artillery includes their two main international media outlets, *RT* (formerly *Russia Today*) and *Sputnik* (formerly *The Voice of Russia*). *RT*'s main platforms consist of television networks, while *Sputnik* comprises a news agency and a radio broadcaster. Both are state controlled and cater to audiences around the world. Together, they operate their channels in several languages and have been accused by numerous sources in the West, as well as by former employee whistleblowers, as mouthpieces of the Russian Federation, used as platforms to deploy disinformation and lacking the impartiality required to be considered respectable global news media outlets (EUvsDisinfo, 2017). For example, in 2016, the Center for European Policy Analysis (CEPA) studied the inner workings of *Sputnik* and noticed that much of its content revolves around disinformation in the Central and Eastern European region, giving plenty of coverage to what CEPA refers to as 'anti-establishment' politicians (CEPA, 2016: 3). Both entities are strongly supported by the Russian Federation, are well funded and attract huge audiences thanks to their infotainment and sensationalist content (CFR, 2018: 41).

Another well-cited entity linked with promoting digital disinformation across Western democracies is the *Internet Research Agency*, a troll factory based in St. Petersburg. According to *Wikipedia* (2020), the entity is owned by the Russian oligarch Yevgeny Prigozhin, known to have strong ties with President Putin. In the West, numerous news outlets have covered stories depicting its deviant activities. Significantly, both *Facebook* and *Twitter* have traced thousands of pieces of content back to the IRA (Chen, 2015; Iosifidis and Nicoli, 2020). One telling story whereby *NBC News* gained access to interview a former employee (at the time a 26-year-old troll named Vitaly Bespalov) clearly illustrate the structure and inner workings of IRA. Bespalov noted:

> Writers were separated by floor, with those on the third level blogging to undermine Ukraine and promote Russia. Writers on the first floor – often former professional journalists like Bespalov – created news articles that referred to blog posts written on the third floor. Workers on the third and fourth floor posted comments on the stories and other sites under fake identities, pretending they were from Ukraine. And the marketing team on the second floor weaved all of this misinformation into social media.
>
> *(Popken and Cobiella, 2017)*

IRA, RT and *Sputnik* use a combination of strategies in their disinformation efforts (for example, the creation of *Facebook* groups and pages, sponsoring content and chatbots). One can assume that the Russian Federation also employs other, more covert channels. Regardless of the channel, the discourse is based on linguistic techniques that have proven to be persuasive drivers of confusion and doubt. The US committee on foreign relations (CFR, 2018: 197–198), citing a study by CEPA, identifies the following disinformation content techniques (CEPA, 2017). The first is altering quotations, sources or context. In such cases, the original source is altered or taken out of context to fit with the overall content strategies of the disinformation message. Another is conspiracy theories, or the use of rumours and myths to anger, confuse, disgust or frighten the public. A conspiracy theory is a unique form of disinformation that can have a history and storytelling element, often connected to social tensions in the world, and it is incredibly hard to disprove. As a general rule it involves a group of deviant agents who plot to change history in their favour against the majority (see Butter and Knight et al., 2020). The use of false visuals is another effective technique that alters content by visually adding more persuasive elements to a story. Drowning facts with emotion that appeals to audiences' sentiments are highly effective since they can stir angry feelings that are thereafter hard to dispute. One technique that can improve the credibility of a story is if it has elements within it that cast a view of being part of the majority. This is known as 'joining a bandwagon'. Other CEPA-identified techniques involve using loaded words and metaphors or substituting accurate words with abstract ones. Misleading titles involve changing the title but keeping the story the same. Since many users only read the titles, this is often enough to help form opinions. Ping-ponging is a well-known technique that consists of Russian platforms using content from lesser known websites on their own sites. Doing so raises the profile of the story. Ridiculing and discrediting are ad hominem approaches that can have persuasive results. 'Whataboutism' allows agents to use content that compares facts that should not be comparable at all. The CFR uses the example of comparing the annexation of Crimea to the invasion of Iraq (CFR, 2018: 198). Finally, the zero-proof approach is merely a statement that offers no proof of its claims.

Digital disinformation interference

A lot has been written regarding Russian interference across the Western hemisphere (see Benkler, Faris and Roberts, 2018; Helmus et al., 2018; Weisburd et al., 2018). In this section, rather than offering a detailed account of each region, we shall highlight examples to illustrate the range of Russia's digital disinformation reach. In Europe, Russia's objectives include destabilising the region, preserving close ties with the Balkan States and impeding Ukrainian and EU relations. Destabilising the EU implies weakening its liberal democratic order, as doing so allows Russia to grow both economically and socially more influential on the global scene. As we have described, apart from digital disinformation, Russia uses other methods to meet these objectives, not least of which involves establishing ties across the region and using them as potential assets when needed. Numerous sources describe the Russian Federation's efforts in achieving this. *The Economist* mentions Russian ties in Italy with right-wing groups such as *Forza Nuova* and the *Northern League*, in Austria the *FPÖ* and in Germany with *Die Linke*, a far-left group (descended from East Germany); in addition, the article states that Russia 'has also cultivated the hard-right *Alternative for Germany* (AFD) party' and further identifies links in the Czech Republic, Hungary, Sweden and the United Kingdom (The Economist, 2018: 16). Through these tie, Russia manages to stay in close proximity with EU affairs. Commentary by *EU vs Disinformation* added that Russian disinformation campaigns have 'an unknown number of channels and speakers' (EUvsDisinfo, 2018; 6). 'The scale encompasses the highest public authorities, diplomatic networks and security services' (ibid.).

An analysis of Russian digital disinformation interference should be neither generalised nor oversimplified. According to Taylor (2019), Putin's plan can be described in three steps: First, to focus on the former Soviet Union states and former communist countries; second, to assault NATO and its presence in the EU[10]; and third, to undermine Western Europe and the US. Consequently, in Eastern Europe, where Russia can take advantage of its influence, the approaches used have been different than those it has used in Western and Northern European countries. In many countries of the Eastern bloc, Russia appeals to a nationalistic sentiment and uses its commonalities in cultural, economic, historical and religious spheres. For example, in Serbia (where anti-NATO sentiments also run high), Russia has strong ties across numerous domains. Russian organisations in the country own over 10 per cent of all entities and, following an incomplete privatisation effort of the media sector, have managed to acquire a stranglehold. *Sputnik's* following and influence are also apparent in Serbia (Meister, et al., 2019; Stefanov and Vladimirov, 2019). In Romania, NATO and the US, the military has extended its reach, and as a consequence, Russian disinformation catering to younger cohorts has increased (Jensen and Rebegea, 2017). In the Balkan states, all of whom have memberships in both the EU and NATO, Russian influence has varied. Its strategy involves painting a picture of divided and fascist states who are gradually corroding Russian ideals. They use a plethora of media outlets in both Russian and the local languages of each respective state. In Estonia, the Russian Federation frequently attempts to establish closer relationships with media outlets that offer Russian-language content to meet their objectives. Barthel (2019: 41) posits that

> One of the two national channels of the Russian Federation, Rossiya, and two private channels, NTV and RTV, are the most popular Russian-based information and entertainment sources among the Russian-speaking population in Estonia.

In the three Balkan States and Ukraine, numerous entities are fighting back against Russian digital disinformation. In Lithuania, for example, one particular software product called *Demaskuok* (debunk), developed by the media group *Delfi*, was created in conjunction with *Google* and is used to trace the source of identified fake news pieces (The Economist, 2019: 75). Ukraine has been Russia's primal focus of disinformation and, following Euromaidan and the annexation of Crimea in 2014, it has stepped up its efforts. Kuzio (2018a) identifies a pattern of ten narratives used by Russia to disseminate disinformation in Ukraine. According to the author, the first six involve Tsarist and White Guard nationalism, while the remaining four centre around USSR sentiments. These are:

1. Ukraine is an artificial country and bankrupt state.
2. Ukrainians are not a separate people to Russians.
3. The Ukrainian language is artificial.
4. The Ukrainian nation was created as an Austrian conspiracy.
5. To belittle, ridicule, and dehumanise Ukrainians.
6. Foment disillusionment in Ukraine's reforms and European integration.
7. Ukraine is a Western puppet.
8. Ukraine is run by 'fascists' and 'Nazis.'
9. Anti-Zionism and Ukrainian oligarchs.
10. Distract attention from accusations made against Russia.

A recurring example of Russian disinformation in Ukraine is that Crimea was not annexed by Russia and that a referendum was held whereby the population voted for accession to Russia (EUvsDisinfo, 2020a).

Following the COVID-19 pandemic, with Russia potentially hit harder than most, one might expect Russian disinformation to be mitigated. Yet its exploits concerning the pandemic, for example, generating or spreading virus conspiracies, have been profound. These conspiracies have no doubt led to a consequent infodemic regarding the outbreak[11]. East StratCom's website *EU vs Disinformation* highlights numerous instances. Among many, one published in *Sputnik Poland* claimed that neoliberal reforms have failed thousands of people in the West regarding how the US and the UK handled the pandemic (EUvsDisinfo, 2020b). The publication revealed that those without insurance in the US were left to die (although according to the debunked response, they were covered by the US government). Jankowicz and Otis (2020) identify *Facebook* groups as the tool of choice for spreading COVID-19 disinformation. These groups were used to spread conspiracy theories about vaccines implanted with microchips and 5G networks as the cause of the pandemic. In our own investigation, we noticed an increased number of *Facebook* groups established to protest against various issues pertaining to the pandemic, for example, groups against the lockdown, or against wearing masks in public places. We should further note that most if not all such groups have since been taken down by *Facebook*. Bots spreading disinformation were also shown to have increased during the early stages of the spread of the pandemic. It is difficult to argue against their role in taking the lives of many victims of the pandemic (Benson, 2020). An array of claims suggesting that China intentionally created the virus as part of its biological warfare strategy, or that Democrats were overstating the threat of the pandemic, were among many fake stories disseminated by these bots.

In the Nordic region, most media outlets where Russia has an influential hold have ceased to exist. Sweden's version of *Sputnik* ran from April 2015 to Spring 2016 but was forced to shut down on account of its sustained attacks and disinformation on the West and NATO (Kragh and Asberg, 2017). In France and in the United Kingdom, reports of Russian interference have also caused significant disruptions in democratic processes. *Facebook* confirmed it had detected accounts that were used to spy on President Macron during the French elections in 2017, during which he faced strong opposition from far-right nationalist Marine Le Pen. According to Menn (2017),

> The spying campaign included Russian agents posing as friends of friends of Macron associates and trying to glean personal information from them … The same GRU unit, dubbed Fancy Bear or APT 28 in the cybersecurity industry, has been blamed for hacking the Democratic National Committee during the 2016 U.S. presidential election and many other political targets.

In the UK, where Brexit was voted in with 52 per cent, many accounts have been cited describing Russian disinformation interference, including the use of trolls and bots on an unprecedented scale. Both *Facebook* (Iosifidis and Nicoli, 2020) and *Twitter* (Lomas, 2017) illustrate the magnitude of the interreference. A report by *The Times* newspaper in the UK identified over 150,000 Russian-based accounts that were at the time being used for Ukraine, switching attention to focus on Brexit only a few days before the vote (Bridge and Gibbons, 2017).

One significant Russian disinformation campaign is that initiated during the 2016 US presidential election. Xiao (2020: 351) posits that Russia's aim in launching the campaign was to attack the public's faith in the US democratic process while also disparaging Secretary Hillary Clinton and, by extension, damaging her chances of being elected president. The campaign's strategy was based on several approaches. These included a hack–and-release operation on the Democratic National Committee (DNC) in March 2016. The operation was apparently launched by the GRU by hacking DNC servers, extracting email accounts of DNC members and releasing the information to various outlets that included *DCLeaks.com* and *WikiLeaks*. *Sputnik* and *RT* launched their own information campaign on their platforms, intensively covering the story and the stolen content (while also supporting the then presidential candidate Donald Trump) (Xiao, 2020). Russia's campaign further included a social media operation by the *IRA*. The agency spent over two million dollars on social media platforms including *Facebook*, *Twitter* and *Instagram* (Carrol, 2017). In this operation, the IRA created and used over 120 *Facebook* groups and accounts and interacted via the fake accounts with voters, swaying opinions toward a pro-Trump decision

(Shane, 2017). Both the Obama and the Trump administrations (following his election) imposed economic sanctions on Russia and exiled numerous Russian government officials.

In the US, an investigation known as the *Report on the Investigation into Russian Interference in the 2016 Presidential Election* was conducted and submitted into record in March 2019. The report, known for short as *The Mueller Report*, did not establish any criminal conspiracy between Moscow and the Trump campaign (BBC, 2019b). Attorney General William Barr noted a lack of evidence regarding American and Russian connections in the interference.[12] Nonetheless, the report did stress that Russian illegal interreference did occur 'in sweeping and systematic fashion' (Mueller, 2019: 1). Volume I of the report mentions IRA's involvement in interfering in *Facebook* and *Twitter* and with the use of individualised accounts and botnet activities. Yet questions over Robert Mueller's decision to choose not to interview Julian Assange of *WikiLeaks*, a potential witness with direct knowledge of the hacking and releasing of DNC email content, remain unanswered (Cohen, 2019).

Russia's take on the Mueller Report

When Mueller's investigation was completed and its results were announced by the US Attorney General, Russian authorities were quick to respond; they noted that the allegations were untrue and that the United States unnecessarily used a significant amount of taxpayer money to refute the story. The Russian Federation Head of the Foreign Ministry's department of North America, Georgy Borisenko, stated, 'the report confirms the absence of any argument that Russia allegedly interfered in the US election', further noting, 'there is no single evidence there. In fact, the authors of the report signed that they did not have such evidence' (TASS, 2019e). Furthermore, Mueller's decision not to interview *WikiLeaks* founder Assange, the central figure who claims that Russia was not behind the hack, might suggest an unwillingness to investigate evidence on fundamental issues (Maté, 2019). Assange claims that Russia was not his source for emails,[13] and previously stated that he would be ready to discuss technical evidence with investigators (Osburn, 2019). Criticism and accusations were nothing more than an attempt to demonise Russia and prevent any US moves towards improving relations with Moscow, noted Alexei Pushkov and Konstantin Kosachev of *The Moscow Times* (Pushkov and Kosachev, 2019). Since the Cold War, relations between Russia and the United States have been complex and tense (Blakemore, 2019), with the investigation of the possible interference of Russia in the US elections significantly worsening them (Ellyatt, 2019).

The positions of heads of state regarding Russia's accusations of interference with US elections were expressed at the Helsinki summit in 2018. Donald Trump condemned his own country's policies, especially the decision to investigate Russian interference in the 2016 election (ABC, 2018). Vladimir Putin denied any interference, saying the allegations were 'complete nonsense'. The

Russian Federation president suggested that US investigators travel to Russia to participate in questioning Russians accused by Washington of US election meddling, as long as Russian investigators were allowed to do the same with US spies operating in Russia (Mason, 2018). He further called the 'Russian threat' a fabrication during a speech at the 'Russia Calling!' Forum. He also added that all the allegations of the US authorities about the so-called Russian threat are a way to get payment from partners for imaginary protection. Despite difficult relations with the United States, Vladimir Putin expressed readiness to further cooperate with Washington (Bratskiy, 2019).

Conclusion

Unfortunately, digital disinformation, as illustrated in this chapter, threatens a period in history many consider as the most collaborative, peaceful and progressive in human history (Pinker, 2018). Nonetheless, such is the nature of current international relations, with contradicting views on the governing of states, that interference is inevitable. Indeed, as we have illustrated throughout the book, digital disinformation is such an effective, cheap (compared to other options) and subtle weapon that it is by far the most obvious means a country can use to destabilise another. Numerous references demonstrate the strategies and the scope of Russia's digital disinformation campaigns from around the world. The approaches it uses that are on record are quite distinct. They have been accused of employing trolls in the so-called Russian troll factories such as the *Internet Research Agency* and *secondary infection*, as well as through the Russian Federation's intelligence agency (*GRU*). Helmus et al. (2018) point to the capabilities of Russian disinformation agents to step up their disinformation efforts when desired. These periods have included Brexit, European parliamentary elections, US elections and Ukrainian protests, to name just four.

The country has directly been involved in interfering in most major Western democracies and its institutions (for example, NATO and the World Health Organisation), as well as the three Baltic States, Serbia and Ukraine (and, to a lesser extent, the Russian-speaking regions of Belarus and Moldova). In these seven regions, the Russian Federation has taken advantage of its shared past in order to create content that caters to the affinities of those willing to confirm those biases. In the western and northern regions of Europe, Russia has allegedly used a variety of strategies in order to undermine democracies and destabilise nations by causing social and political friction and polarisation. In the US, many consider the 2016 Russian interference allegations as an 'act of war' (Xiao, 2020). And in Europe, via Russia's distinctive approaches (depending on the country), Russian interference through digital disinformation is considered one of the highest threats to the region.

While the Russian Federation continues its digital disinformation campaigns around the world, it has attempted to fortify itself internally via a series of policies that protect its sovereignty and information channels from becoming exposed.

It does so by attempting to control not only its legacy media but also its digital platforms with little regard for freedom of expression in the country. *VK*, for example, the most used social media platform in Russia, was created and used by young active citizens but has now been forcefully taken from its founder and placed into the control of an owner with known ties to the Kremlin. In doing so, the platforms can be monitored at all times by the Russian Federation. It is through such examples that President Putin has demonstrated his version of authoritarianism that the West is so clearly desperate to fight off.

Notes

1 Russia's constitution also grants freedom of assembly, although in 2014, a law was introduced stating that all demonstrations require the permission of government authorities to be organised.

2 *Freedom House*, a non-profit organisation in the US that defends human rights and promotes democracy around the world ranks Russia with a 20/100 in terms of press freedom (Freedom House, 2020). With this said, the methodologies used have been criticised in Russia as biased toward the West and worse than other countries that seemingly should rank lower – for example, Russia is ranked 'even below Turkey, which had in 2016, 81 journalists imprisoned' (van de Beek, 2017).

3 *RT* is a Russian state-controlled medium that we describe in the next section of this chapter.

4 *Mail.ru Group* is owned by billionaire Alisher Usmanov, a personal friend of President Putin (Bennetts, 2019).

5 VPN, or virtual private network, allows users to override the securities of private networks. In this case, people in Ukraine could use VK via a VPN.

6 The US has often been criticised for interfering in the democratic process of other countries. *Los Angeles Times* journalist Nina Agrawal cites a study by *Carnegie Mellon University* professor of political science Don Levin. The study points to at least 81 examples of US interferences in foreign democratic processes between 1946 and 2000 (Agrawal, 2016). Xiao (2020) further cites allegations that the US supported the Boris Yeltsin candidacy by intervening in the Russian 1996 presidential election, and *Russia Today* (Bridge, 2011), accused the US of meddling in the Russian Parliamentary elections of 2011 (*Russia Today*, or *RT* as it is known today, is a Russian state-controlled medium we describe in the next section of this chapter).

7 We should note that while similar laws exist in other parts of the world, the manner in which they are enforced differs. Bennetts (2017) describes how a Russian citizen who had protested a decision by the Orthodox Church in Russia to build a series of churches in public parks was forcefully raided inside his home in front of his family and sent to prison.

8 Named as such on account of Irina Yarovaya, a political figure and deputy chairman of the State Duma.

9 See Appendix: Russian Platforms (Nimmo et al., 2020). Examples include, *KOHT*, *Russky Expert*, *Maxpark*.

10 For example, between May and July 2019, 55 per cent of all Russian-language *Twitter* messages regarding NATO's presence in the Baltic States and Poland were generated by disinformation bots (EUvsDisinfo, 2019).

11 On February 15, 2020, *World Health Organisation* (WHO) director-general Tedros Adhanom Ghebreyesus stated, 'we're not just fighting an epidemic; we're fighting an infodemic' (Adhanom, 2020). An infodemic is not yet an established social science term, although its Greek roots (*demos* = 'demon'), and the way it is used today, like the word *pandemic*, pertains to a detrimental and undesirable outcome. As such, the

term can be described as an amplification of conflicting and threatening information that makes it difficult for citizens to critically comprehend and analyse the information they are receiving.

12 According to the *Washington Examiner*, new evidence suggests that Donald Trump might have lied to Mueller during his interview with the president (Dunleavy and Chaitin, 2020).

13 Indicating instead a murdered DNC employee, Seth Rich, as his source (Guo, 2017).

7

UKRAINE AND DIGITAL DEMOCRACY

Introduction

Ukraine is constitutionally one of the youngest existing countries in the world (gaining independence in 1991). Despite its short history, it has witnessed stark oppression and ethnicity challenges from numerous neighbouring states, most notably Russia (Pop-Eleches and Robertson, 2018; Brantly, 2019). Hence, there have been ongoing questions regarding its identity. Owing to its recent history and civil unrest, the country has been divided nationalistically and territorially. Within this context, Ukraine's news media and social media landscapes have been polarising, therefore largely contributing to the instability of the country. Consequently, in any case study on Ukraine's recent history, one should introduce the two supreme fractions pulling the country in opposite directions: pro-European integration and pro-Russian. Both have sought to play a role within the political life of the country. This schism is reflected in the prosecution of a third-year student in Lviv, Ukraine, in 2017. The student was sentenced to two and a half years in prison with a one-year probation term for quoting Lenin on *Facebook* under a controversial 'decommunisation law' (Coynash, 2017). His profile was deleted upon the request of the SBU, the Security Service of Ukraine (Voyko, 2017). The controversial law, № 317-VIII 'on condemning the communist and national-socialist (Nazi) totalitarian regimes in Ukraine and prohibiting the propaganda of their symbolism' (Legislation of Ukraine, 2015), suppresses freedom of expression in the Ukraine and has been scrutinised by the Council of Europe's Venice Commission as well as the OSCE Office for Democratic Institutions and Human Rights (OSCE/ODIHR) (Coynash, 2017). Yet the law reflects persisting political and social divisions within the country as it finds itself caught between two continents. The draconian measures witnessed in the prosecution of the student illustrates high-running tensions between the two divisions, so much so that even those favouring pro-Western ideals have contributed toward repressing freedoms of expression. In doing so, they have disregarded the values they are seemingly fighting for.

While Ukraine's online behaviour will be the primary focus of this chapter, this will be discussed against the backdrop of a tempestuous history following the country's independence in 1991. The chapter will focus on the two significant revolutions that altered the political orientation of the country – the Orange Revolution in 2004 and the Revolution of Dignity (Euromaidan) in 2014. In each, communication outlets have had decisive bearings on the outcomes. Technological communication advancements meant that the 2004 and 2014 revolutions saw the introduction of Web 2.0 tools that played a huge role in deciding the direction of each insurrection. These historical events have reshaped media policies and the overall tone of information delivery and use (Nesteriak, 2019), not just in Ukraine, but also in other parts of the world where recent turmoil has occurred (among others, Egypt, Hungary, Poland, Tunisia, Turkey and the US). In the 2014 revolution in particular, online content consisted of a mixture of real facts and disinformation that ultimately contributed to the international perception of Ukraine as an online deviance and manipulation hub. 'When we want to understand where the future of fake news and political bots is going, we use Ukraine as a case study ... when I ask most people about when they first started noticing widespread disinformation online, they talk about Ukraine', argues computational propaganda expert Samuel Woolley (2020: 18–19).

Contemporary Ukraine is a disinformation haven, owing largely to Russia's efforts to keep the country under its control and influence. Viktor Yanukovych's[1] leanings toward Russia have had a facilitating role in both the Orange Revolution and the Euromaidan. The first was triggered by the announcement of his victory during the presidential elections of 2004, which he eventually lost in the re-vote, and the second by his decision to suspend the signing of an association agreement with the European Union instead choosing closer ties with the Eurasian Economic Union (and Russia). While both uprisings were successful in removing the then serving governments, which in the case of Euromaidan saw Yanukovych flee to Russia, they came at a huge cost. In 2014, Russia stepped up its information warfare on Ukraine and annexed Crimea (Kuzio, 2018b).

The two revolutions of Ukraine and the impact of social media

Due to the limited number of objective sources depicting Ukraine's post-independence history, one is entitled to contextualise an understanding of Ukraine with scepticism. A researcher should take a cautious approach not only toward Russian media but also Ukrainian major media outlets, since they too have been manipulated. To understand the causes of the current situation vis-à-vis an analysis of Ukrainian history and of the two revolutions in particular, we deem it necessary to consider the country's lack of freedom of speech, its partial version of democracy and the political economy of the media. Most media outlets were controlled by incumbent governments, owned by economic oligarchs or manipulated by the political elite of the country. International media were censored, limited and restricted. This leaves an understanding of the country's post-independence era to one's own critical take of the situation as well as the remaining digital posts archived during the period. As Surzhko-Harned and Zahuranec (2017: 758) note in their study on the role of social media during Euromaidan, 'public information posted on social media sites … presents researchers with a unique tool to study protests movements from within'.

Discussing Ukraine's recent history, Kuzio (2018b: 530) posits,

> the overwhelming majority of Western authors writing about the crisis and war have never travelled to Ukraine … while many scholars may not wish to travel to the Donbas frontline of the war, this does not excuse the absence of fieldwork research in Kyiv, and Eastern and southern Ukraine.

The Ukrainian scholar, furthermore, calls for more Ukrainian academics to research the country's recent history as it offers a unique narrative of activism, politics, social media and social movements.

The fall of USSR in 1990

The Glasnost Era[2] gave only an impression of an open society. Examples such as the symbolic opening of *McDonalds* in 1990 were more a misconception rather than the beginnings of a transparent democracy. The reality was that at its core, the Soviet Union was still a controlled society (Belyakov, 2009; History.com, 2018; Encyclopaedia Britannica, 2019). Thus, when the Iron Curtain fell, post-Soviet countries went through an enormous informational surplus that they had never before experienced. Besides influences from the West and newly formed political alliances between former 'brotherly' states, Ukrainian citizens began to engage with the emergent World Wide Web just as it was developing in the 1990s (24tv.ua, 2017; Tregubova, 2017; E-Server, 2018). Yet upon Ukraine's independence, the country soon plummeted into a dark age, characterised by a form of mafia hegemony and crony capitalism (Norwich University, 2017; Nesteriak, 2019). Consequently, at the time, fake news was quite common, predominately affecting print media with no significant fact-checking or debunking options (Nesteriak, 2019). This was despite the adoption of the internet since, at the time, most Ukrainians could not afford to connect to online sources of information. When Leonid Kuchma was elected as the second president of the country in 1994, Ukraine's inflation rate was at a whopping 10,000 per cent (Gorchinskaya, 2020a).

Examples of the difficulties faced by legacy media journalists at the time included the orderings of libellous articles ('jeansa') to diminish exposure of more truthful, well-intentioned opponents and to shape public opinion (Belyakov,

2009; Nesteriak, 2019); and the numerous killings of journalists (for example, Vadim Boyko, Svyatoslav Sosnovsky, Sergiy Shepelev, Viktor Freilikh – overall, 34 journalists were killed from 1991 to 2000, with many others added to that list in the period 2000–2004, mainly from online media and independent radio; see Wikipedia, 2019) (State Committee for Television and Radio-broadcasting of Ukraine, 2005; Yakovlenko, 2013; Gordonua, 2015; Makarenko, 2017). In a study of the country under the presidency of Leonid Kuchma (1994–2005), Katya Gorchinskaya of the independent news organisation *eurasianet* describes an incident linking President Kuchma with the kidnapping and ultimate murder of an outspoken online journalist and film director by the name of Georgiy Gongadze[3] (Gorchinskaya, 2020a):

> Perhaps Kuchma's most difficult political moment occurred in 2000, when, Georgiy Gongadze, a crusading journalist who was working to expose the illicit dealings of the elite, was kidnapped. Months later, his decapitated body was discovered in a wooded area outside Kyiv. In a subsequently leaked audio tape, Kuchma is heard to order an aide, to 'do something' about Gongadze. Kuchma didn't dispute the voice on the tape was his, but claimed the audio was manipulated. The case has never been conclusively solved, but many still believe that Kuchma was somehow complicit in the mafia-style murder.

Gongadze's death became a forerunner to the Orange Revolution, instigating the civic movement 'Ukraine Without Kuchma'. This allowed Viktor Yushchenko (who in the 2002 parliamentary elections won a majority support) to acquire further support. As a consequence, Kuchma decided not to pursue a re-election and to support Viktor Yanukovych (a favourite of Moscow) in the 2004 presidential election, when he was running against Yushchenko.

The Orange Revolution in 2004

In the early noughties, Ukraine was moderately divided into a Western pro-Europe region and an Eastern region, linked in many ways to Russia (language, history, religion). As the country began to lean more to the West, Kuchma's endeavours to maintain control of the media following the death of Gongadze led to the creation of a directive known as *Temnyky*.[4] The directive, first used in 2001, was an attempt by the presidential administration to shape how journalists presented stories across legacy media. It consisted of huge levels of censorship that forced journalists to cover specific stories favouring the government (Human Rights Watch, 2003; Telecriticism, 2005; Dyczok, 2006; Belyakov, 2009).

On account of *Temnyky*, only a few opposition-owned media like *Radio Era* and *Channel 5* showed support for Viktor Yushchenko (Telecriticism, 2005; Gromova, 2008). Other legacy media options, such as *Radio Free Europe/Radio Liberty*, disappeared from the spectrum. This forced people to move online and create a virtual public sphere for debate. Users from various political angles would engage in fierce conversations over online forums on how to make the country better. Such discussions were chaotic as they would often slip off-topic. Slactivists and trolls also entered the scene (described further below), fabricating fake news, offensive comments and assumptions online either for their own agendas (or amusement) or for those of the incumbent government (Rutten, Fedor and Zvereva, 2014; Kurowska and Reshetnikov, 2018). As more people turned to the internet to portray their views, Kuchma signed a law in 2003 mandating internet service providers to maintain specific monitoring equipment that the SBU, Ukraine's security service, could then use accordingly. Drucker and Cox (2004) noted of the period that, apart from legislative changes, intimidation continued in other forms (for instance, rubber bullets were fired at online news media editors-in-chief, while others were arrested and sentenced to jail for not following *Temnyky*).

Nonetheless, online activism grew alongside civic society and non-profit organisations with ties to the West. When a number of media outlets were abruptly shut down in March 2004, roughly 5,000 protestors took to the streets of Kyiv (Drucker and Cox, 2004). Digital media began to have an impact on the formation of new policies and importantly over international affairs. It contributed to the country establishing ties with the West and other regions of the world via international diplomacy. Kyj (2006) describes how supporters of democratic change were able to mobilise activists through online platforms, raise funds, chronicle breaking news and garner support from global democratic communities. Yet, Russia's pull continued to polarise society. By 2004, a further fractioning of the country, driven by a polarised media landscape and corrupt presidential elections, led to the November 2004 revolution that consequently manifested the country's political awakening (Jekel Cik, 2007; Franklin and Brantly 2019). As Viktor Yanukovych was pronounced the winner of the 2004 elections, electoral fraud was exposed online since legacy media continued to be controlled, preventing journalists from covering stories of political deceit and deception. Fatigued with the status quo of government corruption, a national uprising under the slogan 'bandits will go to jail'[5] led to the Orange Revolution[6] (Kuzio, 2010; Önal, 2015).

The subsequent attempt of the newly elected 'orange' government to reinforce the ethno-cultural basis of national identity manifested in a more decisive advancement of the Ukrainian language. At the same time, the use of the Russian language began to decline in legacy media, despite the fact that it was the majority's first language. Narratives also shifted from being friendly toward neighbouring 'big brother' Russia to being more critical and Western-oriented. Combined, these changes toned down the 'political brotherhood' with Russia (Pifer, 2009). This was consequently met with strong resistance from the opposition (Kulyk, 2016). The creation of an inclusive civic Ukrainian identity was not therefore successful. The older post-Soviet generation did not welcome new European and ethnic shifts (Pond, 2017).

Between 2005 and 2009, major informational outlets continued to be owned or controlled by the government – this time, ambivalent towards Russia – caused by the ever-changing parliament membership lists (Telecriticism, 2005; Dyczok, 2006; Belyakov, 2009; Kulyk, 2016,). The frequent shifts in ownership of legacy media from one government to another served to increase online activism as a new way of citizen mobilisation (Aslund and McFaul 2013; Duvanova et al., 2014; Michalchuk, 2019). As a consequence, internet penetration grew by 10 per cent immediately following the 2004 revolution (Brantly, 2019). Social media platforms such as forums, online news boards with comments sections and blogs became a hub for activists to gather and share perspectives (Telecriticism, 2005). The government therefore began to monitor and play a more active role in social media. The impact of digital platforms to campaign for popularising nationalist motives, Ukrainian language and European integration was compounded tremendously between 2005 and 2009 (Gromova, 2008). Russia's social media platform *Vkontakte*[7] entered the scene in 2006 and rapidly grew in popularity. Citizen journalism developed over the platform, as did a struggle to engage with the platforms' users. Attempts to sway opinions came from independent online news media outlets, pro-Kremlin and anti-Kremlin advocates and pro-Ukrainian European integration fractions. All were responsible for spreading disinformation and propaganda over the platform.

#Euromaidan (the Revolution of Dignity) (2013–2014)

The Orange Revolution became the facilitating factor that brought Yushchenko to power in Ukraine in 2004. It was his revolution, the revolution of the orange coalition. Yet ultimately, the Yushchenko era was marred with corruption and stagnation. Under his leadership, rather than liberating the country, Ukraine's problems were further compounded (Gorchinskaya, 2020b). And if that was not enough, according to Pifer (2009), numerous disinformation campaigns sought to discredit Yushchenko between the period 2004 and 2009, further instilling doubt in his ability to lead the country. Eventually, it was his own incompetence that led to his downfall. As a result, Viktor Yanukovych was elected president during the 2010 elections.

Yanukovych immediately changed the pro-European political course of the country. By 2013, the rift amongst Ukrainians had reached a high point. Pro-Maidan and anti-Maidan citizens had conspicuously different views on the European integration process, supporting different leaders and using different media and social network hubs. Integration would have been a major step away from Russia, since it would require Ukraine leaving the Commonwealth of Independent States (CHГ) and adopting legislations dictated by the EU. Such changes were considered an open threat to numerous societal layers, including many wealthy and corrupt families, as well as several traditional agencies, such as the government's pension fund. On the other hand, for less privileged layers of society, joining the EU seemed like a way out of poverty.

As it became more evident that Ukraine would not enter the European Union, unsatisfied citizens and journalists (for example, Afghan-Ukrainian Mustafa Nayem), took to social media, and through their writings and online activism, significantly contributed to what eventually led to the social movements of Euromaidan in 2013 and 2014 (Nayem, 2014; Önal, 2015; Onuch, 2015a; Onuch, 2015b; Brantly, 2019). Contrary to the Orange Revolution, already existing and more established social media platforms like *Facebook, Odnoklassniki, Twitter* and *Vkontakte* had crucial roles to play. Citizens had little trust in legacy media and their political elite owners; 'official' information did not match reality, reminding citizens of Kuchma's *Temnyky*. Due to Yanukovych's anti-protest policies, multiple television channels chose to ignore or discredit events at Maidan Nezalezhnosty[8] – Kyiv's central square – where people began to gather to protest following a decision by the government to suspend the signing of an association agreement with the European Union (Chornokondratenko, 2013; Khmelyovska, 2013; Verkhovna Rada of Ukraine, 2014; Nygren et al., 2016). Surzhko-Harned and Zahuranec (2017), citing Onuch, (2015a) note that in the wake of the decision by Yanukovych to not sign the EU Association Agreement on November 21, 2013, 250 original posts and tweets were immediately uploaded. Yatsenyuk, the opposition leader, straightaway called for protests in Kyiv's Independence Square through his *Twitter* account, while Nayyem followed up with his own support to gather at the square.

On the same day, the Euromaidan *Facebook* page (one of many that were subsequently launched) was created, immediately gaining traction with thousands of posts of activity (Surzhko-Harned and Zahuranec, 2017: 759). By February 22, 2014, the day Yanukovych fled to Russia, social media had contributed with millions of engagements and examples of activism that corresponded to on-ground protests and riots. Pospieszna and Galus (2019) noted that the growth of 'liberation technology' from 2004 to 2014 had given everyone a voice and a place to participate in discussions and policy-making. Moreover, the moving force behind the Revolution of Dignity were millennials – at the time, high-school and university students (Censor, 2013). Indeed, millennials were active, avid users of social media (filled with memories of previous uprisings), the conflict escalated rapidly from online platforms to the streets of Ukraine. #Euromaidan attracted vast attention online, becoming the leading hashtag in Ukraine towards the end of November 2013 on *Facebook* and *Vkontakte*, later reaching the top five on *Twitter* (Makhortykh and Lyebyedyev, 2015; Onuch, 2015a). In addition to the polarisation of citizens, *Vkontakte* and *Facebook* also were noticeably polarised. VK had more people standing for anti-Euromaidan along with strong Russian enforcement, while *Facebook* had more users supporting Euromaidan, with reinforcement from the global community and Ukrainian immigrants (Makhortykh and Lyebyedyev, 2015).

Apart from greater internet penetration, the core difference between the Orange Revolution and the Revolution of Dignity was the increased levels of disinformation spreading over social media platforms during the latter. As the government could not oversee what online users posted, it decided to use #Euromaidan and infiltrate it with false images and information to try and compromise reports from protesters (Chornokondratenko, 2013). Apart from undercover interventions, more traditional media accounts were also obliged to publish information supporting the Yanukovich regime on their social media (Nygren et al., 2016). Many protesters detected fake news due to the amount of people from demonstrations who were exposing online what was actually happening (Chornokondratenko, 2013; Michalchuk, 2019). Because of the obfuscation, it was hard for people to remain objective (Arafa and Armstrong, 2016). Subsequently, as trolls and deviant disinformation agents increased, communication became more disorganised. Inspired users tried to react fast, rarely paying attention to either the sources or the filters the information passed through (Onuch, 2015a). Despite these difficulties, the protestors did manage to overthrow the incumbent government, although it came at a high cost.

In short, the highlights of the revolution were as follows:

- Citizens were empowered by social media platforms where they expressed themselves and mobilised each other to meet their revolutionary objectives (Onuch, 2015a; Onuch, 2015b; Surzhko-Harned and Zahuranec, 2017; Pospieszna and Galus, 2019).
- Due to the significant uptake in global social media platforms such as *Facebook* and *Twitter*, it was easier for users from around the world to cooperate and take part in spreading information (Chornokondratenko, 2013; Placek, 2016).
- There was a significant shift from post-USSR *Vkontakte* (VK) to global *Facebook* and *Twitter*.
- Popular Euromaidan-centered pages become news aggregators.
- Media literacy improved and the number of citizen journalists grew and, together with professional journalists, they demanded that the government not distort information. Ultimately, boundaries between journalism and activism became blurred (Nayem, 2014; Orlova, 2016).
- Public posts and comments often lacked objectiveness and attentiveness and emotions prevailed. Social media moderators failed to deal with it and to weed out open calls for violence and hatred (Onuch, 2015a; Onuch, 2015b).
- Yanukovych was removed from office (fleeing to Russia).
- Russia annexed Crimea.

Social media in the Ukraine after the 2014 revolution

In Ukraine, like in most countries, the digital media landscape includes multiple tradigital entities, that is, legacy media with an online presence (Techopedia, 2019) blended with numerous online-based media and digital publishers (for example, *Ukrainian Truth, Segodnya, Radio Svoboda, 112.ua, Ukraine Crisis Media Centre* and *NewsOne*). They often engage with citizens who submit photos, videos and news stories via social media platforms. Thus, again following trends from around the world, a gradual transition from legacy media toward a more active and social media setting continues to emerge. Nonetheless, we should not neglect the questionable status of freedom of speech, as censorship, disinformation and restrictions remain prevalent in Ukraine. For example, in 2019, *112.ua* was banned from broadcasting due to criticising and highlighting the Trump–Zelensky scandal, unlike numerous other media who chose to remain mute (112.ua, 2019). Such examples undoubtedly stifle other media outlets that might have otherwise chosen to play a more active role in uncovering stories but instead remained silent out of fear of losing their license or being challenged in court for libel.

A ministry watchdog known as the Ministry of Information Policy was created in 2015.[9] Embedded in its logo were four USB flash drives visually portraying where Ukraine feared the threat of information derived from. The ministry's main task was to protect Ukraine from Russian disinformation, but it was also responsible for maintaining freedom of speech in the country. The two duties often contradict each other as understaffed employees of the ministry did their best to keep out Russia's onslaught of fake news without jeopardising its citizens' right to express themselves (Jankowicz, 2019). During its existence, the ministry watchdog implemented various policies affecting citizens, internet intermediaries and journalists, nonetheless ultimately failing to preserve a satisfactory level of freedom of expression.

i. *Vkontakte*

Vkontakte is Russia's and the European regions' largest social network, with over 100 million active users as of August 2019 (see Chapter Six; Duvanova, Semenov and Nikolaev, 2014; Scott, 2014; Tilearcio, 2018; Similar Web, 2019a). According to *Similar Web* (2019a) statistics, *Vkontakte* is ranked the twelfth most visited website globally, with 2.1 billion visits daily on average, of which 77.72 per cent are Russian and 6.22 per cent Ukrainian. *Similar Web*'s '50 top ranking websites – Ukraine' ranks VK fourth (Similar Web, 2019b), while *Facebook*, at the time of writing, is ranked third. In comparison, during 2013–2014, *Vkontakte* was ranked first for Ukrainians, with 27 million accounts registered, as opposed to *Facebook*, which had at the time only 3.2 million Ukrainian users (Yandex, 2014). In contrast, as of August 2019, *Vkontakte* had only five million users from Ukraine (Kantar, 2019). The reason for its 22 million decline in five years is not only the popularity of *Facebook* and *Twitter*, which grew during the revolution in 2013–2014, but also because sanctions implemented by President Poroshenko and the Ministry of Information Policy on May 16, 2017 (The Economist, 2017). The sanctions list included 467 organisations, among them popular sites, software and services, *VKontakte* of Mail.ru, *Odnoklassniky*, *1C*, printed media, radio and television channels such as *First Russian*, *RTR-Planeta*, *NTV*, and others (Poroshenko, 2017). According to *5.ua* (2017), the aftermath of May 16 was called an 'exodus', as all attempts by Ukrainians to enter blocked services were met with the following notification:

> Respected Subscriber!
> Access to this resource was restricted according to Presidential Decree #133/2017 On the Decision of the National Security and Defence Council from April 28, 2017, concerning the application of personal special economic and other restrictive measures.
>
> *(5.ua, 2017).*

President Poroshenko received international criticism for the ban, primarily because it restricted freedom of speech and access to information for Ukrainians (McLaughlin, 2017). Tanya Cooper of Human Rights Watch (Cooper, 2017) commented, 'in a single move Poroshenko dealt a terrible blow to freedom of expression in Ukraine. It is an inexcusable violation of Ukrainians' right to information of their choice'. The report additionally underlined that the ban was against both existing Ukrainian laws at that time and international laws. Specifically, Ukraine is a party to the European Convention on Human Rights and the International Covenant on Civil and Political Rights, both of which guarantee freedom of expression, including access to information (ECHRCE, 1950; Cooper, 2017).

Contrary to those criticising the decree, the Ukrainian government reasoned that Vkontakte was sold to Alisher Usmanov earlier in 2014. Usmanov is President Putin's close ally and controls the MailRu group, which owned 52 per cent of Vkontakte shares before the 2014 deal (Scott, 2014). His media holdings are often referred to as pro-Kremlin, with strong censorship of any criticism of the government's actions (Balmforth, 2019; Deutsche Welle, 2019). Pavel Durov, the creator of Vkontakte, had strong disagreements with the Russian government's online agenda. During the counter-Putin demonstrations that grasped Russia in mid-2012, Durov emerged as a hero of the liberal resistance by declining to shut down groups devoted to organising protest marches and gatherings (Gordonua, 2014; see also Chapter Six). Notably, he also refused to disclose data on the administrators of 39 communities dedicated to the Revolution of Dignity and Euromaidan to the Federal Security Service (FSS) of the Russian Federation. Durov had explained that Russian jurisdiction does not apply to Ukrainian Vkontakte users. As revealed by the latter, with the complete acquisition of Vkontakte by Usmanov's MailRu group, it is questionable if the social network will be loyal to existing laws, as it had been under Durov (Walker, 2014). Furthermore, the Ministry of Information Policy defended its decisions by reminding the world of Russia's disinformation onslaught and that they are at war whereby, 'people are lost every other day, if not every single day' (Jankowicz, 2019). On the day of the censorship, Poroshenko posted the following message on his VK account (see also, Lyah, 2017; Martinets, 2017):

Hybrid warfare requires adequate responses to challenges. Therefore, in order to influence opponents and counter-propaganda, my team used pages on some Russian social networks.

But massive Russian cyberattacks around the world, including the recent interference in the French election campaign, indicate that it is time to act differently and more decisively.

Ukrainian Internet providers should stop providing access to Vkontakte, Odnoklassniki, Yandex and other Russian services. All official pages of the President in these services will be closed. I urge all compatriots to leave Russian servers immediately for security reasons.

Follow my pages on other social networks:

www.facebook.com/petroporoshenko
www.twitter.com/poroshenko
www.instagram.com/PoroshenkoPetro
youtube.com/c/PoroshenkoPetro
www.president.gov.ua

ii. *Facebook*

In 2017, before the ban on *Vkontakte* and other Russian digital media, *Facebook* was ranked the eighth most visited website (Euromaidan Press, 2019). By 2018, *Facebook* had climbed four spots to fourth, while *Vkontakte*'s popularity had decreased, ranking it fifth. As Ukraine took radically pro-West, pro-European courses, joining those societies online was a natural progression. Although many ex-*Vkontakte* users disliked the new interface, VPN was not an option for everybody, therefore leaving them with little choice. According to *Plus One* (2019), *Facebook* had more than 13 million Ukrainian users in 2019, surpassing *Vkontakte*'s 5 million. In comparison, *Facebook*, as of March 2019, had only 7.6 million Russian users (Pokrop, 2019), while *Vkontakte* had 38 million active Russian users in June 2019 (Popsters, 2019). During Euromaidan, *Facebook* had only three million Ukrainian users.

As described above, the reasons behind the sanctioning of *Vkontakte* had to do with hybrid threats and informational warfare between Russia and Ukraine. *Vkontakte* is a Russian social network under the control of a pro-Kremlin owner. Fake news on political issues grew on the platform in a similar manner as Russian state-owned media. The objective of disinformation agents is to use the platform to demoralise Ukrainian national spirit and further fractionalise Ukraine's citizens. Moreover, a blend of push and pull components have created an intensely politicised social atmosphere. Thus, international several cybersecurity agencies have concerns that the FSS of the Russian Federation utilises VK to harvest data, while financially motivated forces make it a rewarding space for entities close to Kremlin's (NATO Strategic Communications Centre of Excellence and Fredheim, 2019). VK is mostly popular among post-USSR countries, the majority of which are in the Commonwealth of Independent States Eurasian Customs Union – two of which are dominated by Russia. By harvesting data of both officials and citizens via VK, the FSS can moderate situations and prevent activism, like the Euromaidan, that might ultimately harm Russian ideals.

Conversely, as we have illustrated in earlier chapters, *Facebook*'s self-regulation policies are comparatively tighter on disinformation, hate speech and bots. BBC (2019c) reported that *Facebook* had deleted 500 pages and personal accounts purportedly associated with disseminating fake news which were mostly situated in Russia and aimed at Ukraine and Eastern Europe. As we have described in the Russian case, endeavouring to pose like independent news pages, Russian disinformation agents have posted on a broad set of issues such as governmental tensions, dissent developments, NATO as a danger and other social matters affecting the country.

In light of the Trump–Zelensky scandal, the Ukrainian-based page 'I love America' was deleted in spite of its 1.1 million followers. In a mixture of engaging posts that included appealing animal content, it had steadily pushed a pro-Trump 2020/anti-Clinton agenda, with pictures highlighting Trump's apparent good deeds (Langlois, 2019; Legum, 2019). Legum (2019) argues that the page was part of an intricate collection of *Facebook* pages and groups all overseen by individuals in Ukraine. Other examples included 'Click Like if you love Donald Trump as much as we do. TRUMP 2020', 'God bless Donald Trump and God bless America' and 'God bless Donald and Melania Trump, and God bless America'. Legum ominously pointed out that the whole Ukrainian network had as much reach as the *New York Times* and *Washington Post* combined.

Kuleba (2019), citing Dek et al. (2019), had noted that the factioning of the country's population became more radical as the number of Ukrainian *Facebook* users grew. VK users became more pro-Russian inside the echo-chambers of the platform that created a burgeoning rhetoric against their country, while the newly formed *Facebook* community created a patriotic haven with more pro-European Ukraine narratives. Moreover, *Facebook*'s globalised Western narratives create a favourable international understanding of the conflict for Ukraine, as well as enabling support from EU citizens, especially former Ukrainian immigrants.

iii. *Twitter*

Twitter is less popular than *Facebook* and *Vkontakte*. Microblogging is not mainstream in Ukraine (nor in Russia). According to DataReportal (2019), *Twitter* was not included in the Alexa top 20 websites by visit in Ukraine and had around 575,000 users. Most Ukrainian accounts were in English and not Ukrainian or Russian. Nonetheless, this has not stopped deviant agents from using the platform to divide opinion in Ukraine. Nadelnyuk (2018) had analysed data concerning Russian propaganda on Ukraine from 2010 to 2018, finding that before the annexation of Crimea, bots were mainly inactive, with only sporadic actions taken, such as during the 2012 elections. An exception to this was the massive bot activity from IRA on July 18, 2014, the day after the accident of MH-17[10]. On this day, bots tweeted more than 44,000 messages, and on the following, more than 25,000. At the time, 297 records promoted data that Ukraine was to blame for shooting down the Boeing, utilising the hashtags #провокациякиев (Kyiv Provocation, with 22.3 thousand references), #киевсбилбоинг (Kyiv Shot The Boeing, with 22.1 thousand references) and #киевскажиправду (Kyiv Tell The Truth, with 21.9 thousand references). In fact, Nadelnyuk discovered that a 'twisofter', a tweet managing service, was utilised for tweeting between July 16 and 19, 2014. The greatest number of posts was made on July 18 and July 19, with 19.3 and 11.2 thousand tweets (or 43 per cent and 40 per cent of the corresponding sum on the relating day) respectively.

In comparison, Charrad and Reith (2019) credited *Twitter* as a mobilising force during the Arab Spring, while also noting an interesting connection that the Arab Spring's alternative name was 'The Revolution of Dignity' (Khamis, 2013; Arafa and Armstrong, 2016). Because the Arab Spring occurred during the period 2010–2013, it is highly possible that Ukrainian protesters took advantage of the movement based on public mobilisation by Arab Spring dissidents (Shveda and Park, 2016). The relation is discussed in more detail by Onuch (2015a) and other scholars on Ukraine in the context of the 'Hashtag Revolution' (Barberá and Metzger, 2014; Bohdanova, 2014; Hermida, Lewis and Zamith, 2014; Nabytovich, 2014; Kuah and Hur, 2018). Activists purposely tweeted in English so the Western world would notice Ukrainian protesters sharing their real experiences online. For this reason, they used trending hashtags, as well as hashtags native only to Ukrainian issues, but in multiple languages. Although anti-Maidaners also took to *Twitter*, it was to no avail by the end of 2013–2014 since disinformation from the pro-Yanukovich camp dominated *Vkontakte* and was infiltrating *Facebook* with less success.

Measures for digital disinformation and freedom of expression violation prevention

Several independent media such as *Ukrainian Truth* work on debunking fake news and informing society via their websites and accounts on social networks. Ukraine is known for its sofa warriors who often act as disinformation agents – they are also known as *sofa activists* and are referred to in English as *slacktivists* (Kiseleva, 2018). The term started as a meme in post-USSR countries, usually depicting a male person of low to middle income, sitting in front of a computer or television set. Sofa warriors were prevalent in the early 2000s and would usually be motivated by their own personal agendas. With the introduction of more advanced digital platforms, sofa warriors acquired an ability to connect with fellow individuals online, forming what is known as 'battalions'. Kiseleva (2018) notes that there is a hierarchy among sofa activists – leaders of sofas (they set topics), scouts (they gather more libellous information) and masses (they support and disseminate). The Ukrainian government has used sofa warriors for their own purposes, framing the news in a context that might attract their loyalty and arouse them to attack users with opposing opinions (Lange Ionatamishvilli, Szwed and NATO Stratcom, 2016). Examples include calling Putin a 'terrorist', which sparks strong negative reactions (Stavichenko, 2014; Censor, 2020,).

More ominous types of slacktivists include trolls (see Chapter Four). With higher coding and digital literacy skills, they are capable of doing more harm than the average sofa activist and are often hired by the government or other influential entities (Saburov, 2015). In more organised examples, trolls are leaders in the sofa activists' hierarchy. Ukrainian trolls, unlike their Russian counterparts, are unorganised, have no particular supervisor and work in small groups or alone, often copy-pasting the same agenda. Ivantsova (2015) characterises their rhetoric distinction as an emotional message that expresses not one's own opinion, but a clear, organised and strategic thesis with a particular appeal. As a general rule, their social media profiles are monotonous, they have few virtual friends and they hardly ever post content of their own, preferring to repost others' (Ivantsova 2015). Woolley (2020: 17–19), describes his involvement with Jasha, 'a self-proclaimed anarchist software engineer' (17) that had experiences with the Euromaidan protests, helping anti-Russian protesters organise themselves by training them to code python. It is through the help of coders like Jasha that Ukraine has become the computational propaganda centre of the world.

Media literate citizens of the country actively ridicule fake news with the support of adequate facts and report publications, particularly if they were posted on *Facebook*. Similarly, *StopFake*, a Ukrainian non-profit fact-checking organisation, assesses reports by columnists, searching for misleading articles dependent on fabricated proof (StopFake, 2014). Its international volunteer base emphasises that they operate exclusively on the basis of 'facts' and not sentiments. Some of the responsibilities of *StopFake* include addressing the below questions:

- Was the photo taken at the time and space the story claims?
- Is the individual cited recognised accurately?
- Does the story mistranslate or distort data in the source on which it claims to be based (Haigh, Haigh and Kozak, 2017)?

Some examples of debunked stories include 'survey shows Ukrainians liked living in the USSR' or, 'Crimean Tatars Deported for deserting the red army and treason' (StopFake, 2020). Besides *StopFake*, other fact-checking entities also operate in Ukraine: *VoxUkraine*, *FactCheck*, and '*Слово і діло*' ('Promise and action') (Hromadske Radio, 2018). Based in Kyiv and a member of the Social Observatory for Disinformation and Social Media Analysis described in Chapter Five, *disinfo.tech* seeks to use digital technology solutions to tackle disinformation. Amid other activities, it bases its technology around big data and software development consisting of tools for fact-checkers, mobile apps and browser plugins (disinfo.tech, 2020). On a government level, Oleg Barna proposed creating a public 'register of liars' – persons who disseminate false information and for whom there is a corresponding court decision. The deputy who represented President Poroshenko (2014–2019) had also suggested that the media should not, for a certain period, have the right to disseminate information from persons on this register, to interview them or to present them on television. This, in his understanding, was to be a preventive action against political forces engaged in discrediting opponents (Zakusylo, 2018). For instance, in September 2017, security authorities appeared at the central office of the online paper *Ukrainska Pravda* to request that an article condemning national military capacities be deleted from the webpage. The views of Ukraine on the matter at the time was that the country continues to be a target of an onslaught of disinformation it receives from Russia (Jankowicz, 2019).

The harsh measures of Poroshenko had not gone down well with voters, and his opponent Volodymyr Zelensky was elected to power by 73 per cent of the people (the highest voter support in the history of Ukraine). The sixth elected president of Ukraine, he seems ideally placed to tackle the media tribulations facing the country. With the support of his new political party 'Servant of the People', Zelensky is equipped with a law degree but is also highly knowledgeable in communication processes (he was a comedian who owned a production company, while his father is a professor of Cybernetics and his mother a trained engineer). One would imagine he has the required experience to tone down computational propaganda and digital disinformation.[11] Although there are positive developments in regard to suppressing digital disinformation, it should be stressed that Ukraine continues to violate freedom of speech and expression with its laws and actions such as stripping media of their license for covering truthful reports (112.ua, 2019).

Conclusion

Kamenetsky and Muradeli (1967) wrote, 'there is a beginning for the revolution, but there is no ending for it'. Thus, what begun in 1991 continues today – a country's search for identity, international standing, a longed-for past and a brighter future. Ukrainian legacy and social media as described in this chapter are reflections of a fractionalised community. Before decommunising a post-Soviet country and demonising what its citizens once worked for and believed in and what is still majorly a part of their ideology, Kyiv should accept the reality of its polarised regions. The government of Ukraine should cater to both factions in order to reach the state's moral integrity. One stands by the opinion that an honest and functioning government should foremost listen to the problems of its citizens. The past 30 years have shown that for as long as the country is divided, split between its European Western and its Eastern past, media will be used as a political tool to sway opinions and mobilise people to take action for or against whatever government happens to be in power.

Ukrainian media, but particularly Russian media and disinformation agents, repeatedly distort information instead of giving adequate reports on Donbas,

Crimea and Ukraine as a whole. Indeed, according to Kuzio (2018a), 'of the 8223 disinformation cases in the EU database collected since January 2015, a high 3329 (or 40 per cent) are on Ukraine', referring to the East StratCom task force archive. Similarly, *StopFake* has identified 500 impactful disinformation stories from Russia on Ukraine. As shown in the previous chapter, Russia is doing all it can to keep its cultural and political ties intact with such a significant former Soviet state. Yet Ukrainian independence is recent enough that most people have their own experiences and memories of its young history. As a result, historical revisionism is difficult to apply regardless of who attempts to do so. The written history the country does have can be found on the digital bulletin boards and social media posts of the past 20 or so years.

If we take a broader perspective of the past 30 years, we notice the evolution of a continuously manipulated media system by subsequent governments attempting to censor and intimidate journalists and editors. During the Kuchma era, Ukrainians were more prone to passively believe whatever was presented to them manifested by old principles of consuming the ruling party views (Siebert, Peterson and Schramm, 1984, pp.105–146; Guevarra, 2015; Nordquist, 2018). Hence, the firm authority of mass media and its use as a mouthpiece of the government in Ukraine in the 1990s was in stark contrast to the decentralised state of 2004 and the communication perplexities of 2014. Of course, there is little to compare between the events of 2004 and 2013–2014 in terms of online penetration. Nonetheless, in both revolutions, the incumbent regimes were anathema to the masses (Way, 2019). And in both, online technologies played their part in ousting previous regimes.

Furthermore, numerous television and print media outlets exacerbated issues of diversity, objectivity and news media trust (Ryabinska, 2011; Belyakov, 2009; Nygren et al., 2016). But unlike in the 1990s, information on media ownership became more accessible to the public as active online users increasingly become a part of watchdog journalism. Ukraine's gradual transition toward democracy and freedom of speech happened during the internet's global expansion. Therefore, many cite the emergence of the internet as a milestone, if not a rebirth, of democracy in Ukraine.

During the 2004 Orange Revolution, albeit still not a smartphone revolution,[12] informal horizontal systems bolstered by advanced digital innovations successfully demonstrated the results of online organisation to street mobilisation (Juris, 2005). The majority of protesters considered digital democracy to be a new, liberating way out of excessive censorship and control. Conversely, Euromaidan illustrated how social media worked to sway behaviours in different directions, framing content that polarises and divides, often without concern as to the true nature of a story (Surzhko-Harned and Zahuranec, 2017). In 2014, Ukraine was more embroiled in an informational war with Russia but also with its own citizens. It has resulted in a country with some of the most capable technologists who either work as disinformation agents or strive to counter deviant content through digital tools and software.

Following the 2014 revolution and Russia's annexation of Crimea, Ukraine took further action to control not only its legacy media but its online media landscape too. While one might justify Ukraine's tight information policy measures as protection from the onslaught of disinformation deriving from Russia, it needs to be constantly checked and rebalanced. Political abuse and the re-emergence of *Temnyky* were recorded not only during Yanukovich's reign (2013–2014 events) but Poroshenko's too (24tv.ua, 2016; *The Ukrainian Truth*, 2017; Goncharova et al., 2017). Despite the use of liberating technologies to trigger its revolutions, the upheaval of the earlier years of Ukraine's independence left huge scars upon the country's cultural, economic, political and social realms (Minich, 2018). Continued informational interference and disinformation from Russia has further dented Ukraine's pursuit of liberalisation. As a consequence, unlike the Baltic States, Ukraine is still unable to stabilise its internal and external affairs and remains torn between its Soviet roots and liberal democracy aspirations of the West (Burke, 2014).

Notes

1 Viktor Yanukovych was prime minister of Ukraine between 2002 and 2004. He ran for the presidency in the 2004 election but upon the announcement of his victory, citizens protested, eventually leading to the Orange Revolution that in turn nullified the election and initiated a recount, which he lost to Viktor Yushchenko. Between August 2006 and December 2007, he served a second term as prime minister. He eventually became president of Ukraine in 2010 but was removed from office in the 2014 Euromaidan revolution. He currently lives in exile in Russia.
2 Contextualised here as a period of time in the mid-1980s that saw the USSR seemingly more open and transparent, popularised by Mikhail Gorbachev, the country's political leader at the time.
3 The incident is known as the Cassette Scandal (or Kuschmagate).
4 *Temnyky* is derived from the Russian word тема which means 'topic'. It consisted of a set of topics and agendas that must be included or avoided by the media, drawn up by president's government. Amendments on media and their function, as well as the acceptable relationship between the state power and the media, were added into constitution (Belyakov, 2009).
5 The phrase was part of a Yushchenko speech he had given in September 2004.
6 Orange was the colour of the Yushenko protestors, while blue was the opposing colour of the pro-Yanukovich supporters.
7 While *Vkontakte* was located in Russia, it was not subordinated to Kremlin at the time.
8 Translated from Ukrainian, *Maidan* (Майдан) means 'public square'. *Nezalezhnosty* (Незалежності) means 'Independence'; because of its symbolic name, it is associated with anti-government or legislation protests, led by people or party leaders.
9 It has since been dissolved (in 2019).
10 MH-17 refers to the Malaysia Airlines Flight 17 from Amsterdam to Kuala Lumpur, which was shot down on July 17, 2014, while flying over Eastern Ukraine, killing all 283 passengers and 15 crew members.
11 We should note here that the previous president, Petro Poroshenko, also had experience in communications processes since he was the owner of the TV channel *5 Kanal*.
12 The first *Apple iPhone*, for example, was launched in 2007.

8

CONCLUSION

The volume has addressed the main conceptual, policy and regulatory issues associated with digital democracy, the network society and the social media and established socio-political and technological methods to tackle disinformation and fake news. These methods were identified as fact-checking, rebuttals and myth-busting, news literacy, policy recommendations, awareness and communication strategies, and the potential of recent technologies such as the blockchain and public interest algorithms to counter disinformation. The book also outlined what has been done up to now to withstand disinformation and fake news by means of a regional analysis. The early chapters intentionally took a more circumspect and open-ended type of approach and offered a balanced view of arguments on combating disinformation and fake news. In addition, a balanced set of arguments was presented from both the sceptics and the optimists concerning the role of social media networks. The sections of the book that followed tested the concepts against the empirical material drawn from various geographical areas of the globe. In addition, the book featured two case studies: Russia and digital disinformation; and Ukraine and digital democracy. These aimed at revealing the nature and the effects of national digital disinformation campaigns and showed the means through which national policies attempt to control both legacy media and digital platforms with little regard to freedom of expression.

The theoretical chapters explored the concepts of the public sphere and citizenship and investigated how these have changed over the past three decades or so following shifts in society and technology. In more recent years, the change has taken these theoretical concepts to a different level thanks to ongoing socio-cultural and technological advances. Specifically, the creation of the internet and the development of social networks impacted communication in both negative and positive ways. By critically engaging with Habermas' idea of the public sphere as well as the limitations of strictly liberal, modernist and rationalist constructions of citizenship, we argued that the understanding of society and the concept of the public sphere are constantly evolving and should therefore be viewed through the constructionist prism of an ever-changing platform. The questions about democracy have become manifold and diverse as technology creates networked publics and introduces new social possibilities that can challenge peoples' assumptions about everyday interactions. At the same time, modes of citizenship evolve, allowing us to witness a gradual shift to so-called mediated citizenship with both positive and negative prospects. The growing literature concerning the sociopolitics of social media and relevant academic debates pay particular attention to the political, social and democratic value of Web 2.0 technologies.

We contributed to this discourse by discussing critically whether social media actually provide new forms of participatory democracy and result in an enhanced public sphere and sense of citizenship. Social media was initially heralded as a means to enhance the public sphere and a powerful drive for freedom of speech and democracy. In 2011, for example, several revolutions and rebellions occurred in many parts of the world. These concerned calls for the replacement of autocratic governments in many Arab countries such as Tunisia, Egypt and Libya, but also involved citizens in southern Europe demanding an end to austerity measures imposed by the European Commission. Activists formed virtual political public spheres conveyed via social media networks that invited citizens' views, aiming to establish a better society. 2011 should have been a year remembered for numerous public sphere examples, a year of Twitter and Facebook revolutions, implying that it was social media that created the protest movements (Fuchs, 2014).

However, social media platforms have come under intense scrutiny for their role in escalating disinformation and fake news, inciting hate speech and violence, triggering the rise of populism and nationalism and lowering levels of trust in media. We devoted space to discussing the rise of populism as a global phenomenon over the course of the 2010s. The election of Donald Trump as US president in November 2016, which followed the 'Brexit' referendum in the United Kingdom in the same year, established an interest in the language and political strategies of populism, including its relationship to the media. We contributed to ongoing debates that have global significance about the relationship of the rise of populism to critiques of globalisation that include nationalist arguments and perspectives. We also attempted to capture the new dynamics of digital and social media, where the much-vaunted openness and horizontal nature of online communication comes up against disinformation and fake news. Our findings are in line with previous research (see Flew and Iosifidis, 2020) that found that such politically and ideologically motivated online campaigns, and the emergence of new actors unconstrained by traditional ethical and professional boundaries of journalism, in turn shapes both the traditional media outlets – which are themselves now dependent upon digital platforms – and the responses of the digital platforms hosting such content, including *Facebook*, *YouTube*, *Twitter* and *WhatsApp*.

The issue of trust in media is also important. A starting point for the consideration of social trust with regards to communication is found in the work of Jürgen Habermas, who introduced the concept of a liberal public sphere, providing both the possibility of the formation of public opinion into political authority that approximates rationality, while at the same time having its own conditions of existence undercut by various interests that distort public communication. The German scholar put forth claims around communicative rationality, proposing that the conditions for truthful statements were threefold: they are propositionally valid, normatively right and expressively sincere (see Flew, 2020). According to Flew (ibid.), we have a global crisis of commercially funded news which has been accelerated by the COVID-19 pandemic and its impact upon advertising expenditure. At the same time, COVID-19 has seen a sharp upturn in news consumption as publics seek information about the pandemic, its societal impact and the nature of restrictions on public activity. As was shown in Chapter Three, levels of public trust in social media are in general lower than trust in traditional media outlets in many national contexts. This has been accompanied by an appetite for regulation that also correlates with beliefs about the extent of the power and influence tech companies have.

Meanwhile, several studies (for example, Bradshaw and Howard, 2019) have demonstrated the ways in which government agencies and political parties have used social media to spread political propaganda, pollute the digital information ecosystem and suppress freedom of speech and freedom of the press. Russia and China have become major players in the global disinformation order. The former stepped up its disinformation efforts during the 2014 crisis that erupted when Russian special forces occupied Ukraine's Crimean peninsula, as well as during the 2016 US election, when the Russian government was widely accused of interfering to boost the candidacy of Donald Trump (see Chapter Six). Vladimir Putin, who has held power since 1999, is set to become 'President for Life' through an array of constitutional amendments that most Russian voters backed, given that opponents were barred from campaigning in the media. Meanwhile China, under the leadership of Xi Jinping, whose term limits of the presidency were abolished in 2018, has more aggressively stirred up nationalist and anti-Western sentiment using state and social media. Disinformation has intensified during the ongoing Hong Kong social arrests and has clearly been aimed at undermining sympathy for the Hong Kong protesters' goals, which now include demands for greater democratic freedoms for its seven million residents.

Our work went on to focus on media intermediaries and the regulatory action that may be required to make them more accountable to the public. Digital platforms such as *Facebook*, *Google* and *Twitter* have become some of the world's fastest growing and most powerful media and communications companies, so new approaches to overseeing these entities in the public interest are required (see, among others, Napoli 2019; Iosifidis and Andrews, 2020). Increasingly, global and regional bodies have introduced strategies to regulate platform power, including the Global Internet Forum to Counter Terrorism (GIFCT) and the

European Commission's Code of Conduct on countering illegal hate speech online. Certain EU Member States have taken initiatives too. As analysed in Chapter Five, a 2019 study by the European Parliament's LIBE Committee identifies several examples of Member States (Germany, France and Italy) combating not just disinformation, but also other detrimental digital content such as hate speech. There has also been an increase in the platforms' own attempts at international, regional and localised forms of self-governance, such as *Facebook*'s Oversight Board and *Twitter*'s Trust and Safety Council. It is clear, then, that new governance initiatives are originating from international, regional and national contexts, often in response to issues of disinformation and harmful content. However, critical questions need to be addressed concerning the accountability, inclusivity and diversity of these strategies, their situated particularity and potential universal applications.

Platform governance should take shape worldwide and involve multiple formal and informal arrangements between global entities, corporations, states and civil society actors. It is even more important today, in the midst of an unprecedented global health crisis, that diverse actors, coalitions and partnerships come together to design workable approaches to policy formation around the world's tech giants and control over user data, privacy and security, speech rights and dis(information) distribution. Examining the effects of disinformation is key during a pandemic, given the significant consequences of misinformed behaviour for individuals' health and for the health-care system as a whole. We asked specifically if a new generation of internet regulation is needed to counter these trends and overturn a situation whereby platforms have amassed great power but have 'limited responsibility' for the illegal and harmful content available via their services. We contended that the articulation of a public interest framework in a regime of social media governance needs to consider both traditional concerns (such as access, media plurality and freedom of expression) and new emerging concerns, including privacy and intellectual property rights, transparency about data processing and protection of users from harmful content (violence, sexually explicit content, hate speech and harassment).

It is our firm belief that the focus on different regions allows the drawing of comparative aspects and strengthens the international character of the project. In this sense, it contributes to the burgeoning literature on fake news and post-truth politics, disinformation, social media, democracy and the public sphere. This publication has brought together theoretical analysis with empirical findings to make sense of the key contemporary debates and tensions in the rapidly shifting communications ecology. Its intention has been to contribute to the understanding of the dynamics of media and communications policy at a global level. Media policy has always been controversial, since it assumes state intervention which limits freedom of expression and the right to communication. While we acknowledge this, we have taken an expansive approach to the debates surrounding media and communication platform governance. The reader will judge as to whether this has been achieved.

REFERENCE LIST

5.ua (2017) 'Volya internet provider announcement upon entry to blocked Russian websites', 5.ua, May 31. Available at: https://www.5.ua/regiony/v-okupovanomu-s evastopoli-ukrainskyi-provaider-zablokuvav-yandeks-mailru-ta-vkontakte-146765 .html, (Accessed 1 Sep. 2019).

112.ua (2019) 'Нацсовет по ТВ завтра лишит 112 Украина лицензий на цифровое вещание', 112.ua, Sep. 25. Available at: https://112.ua/glavnye-novosti/nacsovet- po-tv-zavtra-lishit-112-ukraina-licenziy-na-cifrovoe-veshhanie-508721.html, (Accessed 24 June 2020).

24tv.ua (2016) 'Poroshenko journalists made temniki after offshore scandal | Журналисты Порошенко составили темники после оффшорного скандала', 24tv, 24 Канал, Apr. 4. Available at: https://24tv.ua/ru/zhurnalisty_poroshenko_sostavili_temniki_ posle_offshornogo_skandala_n673818, (Accessed 20 Sep. 2019).

24tv.ua (2017) 'Вспомнить все. Интернет 90-х в Украине — Телеканал новостей', 24tv, 24 Канал, Apr. 4. Available at: https://24tv.ua/ru/vspomnit_vse_internet _90h_v_ukraine_n801888, (Accessed 9 Sep. 2019).

ABC (2018) 'Donald Trump sides with Russia against FBI on election meddling', ABC News, July 16. Available at: https://www.abc.net.au/news/2018-07-17/donald-trump-attacked -weak-summit-vladimir-putin-denies-meddling/10001770, (Accessed 28 Nov. 2019).

Abdulkader, A., Lakshmiratan, A. and Zhang, J. (2016) 'Introducing deeptext: Facebook's text understanding engine', *Facebook Engineering*, June 1. Available at: https://enginee ring.fb.com/core-data/introducing-deeptext-facebook-s-text-understanding-en gine/, (Accessed 30 Apr. 2020).

Adhanom, T. (2020) 'Munich security conference', World Health Organization DG Speech, Feb 15. Available at: https://www.who.int/dg/speeches/detail/munich-secu rity-conference, (Accessed 24 May).

Adorno, T. and Leppert, R. (2002) *Essays on Music*. California: University of California Press.

Agrawal, N. (2016) 'The US is no stranger to interfering in the elections of other countries', *Los Angeles Times*, Dec. 21. Available at: http://www.latimes.com/nation/la-na-us-i ntervention-foreign-elections-20161213-story.html, (Accessed 22 June 2020).

Ahval (2019) 'The populist rise of Turkey's Erdogan', *Ahval*, Mar. 11. Available at: https://ahvalnews.com/recep-tayyip-erdogan/populist-rise-turkeys-erdogan, (Accessed 30 Apr. 2020).

Allcott, H., Gentkow, M. and Yu, C. (2019) 'Trends in the diffusion of misinformation on social media', *Research and Politics* April-June, 1–8.

Alter, A. (2017) *Irresistible: The Rise of Addictive Technology and the Business of Keeping us Hooked*. New York: Penguin Random House.

Ananny, M. (2018) 'Checking in with the Facebook fact-checking partnership', *Columbia Journalism Review*, Apr. 4. Available at: https://www.cjr.org/tow:center/facebook-fact-checking-partnerships.php, (Accessed 3 May 2020).

Arafa, M. and Armstrong, C. (2016) 'Facebook to mobilize, twitter to coordinate protests, and YouTube to tell the world: New media, cyberactivism, and the Arab spring', *Journal of Global Initiatives: Policy, Pedagogy, Perspective*, 10(1), 74–89. Available at: https://digitalcommons.kennesaw.edu/cgi/viewcontent.cgi?article=1187&context=jgi, (Accessed 22 Sep. 2019).

Arutunyan, A. (2020) 'Putin is not smiling', *Foreign Affairs*, June 17. Available at: https://www.foreignaffairs.com/articles/russian-federation/2020-06-17/putin-not-smiling, (Accessed 22 June 2020).

Ascott, T. (2020) 'Microfake: How small-scale deepfakes can undermine society', *Journal of Digital Media & Policy*, 11(2): 215–222. DOI: 10.1386/jdmp_00018_1

Aslund, A. and Mcfaul, M. (2013) *Revolution in Orange: The Origins of Ukraine's Democratic Breakthrough*. New York: Brookings Institution Press.

Bagdigian, B. (1983) *Media Monopoly*. Boston: Beacon Press.

Balmforth, T. (2019) 'Russian reporters resign en masse in row over Putin ally report', *Reuters*, May 20. Available at: https://www.reuters.com/article/russia-politics-kommersant/russian-reporters-resign-en-masse-in-row-over-putin-ally-report-idUSL5N22W39A, (Accessed 11 Sep. 2019).

Baran, K. and Stock, W. (2015) 'Acceptance and quality perceptions of social network services in cultural context: *Vkontakte* as a case study', *Systemics, Cybernetics and Informatics*, 13(3), 41–46. Available at: http://www.iiisci.org/journal/CV$/sci/pdfs/HA408OW15.pdf, (Accessed 15 June 2020).

Barber, L., Foy, H. and Barker, A. (2019) 'Vladimir Putin says liberalism has "become obsolete"', *Financial Times*, June 28. Available at: https://www.ft.com/content/670039ec-98f3-11e9-9573-ee5cbb98ed36, (Accessed 15 June 2020).

Barberá, P. and Metzger, M. (2014) 'Tweeting the revolution: Social media use and the #Euromaidan protests', *HuffPost*, Feb. 21. Available at: https://www.huffpost.com/entry/tweeting-the-revolution-s_b_4831104?guccounter=1, (Accessed 5 July 2019).

Barros, L. and Santos Silva, M. (2020) 'Right-wing populism in the tropics: The rise of Jair Bolsonaro', VOX EU, Jan. 24. Available at: https://voxeu.org/article/right-wing-populism-tropics-rise-jair-bolsonaro, (Accessed 30 Apr. 2020).

Barry, E. (2011) 'Young and connected, "Office Plankton" protesters surprise Russia', *The New York Times*, Dec. 23. Available at: https://www.nytimes.com/2011/12/24/world/europe/young-and-connected-office-plankton-protesters-stir-russia.html, (Accessed 20 June 2020).

Bartel, J. (2019) 'Communication strategy of Russia: A case study of Estonia', in Meister, S. (ed.), *Understanding Russian Communications Strategy: Case Studies of Serbia and Estonia*. IFA Edition Cultural and Foreign Policy, 31–50. Available at: https://ifa-publikationen.de/out/wysiwyg/uploads/70edition/understanding-russian_meister.pdf.

BBC (2012) 'Russia internet blacklist law takes effect', BBC News, Nov. 1. Available at: https://www.bbc.com/news/technology-20096274, (Accessed 30 Nov. 2019).

BBC (2017a) 'Ukraine's Poroshenko to block Russian social networks', BBC News, May 16. Available at: https://www.bbc.com/news/world-europe-39934666, (Accessed 30 Nov. 2019).

BBC (2017b) 'Putin bans VPNs in web browsing crackdown', BBC News, July 31. Available at: https://www.bbc.com/news/technology-40774315, (Accessed 30 Nov. 2019).

BBC (2019a) 'Russia protests: Thousand arrests at Moscow rally', BBC News, July 27. Available at: https://www.bbc.com/news/world-europe-49125045, (Accessed 15 June 2020).

BBC (2019b) 'Mueller report: Criminal probe into Russia inquiry begins', BBC News, Oct. 25. Available at: https://www.bbc.com/news/world-us-canada-50178197, (Accessed 17 Nov. 2019).

BBC (2019c) 'Facebook tackles Russians making fake news stories', BBC News, Jan. 17. Available at: https://www.bbc.com/news/technology-46904935, (Accessed 28 Sep. 2019).

BBC (2020) 'Mark Zuckerberg: Facebook boss urges tighter regulation', BBC News, Feb. 15. Available at: https://www.bbc.com/news/technology-51518773, (Accessed 1 Mar 2020).

BBC Russian Service (2013)'*Duma approves law on extra-judicial blocking of websites. BBC Russian Service', (in Russian)*, 'Русская служба. Дума одобрила закон о внесудеб ной блокировке сайтов', BBC Russian Service, Dec. 20. Available at: https://ww w.bbc.com/russian/russia/2013/12/131220_duma_websites_block.shtml, (Accessed 30 Nov. 2019).

Beaufort, M. (2018) 'Digital media, political polarization and challenges to democracy', *Information, Communication & Society*, 21(7), 915–920, doi:10.1080/13691 18X.2018.1451909.

Beck, U. (1992) *Risk Society*. London: Sage Publications.

Belyakov, A. (2009) 'The influence of "Censorship by Money" on freedom of speech in Ukraine', *Critique*, 37(4), 601–617. Available at: https://www.tandfonline.com/doi/full/10.1080/03017600903205740, (Accessed 20 Sep. 2019).

Benkler, Y, Farris, R and Roberts, H (2018) *Network Propaganda*. New York: Oxford University Press.

Bennett, L.W. and Entman, R.M. (eds.) *Mediated Politics, Communications in the Future of Democracy*. Cambridge: Cambridge University Press, 33–55.

Bennett, L.W. and Livingston, S. (2018) 'The disinformation order: Disruptive communication and the decline of democratic institutions', *European Journal of Communication*, 33(2), 122–139.

Bennetts, M. (2017) 'Putin's holy war', *Politico*, Feb. 21. Available at: https://www.pol itico.eu/article/putins-holy-war/, (Accessed 15 June 2020).

Bennetts, M. (2019) 'Facebook and twitter could be blocked in Russia in data storage row', *The Guardian*, Apr. 17. Available at: https://www.theguardian.com/world /2019/apr/17/facebook-and-twitter-face-russian-sanctions-in-data-storage-row, (Accessed 20 June 2020).

Benson, T. (2020) 'Bots are waging a coronavirus disinformation campaign on social media', *Inverse*, Feb. 28. Available at: https://www.inverse.com/innovation/bots-are-spreading-lies-about-the-coronavirus-on-social-media, (Accessed 20 June 2020).

Bickert, M. (2020) 'Enforcing against manipulated media', *Facebook Newsroom*, Jan. 6. Available at: https://about.fb.com/news/2020/01/enforcing-against-manipulated-m edia/, (Accessed 30 Apr. 2020).

Blakemore, E. (2019) 'What was the Cold War?', *National Geographic*. Available at: https ://www.nationalgeographic.com/culture/topics/reference/cold-war/ (Accessed 27 Nov. 2019).

Bodner, M. (2020) 'Kremlin hails "triumph" as Russians clear way for Vladimir Putin to rule until 2036', *NBC News*, July 2. Available at: https://www.nbcnews.com/n ews/world/vladimir-putin-headed-victory-reform-vote-could-keep-him-power-n1 232688, (Accessed 4 July 2020).

Bohdanova, T. (2014) 'Unexpected revolution: The role of social media in Ukraine's Euromaidan uprising', *European View*, 13(1), 133–142.

Bok, S. (1978) *Lying: Moral Choice in Public and Private Life*. New York: Pantheon Publishing.

Borger, J. (2019) 'Donald Trump Denounces "Globalism" in nationalist address to UN', *The Guardian*, Sep. 24. Available at: https://www.theguardian.com/us-news/2019/ sep/24/donald-trump-un-address-denounces-globalism, (Accessed 12 May 2020).

Bourdieu, P. (1977) *Outline of a Theory of Practice*. Cambridge: Cambridge University Press.

Boyd, D. (2014) *It's Complicated: The Social Lives of Networked Teens*. New Haven: Yale University Press.

Bradshaw, S. and Howard, P. (2017) 'The global organization of social media disinformation campaigns', *Journal of International Affairs*, 71(1), 5.

Bradshaw, S. and Howard, P. (2019) *The Global Disinformation Order: 2019 Global Inventory of Organized Social Media Manipulation*. Oxford: Oxford University.

Brantly, A.F. (2019) 'From cyberspace to independence square: Understanding the impact of social media on physical protest mobilization during Ukraine's Euromaidan revolution', *Journal of Information Technology & Politics*, 16(4), 360–378.

Bratskiy, Y. (2019) 'Putin called the "Russian threat" fiction. Путин назвал «российск ую угрозу» выдумкой', Zvezda TV *Channel, Телеканал «Звезда*. Available at: https ://tvzvezda.ru/news/vstrane_i_mire/content/201911201514-08fuP.html, (Accessed 28 Nov. 2019).

Bridge, R. (2011) 'Election-meddling Fiasco hits US-Russia relations', *Russia Today*, Dec. 9. Available at: https://www.rt.com/russia/russia-us-elections-clinton-putin-2012-usaid-427/, (Accessed 20 June 2020).

Bridge, M. and Gibbons, K. (2017) 'Russia used twitter bots and trolls "to disrupt" Brexit vote', *The Times*, Nov. 15. Available at: https://www.thetimes.co.uk/edition/ news/russia-used-web-posts-to-disrupt-brexit-vote-h9nv5zg6c, (Accessed 22 June 2020).

Brown, B.T., Mann, B., Ryder, N., et al. (2020) 'Language models are few-shot learners', arxiv. Available at: https://arxiv.org/pdf/2005.14165.pdf, (Accessed 3 June 2020).

Burke, J. (2014) 'Post-Soviet world: What you need to know about the 15 states', *The Guardian*, June 9. Available at: https://www.theguardian.com/world/2014/jun/09/ -sp-profiles-post-soviet-states, (Accessed 19 Sep. 2019).

Butter, M. and Knight, P. (eds.) (2020) *Routledge Handbook of Conspiracy Theories*. Routledge: London.

Buckingham, D. (2019) *The Media Education Manifesto*. Cambridge: Polity.

Cairncross, F. (2019) 'The cairncross review: A sustainable future for journalism', *GOV. UK*, Feb. 12. Available at: https://www.gov.uk/government/publications/the-cai rncrossreview-a-sustainable-future-for-journalism, (Accessed 15 Mar. 2019).

Calhoun, C. (1966) *Habermas and the Public Sphere*. Cambridge: MIT Press.

Cammaerts, B. (2007) 'Citizenship, the public sphere and media', in Cammaerts, Bart and Carpentier, Nico, (eds.), *Reclaiming the Media: Communication Rights and Democratic*

Media Roles. European Communication Research and Education Association Series,3. Bristol: Intellect, 1–8.

Carlson, M. (2018) 'Fake news as an informational moral panic: The symbolic deviancy of social media during the 2016 US presidential election', *Information, Communication & Society*, 23(3), 374–388.

Carpentier, N. and Bart, C. (2006) 'Hegemony, democracy, agonism and journalism: An interview with Chantal Mouffe', *Journalism Studies*, 7(6), 964–975.

Carr, N. (2010) *The Shallows: What the Internet is Doing to Our Brains.* New York: W.W. Norton.

Carrol, C. (2011) 'Media relations and corporate social responsibility', in Ihlen, Ø., Bartlett, J. and May, S., (eds.), *The Handbook of Communication and Corporate Social Responsibility.* New Jersey: Wiley, Blackwell, 423–444.

Carroll, O. (2017) 'St. Petersburg "Troll Farm" had 90 dedicated staff working to influence US election campaign', *Independent*, Oct. 17. Available at: https://perma.cc /BL34-WK9F, (Accessed 16 June 2020).

Castells, M. (1996) *The Rise of the Network Society.* Oxford: Blackwell.

Castells, M. (2012) *Networks of Outrage and Hope: Social Movements in the Internet Age.* Cambridge: Polity.

Cederberg, P. and Erosen, A. (2015) 'How can Societies be Defended against Hybrid Threats?' *Geneva Centre for Security Policy*, September. Available at: https://s3.us-east -2.amazonaws.com/defenddemocracy/uploads/documents/GCSP_Strategic_Securi ty_Analysis_-_How_can_Societies_be_Defended_against_Hybrid_Threats.pdf, (Accessed 15 May 2020).

Censor (2013) '90% of participants euromaidan willing to stand up to the end – sociology', *Censor.net*, Dec. 25. Available at: https://censor.net.ua/news/264746/90_uchastni kov_evromayidana_gotovy_stoyat_do_kontsa_sotsiologiya, (Accessed 16 Sep. 2019).

Censor (2020) 'Russia sends a signal: The terrorist Putin can be for life on the Russian throne, and now everyone will have to reckon with him, - Butusov | Россия посылает сигнал: террорист Путин может быть пожизненно на российском троне, и теперь всем придется с ним считаться, – Бутусов. Цензор.НЕТ', *Censor .net*, Mar. 10. Available at: https://censor.net.ua/news/3180545/rossiya_posylaet_sig nal_terrorist_putin_mojet_byt_pojiznenno_na_rossiyiskom_trone_i_teper_vsem_ pridetsya, (Accessed 25 June 2020).

Centre for Data Ethics and Innovation (2019) 'Covid-19 Repository', Part of Department for Digital, Culture, Media & Sport, UK Government.

CEPA (2016) 'Sputnik: Propaganda in a new orbit: Information warfare initiative paper no. 2', *The Center for European Policy Analysis (CEPA)*, Jan. Available from http://inf owar.cepa.org/files/?id_plik=2083, (Accessed 16 June 2020).

CEPA (2017) 'Disinformation techniques', *The Center for European Policy Analysis (CEPA)*. Available from https://www.cepa.org/disinfo-techniques, (Accessed 16 June 2020).

CFR (2018) 'Putin's asymmetric assault on democracy in Russia and Europe: Implications for U.S. national security', *Committee of Foreign Relations United States Senate (CFR)*, Jan 10. Available from: https://www.foreign.senate.gov/imo/media/doc/FinalRR .pdf, (Accessed 16 June 2020).

Chadwick, A. (2006) *Internet Politics: States, Citizens and New Communications Technologies.* Oxford: Oxford University Press.

Charrad, M.M. and Reith, N.E. (2019) 'Local solidarities: How the arab spring protests started', *Sociological Forum*. Available at: https://onlinelibrary.wiley.com/doi/10.1111/ socf.12543, (Accessed 26 Sep. 2019).

Chee, F.Y. (2019) 'Facebook in EU antitrust crosshairs over data collection', *Reuters*, Dec. 2. Available at: https://www.reuters.com/article/us-eu-facebook-antitrust/facebook -in-eu-antitrust-crosshairs-over-data-collection-idUSKBN1Y625J, (Accessed 3 May 2020).

Chen, A. (2015) 'The agency', *New York Times Magazine*, June 2. Available from https ://www.nytimes.com/2015/06/07/magazine/the-agency.html., (Accessed 16 June 2020).

Chomsky, N. and Herman, E.S. (1988) *Manufacturing Consent: The Political Economy of the Mass Media*. New York: Pantheon Books.

Chornokondratenko, M. (2013) 'The phenomenon of Euromaidan in media', *The European Journalism Observatory – EJO*. Available at: https://ua.ejo-online.eu/1583/ sfery-vysvitlennya, (Accessed 14 June 2019).

Choy, M. and Chong, M. (2018) 'Seeing through misinformation: A framework for identifying fake online news', *Deep AI*, Mar. 31. Available at: https://deepai.org/ publication/seeing-through-misinformation-a-framework-for-identifying-fake-o nline-news, (Accessed 5 May 2020).

Cialdini, R.B. (2006) *Influence: The Psychology of Persuasion*. New York: Harper Business.

Cohen, M. (2019) 'Exclusive: Assange turned embassy into command post in 2016', *CNN*. Available at: https://edition.cnn.com/2019/07/15/politics/assange-embassy-exclusive-documents/index.html, (Accessed 21 Nov. 2019).

Coleman, S. and Blumler, J. (2009) *The Internet and Democratic Citizenship: Theory, Practice and Policy*. New York: Cambridge University Press.

Cooper, T. (2017) 'Ukraine: Revoke Ban on Dozens of Russian web companies', *Human Rights Watch*. Available at: https://www.hrw.org/news/2017/05/16/ukraine-revoke -ban-dozens-russian-web-companies, (Accessed 22 Sep. 2019).

Corner, J. (1997) 'Television in theory', *Media, Culture and Society*, 19(2), 247–262.

Couldry, N. (2008) 'Mediatization or mediation? Alternative understandings of the emergent space of digital storytelling', *New Media & Society*, 10(3), 373–391.

Couldry, N. and Hepp, A. (2017) *The Mediated Construction of Reality*. London: Polity Press.

Coynash, H. (2017) 'Ukrainian student sentenced for "propaganda of communism" on Facebook', *Kharkiv Human Rights Protection Group*, May 15. Available at: http://khpg .org/en/index.php?id=1494505913, (Accessed 26 Sep. 2019).

Craft, S., Ashley, S. and Maksl, A. (2017) 'News media literacy and conspiracy theory endorsement', *Communication and the Public*, 2(4), 388–401.

Cummings, D. (2017) 'How the Brexit referendum was won', *Spectator*, Jan. 9. Available at: https://www.spectator.co.uk/article/dominic-cummings-how-the-brexit-re ferendum-was-won, (Accessed 30 May 2018).

Curran, J. (1991) 'Rethinking the media as a public sphere', in Dahlgren, P. and Sparks, C. (eds.), *Communication and Citizenship: Journalism and the Public Sphere in the New Media Age*. London: Routledge, 27–57.

Dahlgren, P. (1991) 'Introduction', in Dahlgren, P. and Sparks, C. (eds.), *Communication and Citizenship: Journalism and the Public in the Media*. London: Routledge: 1–24.

Dahlgren, P. (2001) 'The public sphere and the net: Structure, space, and communication', in Lance Bennett, W. and Entman, Robert M. (eds.), *Mediated Politics: Communication in the Future of Democracy*. Cambridge: Cambridge University Press, 33–55.

Dahlgren, P. (2009) *Media and Political Engagement*. Cambridge: Cambridge University Press.

Dahlgren, P. (2018) 'Media, knowledge and trust: The deepening epistemic crisis of democracy', Yavnost – The Public, 25(1–2), 20–27.

D'Ancona, M. (2017) *Post Truth: The New War on Truth and how to Fight Back*. London: Ebury Press.

DataReportal (2019) 'Digital 2019 Ukraine (January 2019) v01', *Slideshare*. Available at: https://www.slideshare.net/DataReportal/digital-2019-ukraine-january-2019-v01, (Accessed 23 Sep. 2019).

DCMSC (2019) 'House of commons digital, culture, media and sport committee, disinformation and "Fake News": Final report, eighth report of session 2017–19', *Digital, Culture, Media and Sport Committee*, Feb. 14. Available at: https://www.par liament.uk/business/committees/committees-a-z/commons-select/digital-culture -media-and-sport-committee/news/fake-news-report-published-17-19/, (Accessed 28 Mar. 2019).

De Angelis, R. (1998) 'Pauline Hanson's one nation party: Xenophobic populism compared', *Policy, Organisation and Society*, 16(1), 1–27. doi:10.1080/10349952.1998. 11876687.

Dek, A., Kononova, K., Marchenko, T. and NATO STRATCOM (2019) 'Responding to cognitive security challenges', *StratCom*. Available at: https://stratcomcoe.org/r esponding-cognitive-security-challenges?fbclid=IwAR0GXWFWyH703cBbthr2x ejv8qxvXxe_hCRxp1u8DLGeckkEOZ7khw5sKTo, (Accessed 26 Sep. 2019).

De Sola Pool, I. (1983) *Technologies of Freedom*, Massachusetts: Harvard University Press.

Deutsche Welle (2019) '"Kommersant" Russian journalists quit over censorship', *Deutsche Welle*, May 20. Available at: https://www.dw.com/en/kommersant-russian-journalis ts-quit-over-censorship/a-48809394, (Accessed 3 Sep. 2019).

Dickson, B (2017) 'How blockchain helps fight fake news and filter bubbles', *The Next Web*, Aug. 24. Available at: https://thenextweb.com/contributors/2017/08/24/blo ckchain-helps-fight-fake-news-filter-bubbles/, (Accessed 12 Apr. 2018).

Disinfo.tech (2020) 'Design, development & training', disinfo.tech. Available at: https:// disinfo.tech/we-do/ (Accessed 13 June 2020).

DQ Institute (2019) 'Leading digital education, culture, and innovation', *DQ Institute*. Available at: https://www.dqinstitute.org, (Accessed 20 Apr. 2020).

Drucker, J. and Cox, D. (2004) 'Under assault: Ukraine's news media and the 2004 presidential elections', *Freedom House*. Available at: https://freedomhouse.org/ sites/default/files/Essay%20Ukraine%206-18-04%20final.pdf, (Accessed 13 June 2020).

Dunleavy, J. and Chaitin, D. (2020) 'Robert Mueller: Trump may have lied', *Washington Examiner*, June 19. Available from: https://www.washingtonexaminer.com/news/ robert-mueller-trump-may-have-lied, (Accessed 22 June 2020).

Duvanova, D., Semenov, A. and Nikolaev, A. (2014) 'Do social networks bridge political divides? The analysis of *VKontakte* social network communication in Ukraine', *Post-Soviet Affairs*, 31(3), 224–249. https://doi.org/10.1080/1060586X.2014. 918453.

Dyczok, M. (2006) 'Was Kuchma's censorship effective? mass media in Ukraine before 2004', *Europe-Asia Studies*, 58(2), 215–238.

Eatwell, R. and Goodwin, M. (2018) *National Populism: The Revolt Against Liberal Democracy*. London: Penguin.

EBU (2018a) 'Market insights: Trust in media 2018', *European Broadcasting Union*, Feb. Available at: https://www.ebu.ch/files/live/sites/ebu/files/Publications/MIS/lo gin_only/market_insights/EBU-MIS%20-Trust%20in%20Media%202018.pdf, (Accessed 3 May 2020).

EBU (2018b) 'The sounding board's unanimous final opinion on the so-called code of practice', *European Broadcasting Union*, Sep. 24. Available at: https://www.ebu.ch

/files/live/sites/ebu/files/News/2018/09/Opinion%20of%20the%20Sounding%2 0Board.pdf, (Accessed 3 May 2020).

EC (2016) 'European commission, joint communication to the European parliament and the council: Joint framework on countering hybrid threats. A European union response', *European Commission*. Available at: https://eur-lex.europa.eu/legal-con tent/EN/TXT/PDF/?uri=CELEX:52016JC0018&from=EN, (Accessed 7 May 2020).

EC (2018a) 'European commission, a multi-dimensional approach to disinformation: Report of the independent high level group on fake news and online disinformation', *European Commission*. Available at: https://ec.europa.eu/digital-single-market/en/ news/final-report-high-level-expert-group-fake-news-and-online-disinformation, (Accessed 1 Feb. 2020).

EC (2018b), 'Tackling online disinformation: A European approach', *European Commission*. Available at: https://eur-lex.europa.eu/legal- content/EN/TXT/PDF/ ?uri=CELEX:52018DC0236&from=EN, (Accessed 1 Feb 2020).

EC (2018c), 'Code of practice on disinformation', *European Commission*. Available at: https://ec.europa.eu/digital-single-market/en/news/code-practice-disinformation, (Accessed 7 Feb. 2020).

EC (2018d) 'Increasing resilience and bolstering capabilities to address hybrid threats', *European Commission*. Available at: https://eur-lex.europa.eu/legal-content/EN/TX T/PDF/?uri=CELEX:52018JC0016, (Accessed 7 May 2020).

EC (2018e) 'Meeting of the multistakeholder forum on disinformation', *European Commission*. Available at: https://ec.europa.eu/digital-single-market/en/news/meet ing-multistakeholder-forum-disinformation, (Accessed 7 May 2020).

EC (2018f) 'Joint communication to the European parliament, the European council, the council, the European economic and social committee and the committee of the regions: Action plan against disinformation', *European Commission*. Available at: https://eeas.europa.eu/sites/eeas/files/action_plan_against_disinformation.pdf, (Accessed 7 May 2020).

EC (2019) 'Shaping Europe's digital future: Tackling online disinformation', *European Commission*. Available at: https://ec.europa.eu/digital-single-market/en/tackling-online-disinformation, (Accessed 7 May 2020).

EC (2020a) 'Shaping Europe's digital future: Commission presents strategies for data and artificial intelligence', *European Commission*. Available at: https://ec.europa.eu/comm ission/presscorner/detail/en/ip_20_273, (Accessed 24 May 2020).

EC (2020b) 'European media literacy week', *European Commission*. Available at: https ://ec.europa.eu/digital-single-market/en/news/european-media-literacy-week, (Accessed 4 May 2020).

EC (2020c) 'Roadmaps to implement the code of practice on disinformation', *European Commission*. Available at: https://ec.europa.eu/digital-single-market/en/news/road maps-implement-code-practice-disinformation, (Accessed 24 May 2020).

EC (2020d) 'The European digital media observatory kicks off', *European Commission*, June 4. Available at: https://ec.europa.eu/inea/en/news-events/newsroom/european -digital-media-observatory-kicks, (Accessed 25 June 2020).

ECHRCE (1950) 'European convention on human rights', *European Court of Human Rights and Council of Europe*. Available at: https://www.echr.coe.int/Documents/ Convention_ENG.pdf, (Accessed 21 Sep. 2019).

Ecker, U. (2018) 'Why rebuttals may not work: The psychology of misinformation', *Media Asia*, 44(2), 79–87.

Ecker, U., Hogan, L. and Lewandowsky, S. (2017) 'Reminders and repetition of misinformation: Helping or hindering its retraction?', *Journal of Applied Research in Memory and Cognition*, 6, 185–192.

Ecker, U.K.H. (2017) 'Why rebuttals may not work: The psychology of misinformation', *Media Asia*, 44(2), 79–87, doi:10.1080/01296612.2017.1384145.

Ecker, U.K.H., Hogan, J.L. and Lewandowsky, S. (2017) 'Reminders and repetition of misinformation: Helping or hindering its retraction?', *Journal of Applied Research in Memory and Cognition*, 6, 185–192.

Edwards, L. (2018) *Understanding Public Relations*. London: Sage Publications.

EEAS (2019) 'Rapid alert system: Strengthening coordinated and joint responses to disinformation', *European External Action Service*, Mar. Available at: https://eeas.eu ropa.eu/sites/eeas/files/ras_factsheet_march_2019_0.pdf, (Accessed 25 June 2020).

Elis, G.E. (2017) 'Fake think tanks fuel fake news – and the president's tweets', *Wired*, Jan. 24. Available at: https://www.wired.com/2017/01/fake-think-tanks-fuel-fake-news -presidents-tweets/, (Accessed 23 May 2020).

Ellyatt, H. (2019) 'After Mueller findings, US-Russian relations can hopefully "start again" VTB's Kostin says', *CNBC*. Available at: https://www.cnbc.com/2019/04 /24/kostin-mueller-report-can-lead-to-new-start-for-us-russia-relations.html, (Accessed 28 Nov. 2019).

Encyclopedia Britannica (2019) 'Glasnost | Soviet government policy', *Encyclopædia Britannica*. Available at: https://www.britannica.com/topic/glasnost, (Accessed 28 Mar. 2019).

EP (2018) 'Directive (eu) 2018/1808 of the European parliament and of the council', European Parliament, Nov. 14. Available at: https://eur-lex.europa.eu/legal-con tent/EN/TXT/PDF/?uri=CELEX:32018L1808&from=EN, (Accessed 3 May 2020).

EP (2019a) 'Disinformation and propaganda – impact on the functioning of the rule of law in the EU and its member states', European Parliament, Feb Available at: https ://www.europarl.europa.eu/RegData/etudes/STUD/2019/608864/IPOL_ST U(2019)608864_EN.pdf, (Accessed 20 May 2020).

EP (2019b) 'Regulating disinformation with artificial intelligence', European Parliament, Mar. Available at: https://www.europarl.europa.eu/RegData/etudes/STUD/2019 /624279/EPRS_STU(2019)624279_EN.pdf, (Accessed 20 May 2020).

EPRS (2019) 'Automated tackling of disinformation', *European Parliamentary Research Service*, Mar. Available at: https://www.europarl.europa.eu/RegData/etudes/STUD /2019/624278/EPRS_STU(2019)624278_EN.pdf, (Accessed 16 May 2020).

E-Server (2018) 'History of internet development', EServer, Dec. 28. Available at: https://e-server.com.ua/sovety/240-istoriya-razvitiya-interneta, (Accessed 13 Sep. 2019).

EUInfoCenter (2017) 'Fake news' and the EU's response', The Delegation of the European Union to the Republic of Serbia, Apr. 4. Available at: https://europa.rs/fa ke-news-and-the-eus-response/?lang=en, (Accessed 26 Feb. 2020).

Euromaidan Press (2019) 'Two important results of Ukraine's ban of *VKontakte* Russian social network', *Euromaidan Press*, Mar. 24. Available at: http://euromaidanpress.co m/2019/03/24/ukraines-vkontakte-ban-led-to-drop-in-users-but-die-hards-now- more-radicalized/, (Accessed 23 Sep. 2019).

European Council (2015) 'European council meeting (19 and 20 March 2015) – conclusions', European Council, Mar. 20. Available at: http://data.consilium.europa .eu/doc/document/ST-11-2015-INIT/en/pdf, (Accessed 4 Sep. 2018).

European Sources Online (2015) 'Action plan on strategic communication', *Eastern Partnership Civil Forum*, June 22. Available at: http://archive.eap-csf.eu/assets/files/A ction%20PLan.pdf, (Accessed 26 Feb. 2020).

EUvsDisinfo (2017) 'Three things you should know about RT and Sputnik', EU vs Disinformation, Sept. 11. Available at: https://euvsdisinfo.eu/three-things-you-shoul d-know-about-rt-and-sputnik/, (Accessed 16 June 2020).

EUvsDisinfo (2018) 'The strategy and tactics of the pro-Kremlin disinformation campaign', EU vs Disinformation, Jun. 27. Available at: https://euvsdisinfo.eu/the-str ategy-and-tactics-of-the-pro-kremlin-disinformation-campaign/, (Accessed 17 June 2020).

EUvsDisinfo (2019) 'Figure of the week: 55%', EU vs Disinformation, Sept. 3. Available at: https://euvsdisinfo.eu/figure-of-the-week-55/?highlight=bot, (Accessed 17 June 2020).

EUvsDisinfo (2020a) 'Disinfo: Crimea was not annexed, the people voted for accession to russia in a referendum', EU vs Disinformation. Available at: https://euvsdisinfo. eu/report/crimea-was-not-annexed-the-people-voted-for-accession-to-russia-in-a -referendum/, (Accessed 17 June 2020).

EUvsDisinfo (2020b) 'Disinfo: Socialist countries such as cuba deal with the epidemic much better than rich capitalistic western states', EU vs Disinformation. Available at: https://euvsdisinfo.eu/report/the-socialist-countries-such-as-cuba-deal-with-the -epidemic-in-a-much-better-way-than-rich-capitalistic-western-states/, (Accessed 17 June 2020).

Falkheimer and Heide (2018) *Strategic Communications: An Introduction*. London: Routledge.

Ferrara, E., Varol, O., Davis, C., Menczer, F. and Flammini, A. (2016) 'The rise of social bots', *Communications of the ACM*, 59(7), 96–104.

Fetzer, J.H. (2014) 'Disinformation: The use of false information', *Minds and Machines*, 14(2), 231–240.

Field, M. (2020) 'WhatsApp imposes strict limit on messages to combat fake news', *The Telegraph*, Apr. 7. Available at: https://www.telegraph.co.uk/technology/2020/04 /07/whatsapp-imposes-strict-limit-messages-combat-fake-news/, (Accessed 11 June 2020).

Flew, T. (2020) 'The global trust deficit disorder: A communications perspective on digital trust in the time of global pandemics', May. 23. Available at: https://www.you tube.com/watch?v=tkdTXwbpAWs, (Accessed 7 July 2020).

Flew, T. and Iosifidis, P. (2020) 'Populism, globalisation and social media', *International Communications Gazette*, 82(1), 7–25.

Flew, T., Martin, F. and Suzor, N.P. (2019) 'Internet regulation as media policy: Rethinking the question of digital communication platform governance', *Journal of Digital Media and Policy*, 10(1), 33–50. https://doi.org/10.1386/jdtv.10.1.33_1.

Fraser, N. (1990) 'Rethinking the public sphere: A contribution to the critique of actually existing democracy', 25/26, 56–80. Available at: https://www.jstor.org/ stable/466240, (Accessed 28 Nov. 2019). doi:10.2307/466240.

Freedman, D. (2018) 'Populism and media policy failure', *European Journal of Communication,* 33(2), 122–139.

Freedom House (2019) 'Democracy in retreat: Freedom in the world 2019', *Freedom House*, Feb 2. Available at: https://freedomhouse.org/sites/default/files/2020-02/Fe b2019_FH_FITW_2019_Report_ForWeb-compressed.pdf, (Accessed 7 May 2020).

Freedom House (2020) 'Countries and territories', *Freedom House*. Available from https:/ /freedomhouse.org/countries/freedom-world/scores, (Accessed 16 June 2020).

Freistad and Wright (1984) 'Persuasion model: How people cope with Persuasion attempts', *Journal of Consumer Research*, 21(1), 1–31.

Friedersdorf, C. (2019) 'Doubt anyone who's confident that Facebook should ban political ads', *The Atlantic*, Nov. 1. Available at: https://www.theatlantic.com/ideas /archive/2019/11/twitter-facebook-political-ads/601174/, (Accessed 11 June 2020).

Fuchs, C. (2014) 'Social media and the public sphere', triple-C, 12(1), https://doi.org/10 .31269/triplec.v12i1.552.

Fuchs, C. (2017) 'Donald Trump: A critical theory-perspective on authoritarian capitalism', triple-C, 15(1), 1–72.

Fuchs, C. (2018) 'Social media, big data, and critical marketing', in Todajewski, M., Higgins, M, Denedri-Knott, J. and Varman, R. (eds.), *The Routledge Companion to Critical Marketing*, London: Routledge, 467–481.

Fukuyama, F. (2018) 'Against identity politics: The new tribalism and the crisis of democracy', *Foreign Affairs*, 97(5), 90–114.

Funke, D. and Benkelman, S. (2019) '19 fact-checkers are teaming up to fight misinformation about the EU elections', *Poynter*, Mar 21. Available at: https://www .poynter.org/fact-checking/2019/19-fact-checkers-are-teaming-up-to-fight-misinf ormation-about-the-eu-elections/, (Accessed 7 May 2020).

Garnhman, N. (1990) *Capitalism and Communication: Global Culture and the Economics of Information*. London: Sage Publications.

Gaydareva, I.N., Eshev, M.A. and Markov, P.N. (2020) 'Internet censorship in the context of legal regulation in Russia', *Advances in Economics, Business and Management Research*, 138, 264–270.

Gessen, M. (2020) *Surviving Autocracy*. New York: Riverhead Books.

Ghosh, D. and Scott, B. (2018) '#Digital deceit: The technologies behind precision propaganda on the internet', *Harvard Kennedy School: Shorenstein Center on Media, Politics and Public Policy*, Jan. Available at: https://d1y8sb8igg2f8e.cloudfront.net/do cuments/digital-deceit-final-v3.pdf, (Accessed 6 June 2020).

Giddens, A. (1991) *The Consequence of Modernity*. Stanford: Stanford University Press.

Giles, K. (2019) 'The next phase of Russian information warfare', *NATO Strategic Communications Centre of Excellence*. https://www.stratcomcoe.org/next-phase-russia n-information-warfare-keir-giles, (Accessed 15 June 2020).

Goncharova, T., Turkevich, I., Rudik, O., Smetana, V., Dikiy, V. and Derkach, A. (2017) 'Stop the destruction of freedom of speech in Ukraine! | Зупинити знищення свободи слова в Україні!', Good *Morning, Country | Доброго ранку, Країно*. Available at: http://eramedia.com.ua/273632-zupiniti_znischennya_svobodi_slova_ v_ukran/, (Accessed 21 Sep. 2019).

Gorchinskaya, K. (2020a) 'A brief history of corruption in Ukraine: The Kutchma era', May 20. Available at: https://eurasianet.org/a-brief-history-of-corruption-in-ukra ine-the-kuchma-era, (Accessed 26 June 2020).

Gorchinskaya, K. (2020b) 'A brief history of corruption in Ukraine: The Yanukovych era', Jun. 3. Available at: https://eurasianet.org/a-brief-history-of-corruption-in -ukraine-the-yanukovych-era, (Accessed 26 June 2020).

Gordon, A., Ecker, U. K.H. and Lewandowsky, S. (2019) 'Polarity and attitude effects in the continued-influence paradigm', *Journal of Memory and Language*, 108, , 104028, https://doi.org/10.1016/j.jml.2019.104028.

Gordonua (2014) 'Durov refused to give FSB data on administrators of the Euromaidan dedicated communities and deleting Navalny's pages | Дуров отказался выдать ФСБ данные админов сообществ Евромайдана и закрыть группу Навального', *Gordonua*, Apr. 16. Available at: https://gordonua.com/news/worldnews/durov-otk

azalsya-vydat-fsb-dannye-adminov-soobshchestv-evromaydana-i-zakryt-gruppu-n avalnogo-18673.html, (Accessed 17 Sep. 2019).

Gordonua (2015) 'Самые резонансные смерти в независимой Украине', *Gordonua*. Available at: https://gordonua.com/specprojects/dead.html, (Accessed 11 Sep. 2019).

Graves, L. and Cherubini, F. (2016) 'The rise of fact-checking sites in Europe', *Reuters Institute for the Study of Journalism*. Available at: https://reutersinstitute.politics.ox.ac. uk/sites/default/files/research/files/The%2520Rise%2520of%2520Fact-Checking %2520Sites%2520in%2520Europe.pdf, (Accessed 6 June 2020).

Greenwood, S. (2018) *Future Journalism: Where We Are and Where We're Going*. London: Routledge.

Gregory, A. (2013) *Planning and Managing Public Relations Campaigns: A Strategic Approach*. London: Kogan Press.

Gromova, A. (2008) 'The role of media in the implementation of the "Color Revolutions"', *The Herald of People's Friendship University* of Russia, 2, 46–56. Available at: https:// cyberleninka.ru/article/n/rol-smi-v-osuschestvlenii-tsvetnyh-revolyutsiy, (Accessed 16 Aug. 2019).

Guarino, S., Trino, N., Chessa, A. and Riotta, G. (2020) 'Beyond fact-checking: Network analysis tools for monitoring disinformation in social media', in Cherifi, H., Gaito, S., Mendes, J., Moro, E. and Rocha, L. (eds.), *Complex Networks and Their Applications VIII. COMPLEX NETWORKS 2019. Studies in Computational Intelligence*, vol. 881. Cham: Springer, 436–447.

Guevarra, R. (2015) 'Communist theory of mass communication', Academia.edu. Available at: https://www.academia.edu/35783893/Communist_Theory_of_Mass _Communication, (Accessed 23 Sep. 2019).

Guo, J. (2017) 'The bonkers seth rich conspiracy theory, explained', Vox, May 24. Available at: https://www.vox.com/policy-and-politics/2017/5/24/15685560/seth-r ich-conspiracy-theory-explained-fox-news-hannity, (Accessed 1 July 2020).

Habermas, J. (1984) *The Theory of Communicative Action*. Cambridge: Polity Press.

Habermas, J. (1989) [1962], *The Structural Transformation of the Public Sphere: An Inquiry into a Category of Bourgeois Society*. Cambridge: Polity Press.

Hågvar, Y.B. (2019) 'New media's rhetoric on Facebook', *Journalism Practice*, 13(7), 853–872.

Haigh, M., Haigh, T. and Kozak, N.I. (2017) 'Stopping fake news', *Journalism Studies*, 19(14), 2062–2087.

Halperin, J. (1996) *The Truth Machine*. New York: Random House.

Harari, Y.N. (2015) *Sapiens: A Brief History of Humankind (First U.S. Edition.)*. New York: Harper.

Harper's Magazine (2020) 'A letter on justice and open debate', *Harper's Magazine*, Jul 7. Available at: https://harpers.org/a-letter-on-justice-and-open-debate/, (Accessed 11 July 2020).

Harris (2020) 'EU should regulate Facebook and google as "attention utilities"', *Financial Times*, Mar. 1. Available at: https://www.ft.com/content/abd80d98-595e-11ea-abe5 -8e03987b7b20, (Accessed 3 May 2020).

Harwell, D. (2018) 'AI will solve Facebook's most vexing problems Mark Zuckerburg says. Just don't ask when or how', *The Washington Post*, Apr. 11. Available at: https ://www.washingtonpost.com/news/the-switch/wp/2018/04/11/ai-will-solve-faceb ooks-most-vexing-problems-mark-zuckerberg-says-just-dont-ask-when-or-how/, (Accessed 16 May 2020).

Heinrich, A. (2019) 'How to build resilient news infrastructures? Reflections on information provision in times of "Fake News"', in Linkov, I., Roslycky, L. and

Trump, B.D. (eds.), *Resilience and Hybrid Threats: Security and Integrity for the Digital World*. Amsterdam: IOS Press: 174–187.

Helmus, T., Bodine-Baron, E., Radin, A., Magnuson, M., Mendelsohn, J., Marcellino, W., Bega, A. and Winkelman, Z. (2018) *Russian Social Media Influence: Understanding Russian Propaganda in Eastern Europe*. California: RAND Corporation.

Hermida, A., Lewis, S.C. and Zamith, R. (2014) 'Sourcing the Arab spring: A case study of Andy Carvin's sources on twitter during the Tunisian and Egyptian revolutions', *Journal of Computer-Mediated Communication*, 19(3), 479–499.

Heyamoto, L. and Milbourn, T. (2018) '6 ways to increase the public's trust in journalism', *Digital Content Next*, Aug. 15. Available at: https://digitalcontentnext.org /blog/2018/08/15/6-ways-to-increase-the-publics-trust-in-journalism/, (Accessed 30 May 2020).

History.com (2018) 'Perestroika', History.com. Available at: https://www.history.com/t opics/cold-war/perestroika-and-glasnost, (Accessed 20 Aug. 2019).

Hoffman, D. (2013) 'Citizens: The New Forth Estate', *HuffPost*, Nov 10. Available at: https://www.huffpost.com/entry/citizens-the-new-fourth-e_b_3894819?guccount er=1&guce_referrer=aHR0cHM6Ly9kdWNrZHVja2dvLmNvbS8&guce_refer rer_sig=AQAAACWRsn4WZ220SYG5BEA_813m3roRJnZIap_KPtBKvN5w84II wkSPePBUwvJAvVLlILeRJAubilserVzBFKFfCM6ZittyqD7Mr5F2Yi8d-2yTx1dHV F6bKda-dTBhwN0l13DnwZO5XT_cAQMe8bdQPyO99lGUlb8CnNlRJJ-laaKk/, (Accessed 12 June 2020).

Hoffman, F.G. (2010) '"Hybrid Threats": Neither omnipotent nor unbeatable', *Orbis*, 54(3), 441–455.

Horowitz, M. (2018) 'Public service media and information disorder: Public media institutions at a crossroads: Visions, strategies, tactics', *Center for Media, Data and Society Central European University*, Aug. Available at: https://cmds.ceu.edu/sites/cmc s.ceu.hu/files/attachment/article/1367/publicservicemediaandinformationdisorder. pdf, (Accessed 12 Dec. 2019).

House of Commons Select Committee on Culture, Media and Sport (2017) 'Fake news inquiry launched', *House of Commons Select Committee on Culture, Media and Sport*. Available at: http://www.parliament.uk/business/committees/committees-az/c ommons-select/culture-media-and-sport-committee/news-parliament-2015/fake-n ewslaunch-16-17/, (Accessed 3 Sep. 2018).

Hromadske Radio (2018) 'How does fact-checking fight lies in the media? | Як фактчекінг бореться з брехнею у ЗМІ?', *Громадське радіо*. Available at: https:/ /hromadske.radio/podcasts/dno/yak-faktcheking-boretsya-z-brehneyu-v-zmi, (Accessed 10 Sep. 2019).

Human Rights Watch (2003) 'Unofficial state censorship on Ukrainian television', *Human Rights Watch*. Available at: https://www.hrw.org/legacy/russian/reports/ru ssia/2003/fight1/t3.html, (Accessed 17 Sep. 2019).

Humprecht, E. (2018) 'Where "fake news" flourishes: A comparison across four Western democracies', *Information, Communication & Society*, 22(13), 1973–1988, doi:10.1080/1 369118X.2018.1474241.

Ibrahim, Y. and Safieddine, F. (eds.) (2020) Fake News in an Era of Social Media: Tracking Viral Contagion. Maryland: Rowman & Littlefield International.

Idrisova, K. (2017) 'Explainer: What is Russia's new VPN law all about?', BBC News, Nov 1. Available at: https://www.cepa.org/copy-of-powering-influence, (Accessed 16 June 2020).

IFCN (2020) 'Code of principles', *International Fact-Checking Network*. Available at: https ://ifcncodeofprinciples.poynter.org/, (Accessed 4 May 2020).

Ingelhart, R. and Norris, P. (2016) 'Trump, Brexit, and the rise of populism: Economic have-nots and cultural Backlash', Faculty Research Working Paper Series RWP-16. Cambridge: Harvard Kennedy School - John FR. Kennedy School of Government. Aug. Available at: https://www.hks.harvard.edu/publications/trump-brexit-and-rise -populism-economic-have-nots-and-cultural-backlash#citation, (Accessed 20 May 2019).

Iosifidis, P. (2020) 'Public sphere', in *Routledge Encyclopaedia of Citizen Media*. Routledge.

Iosifidis, P. and Andrews, L. (2020) 'Regulating the internet intermediaries in a post-truth world: Beyond media policy?', *International Communication Gazette*, 82(3), 211–230. doi:10.1177/1748048519828595.

Iosifidis, P. and Nicoli, N. (2020) 'The battle to end fake news: A qualitative content analysis of Facebook announcements on how it combats disinformation', *International Communication Gazette*, 82(1), 60–81. doi:10.1177/1748048519880729.

Iosifidis, P. and Wheeler, M. (2016) *Public Spheres and Mediated Social Networks in the Western Context and Beyond*. London: Palgrave Macmillan.

Iosifidis, P. and Wheeler, M. (2018) 'Modern political communication and web 2.0 in representative democracies', *Javnost/The Public*, 25(1–2). E-pub ahead of print 29 January 2018. doi:10.1080/13183222.2018.1418962.

Ivaldi, G. (2018) 'Populism in France', in Stockemer, D. (ed.), *Populism Around the World. A Comparative Perspective*. Cham: Springer, 27–48.

Ivancsics, B. (2019) 'Blockchain in journalism', *Columbia Journalism Review*, Jan. 25. Available at: https://www.cjr.org/tow:center_reports/blockchain-in-journalism.p hp, (Accessed 21 May 2020).

Ivantsova, A. (2015) 'Особенности украинского троллинга', *RFL/RL | Радио Свобода*. Available at: https://www.svoboda.org/a/27043105.html, (Accessed 1 Aug. 2019).

Iyengar and Hahn (2009) 'Red media, blue media: Evidence of ideological selectivity in media use', *Journal of Communication*, 59, 19–39.

Jankowicz, N. (2019) 'Ukraine's election is an all-out disinformation battle', *The Atlantic*, Apr. 17. Available at: https://www.theatlantic.com/international/arc hive/2019/04/russia-disinformation-ukraine-election/587179/, (Accessed 26 June 2020).

Jankowicz, N. and Otis, C. (2020) 'Facebook groups are destroying America', *Wired Magazine*, Jun. 17. Available at: https://www.wired.com/story/facebook-groups-are -destroying-america/#intcid=recommendations_wired-right-rail_15e3d3aa-d6aa -4092-b050-8d342dcd1c4f_popular4-1, (Accessed 20 June 2020).

Jekel Cik, S. (2007) *Ukraine: Birth of a Modern Nation*. Oxford: Oxford University Press.

Jenkins, H., Ford, S. and Green, J. (2013) *Spreadable Media: Creating Value and Meaning in a Networked Culture*. New York: NYU Press.

Jensen, D. and Rebegea, C. (2017) 'Russian disinformation and anti-Western narratives in Romania: How to fight back?', *Center for European Policy Analysis*, Nov. 2. Available at: https://www.cepa.org/copy-of-powering-influence, (Accessed 16 June 2020).

Jones, J. (2018) 'U.S. media trust continues to recover from 2016 low', Gallup, Oct. 12. Available at: https://news.gallup.com/poll/243665/media-trust-continues-recover -2016-low.aspx, (Accessed 12 May 2020).

Jones, S. (1998) 'Understanding micropolis and compunity', *Journal of Electronic Communication*, 8(3/4).

Jowett, G. and O'Donnell, V. (2019) *Propaganda & Persuasion*, 7th Edition, California: Sage Publications.

Ju, A, Jeong, S and Chyi, H (2014) 'Will social media save newspapers?', *Journalism Practice*, 8(1), 1–17. doi:10.1080/17512786.2013.794022.

Judis, J. (2016) *The Populist Explosion: How the Great Recession Transformed American and European Politics*. New York: Columbia Global Reports.

Juris, J.S. (2005) 'The new digital media and activist networking within anti–corporate globalization movements', *The ANNALS of the American Academy of Political and Social Science*, 597(1), 89–208.

Kahneman, D. (2011) *Thinking Fast and Slow*. New York: Farrar, Straus and Giroux

Kamenetsky, Y. and Muradeli, V. (1967) *There is a Beginning for the Revolution*. Есть у революции начало.

Kantar (2019) 'Top sites and apps ranking August 2019 | Рейтинг популярних сайтів та додатків за серпень 2019', Tns-ua.com. Available at: https://tns-ua.com/news/r eyting-populyarnih-saytiv-za-serpen-2019, (Accessed 21 Sep. 2019).

Kaplan, A.M. and Haenlein, M. (2010) 'Users of the world, unite! The challenges and opportunities of social media', *Business Horizons*, 53(1), 59–68.

Kelion, L. (2020) 'Coronavirus: YouTube tightens rules after David Icke 5G interview', BBC News, Apr. 7. Available at: https://www.bbc.com/news/technology-52198946, (Accessed 4 May 2020).

Kelly, M. (2020) 'Twitter labels Trump tweets as "potentially misleading" for the first time', *The Verge*, May 26. Available at: https://www.theverge.com/2020/5/26/21271 207/twitter-donald-trump-fact-check-mail-in-voting-coronavirus-pandemic-cal ifornia, (Accessed 20 June 2020).

Kemp, S. (2020) 'Digital 2020: 3.8 billion people use social media', We *Are Social*, Jan. 30. Available at: https://wearesocial.com/blog/2020/01/digital-2020-3-8-billion -people-use-social-media (accessed 9 May 2020).

Khamis, S. (2013) '"Cyberactivism" in the Arab spring: What social media can and cannot do', *International Affairs Forum*, 4(1). Available at: https://www.tandfonline.c om/doi/full/10.1080/23258020.2013.824258, (Accessed 22 July 2019).

Khmelyovska, O. (2013) 'Mass media during the Maidan protests: The beating of journalists, attacks on editorial boards and hacking attacks', *Tyzden (Week)*, Jan. Available at: https://tyzhden.ua/News/96293, (Accessed 16 Sep. 2019).

King, G., Pan, J. and Roberts, M.E. (2017) 'How the Chinese government fabricates social media posts for strategic distraction, not engaged argument', *American Political Science Review*, 111(3), 484–501.

Kiseleva, M. (2018) '"Sofa Warriors". Do not confuse with the civilians |"Диванные войска", *Не путать с народом. РИА Новости*. Available at: https://ria.ru /20180627/1523463510.html, (Accessed 18 June 2019).

Kellner, Douglas (ed.) (1997) 'Intellectuals, the new public spheres, and technopolitics', *New Political Science*, 41–42:169–88.

Kragh, M.Å.S. (2017) 'Russia's strategy for influence through public diplomacy and active measures: The Swedish case', *Journal of Strategic Studies*, 40(6), 773–816.

Krasnoboka, N. (2017) ' Media landscapes: Russia', *European Journalism Centre*. Available at: https://web.archive.org/web/20180311235132/http://ejc.net/media_landscapes/ russia, (Accessed 16 June 2020).

Kreps and Nyhan (2020) 'Coronavirus fake news isn't like other fake news', *Foreign Affairs*, Mar. 30. Available at: https://www.foreignaffairs.com/articles/2020-03-30 /coronavirus-fake-news-isnt-other-fake-news?utm_source=facebook_posts&utm _medium=social&utm_campaign=fb_daily_soc&fbclid=IwAR18TbzsNc7XdnW9 cRfnqwfuloHg-mE_3ncK1S7aERuC1vcry9FJB9hozMA, (Accessed 3 Apr. 2020).

Kuah, W. and Hur, Y. (2018) 'Hashtag warriors: The influence of social media on collective violence in Ukraine', *Nps.edu*. Available at: https://calhoun.nps.edu/h andle/10945/61332, (Accessed 30 Aug. 2019).

Kuleba, D. (2019) 'Ban of *VKontakte.* How Ukrainians behave now | Дмитрий Кулеба Вице-премьер-министр по европейской и евроатлантической интеграции Украины Запрет ВКонтакте. Как ведут себя украинцы сейчас', *Ukrainian News | Українські Новини.* Available at: https://nv.ua/opinion/zapret-vkontakte-kak-vedut-s ebya-ukraincy-seychas-50008022.html, (Accessed 10 Sep. 2019).

Kulyk, V. (2016) 'National identity in Ukraine: Impact of Euromaidan and the war', *Europe-Asia Studies,* 68(4), 588–608.

Kurowska, X. and Reshetnikov, A. (2018) 'Neutralization: Industrialized trolling as a pro-Kremlin strategy of desecuritization', *Security Dialogue,* 49(5), 345–363.

Kuzio, T. (2010) 'Ukraine's controversial transition: How it became a market democracy', *Journal of Communist Studies and Transition Politics,* 26(2), 306–314.

Kuzio, T. (2018a) 'Russia–Ukraine crisis: The blame game, geopolitics and national identity', *Europe-Asia Studies,* 70(3), 462–473.

Kuzio, T. (2018b) 'Euromaidan revolution, crimea and Russia–Ukraine war: Why it is time for a review of Ukrainian–Russian studies', *Eurasian Geography and Economics,* 59(3–4), 529–553.

Kyj, M.J. (2006) 'Internet use in Ukraine's orange revolution', *Business Horizons,* 49, 71–80.

Lambert (2009) *Digital Storytelling.* New York: Routledge.

Landon-Murray and Anderson (2013) 'Thinking in 140 characters: The internet, neuroplasticity, and intelligence analysis', *Journal of Strategic Security,* 6(3), 73–82.

Lange Ionatamishvilli, E., Szwed, R. and NATO Stratcom (2016) 'Framing of the Ukraine–Russia conflict in online and social media', *StratCom.* Available at: https ://www.stratcomcoe.org/framing-ukraine-russia-conflict-online-and-social-media, (Accessed 14 Aug. 2019).

Langlois, S. (2019) 'Facebook shuts several pro-Trump pages that were managed by Ukrainians', MarketWatch, Sep. 28. Available at: https://www.marketwatch.com/st ory/these-are-the-pro-trump-memes-that-ukraines-facebook-network-is-spreading -2019-09-23, (Accessed 29 Sep. 2019).

Leathern, R. (2020) 'Expanded transparency and more control for political ads', *Facebook Newsroom,* Jan. 9. Available at: https://about.fb.com/news/2020/01/political-ads/, (Accessed 4 May 2020).

Legislation of Ukraine (2010) 'On personal data protection', zakon.rada.gov.ua. Available at: https://zakon.rada.gov.ua/laws/show/2297-17, (Accessed 12 Sep. 2019).

Legum, J. (2019) 'Massive "I Love America" Facebook page, pushing pro-Trump propaganda, is run by Ukrainians', *Popular.info.* Available at: https://popular.info/p/ massive-i-love-america-facebook-page, (Accessed 28 Sep. 2019).

Lewandowsky, S., Ecker, U.K.H. and Cook, J. (2017) 'Beyond misinformation: Understanding and coping with the "Post-Truth" era', *Journal of Applied Research in Memory and Cognition,* 6, 353–369.

Lewis, P., Clarke, S., Barr, C., Kommenda, N. and Holder, J. (2018) 'Revealed: One in four Europeans vote populist', *The Guardian,* Nov. 20. Available at: https://www.the guardian.com/world/ng-interactive/2018/nov/20/revealed-one-in-four-europeans -vote-populist, (Accessed 12 May 2020).

Li, A. (2020) 'Sundar Pichai details google, alphabet response to coronavirus and this "unprecedented moment"', 9to5goole.com, May 6. Available at: https://9to5google.c om/2020/03/06/google-coronavirus-response/, (Accessed 8 May 2020).

Livingstone, S. (2011) 'Digital learning and participation among youth: Critical reflections on future research priorities', *International Journal of Learning and Media,* 2, 1–13.

Lomas, N. (2017) 'Study: Russian twitter bots sent 45k Brexit tweets close to vote', *Techcrunch*, Nov. 15. Available at: https://techcrunch.com/2017/11/15/study-russian -twitter-bots-sent-45k-brexit-tweets-close-to-vote/, (Accessed 19 June 2020).

Lua, A. (2020) 'How the twitter timeline works (and 6 simple tactics to increase your reach', *Buffer*. Available at: https://buffer.com/library/twitter-timeline-algorithm/, (Accessed 6 June 2020).

Luceri, L., Deb, A., Giordano, S. and Ferrara, E. (2019) 'Evolution of bot and human behavior during elections', *First Monday*, 24(9), Sep. 2. http://dx.doi.org/10.5210/fm .v24i9.10213.

Lyah, K. (2017) 'Poroshenko decided to delete his accounts from *Vkontakte* and Odnoklassniki | Порошенко решил удалить свои аккаунты из *Вконтакте* и *Одноклассников*', dp.informator.ua. Available at: https://dp.informator.ua/2017/ 05/16/poroshenko-reshil-udalit-svoi-akkaunty-iz-vkontakte-i-odnoklassnikov/, (Accessed 24 June 2020).

Makarenko, V. (2017) 'Первое убийство журналиста в Украине так и не раскрыли', Kp.ua. Available at: https://kp.ua/politics/566997-pervoe-ubyistvo-zhurnalysta-v- ukrayne-tak-y-ne-raskryly, (Accessed 13 Sep. 2019).

Makhortykh, M. and Lyebyedyev, Y. (2015) '#SaveDonbassPeople: Twitter, propaganda, and conflict in Eastern Ukraine', *The Communication Review*, 18(4). Available at: https ://doi.org/10.1080/10714421.2015.1085776, (Accessed 12 Sep. 2019).

Manjoo, F. (2017) 'Can Facebook fix its own worst bug?', *The New York Times Magazine*, Apr. 25. Available at: https://www.nytimes.com/2017/04/25/magazine/can-faceboo k-fix-its-own-worst-bug.html, (Accessed 5 Jan 2020).

Mansell, R. (2012) *Imagining the Internet: Communication, Innovation and Governance*. Oxford: Oxford University Press.

Marantz, A. (2019) *Antisocial: Online Extremists, Techno-Utopians and the Hijacking of the American Conversation*. New York: Viking Publishing.

Marcus, G.E., Neuman, W.R. and MacKuen, M. (2000) *Affective Intelligence and Political Judgement*. Chicago: University of Chicago Press.

Marcuse, H. (1968) 'Industrialization and capitalism in the work of max weber', in Bohm, S. (ed.), *Negations: Essays in Critical Theory*. Boston: Beacon Press, 201–226.

Maréchal, N. (2017) 'Networked authoritarianism and the geopolitics of information: Understanding russian internet policy', *Media and Communication*, 5(1), 29.

Marrow, A. (2019) 'Russian parliament backs law to label individuals "Foreign Agents"', *The Moscow Times*. Available at: https://www.themoscowtimes.com/2019/11/21/rus sian-parliament-backs-law-to-label-individuals-foreign-agents-a68272, (Accessed 30 Nov. 2019).

Marshall, J. P. (2017) 'Disinformation society, communication and cosmopolitan democracy', *Cosmopolitan Civil Societies: An Interdisciplinary Journal*, 9(2),1–24.

Marshall, T.H. (1950) *Citizenship and Social Class: And Other Essays*. Cambridge: Cambridge University Press.

Martinets, S. (2017) 'Порошенко решил удалить свою страницу из "ВКонтакте', *Segodnya*. Available at: https://www.segodnya.ua/politics/poroshenko-reshil-udalit -svoyu-stranicu-iz-vkontakte-1021414.html, (Accessed 24 June 2020).

Mason, J. (2018) 'Trump backs Putin on election meddling at summit, stirs fierce criticism', *Reuters*. Available at: https://www.reuters.com/article/us-usa-russia -summit/trump-backs-putin-on-election-meddling-at-summit-stirs-fierce-criti cism-idUSKBN1K601D, (Accessed 28 Nov. 2019).

Maté, A. (2019) 'CrowdStrikeOut: Mueller's own report undercuts its core Russia-meddling claims', *Real Clear Investigations*. Available at: https://www.realclearinvestigations.com/articles/2019/07/05/crowdstrikeout_muellers_own_report_undercuts_its_core_russia-meddling_claims.html, (Accessed 21 Nov. 2019).

Matsa, K.E., Silver, L., Shearer, E. and Walker, M. (2018) 'Despite overall doubts about the news media, younger Europeans continue to trust specific outlets', *Pew Research Center*, Oct. 30. Available at: https://www.journalism.org/2018/10/30/despite-overall-doubts-about-the-news-media-younger-europeans-continue-to-trust-specific-outlets/, (Accessed 14 May 2020).

McDermott, B. (2019) 'Trust is at breaking point. It's time to rebuild it', *World Economic Forum*, Jan. 14. Available at: https://www.weforum.org/agenda/2019/01/trust-is-at-breaking-point-it-s-time-to-rebuild-it/, (Accessed 8 June 2020).

McGee, M. (2013) 'EdgeRank is dead: Facebook's news feed algorithm now has close to 100k weight factors', *Social Media Marketing*, Aug. 16. Available at: https://marketingland.com/edgerank-is-dead-facebooks-news-feed-algorithm-now-has-close-to-100k-weight-factors-55908, (Accessed 16 May 2020).

McKelvey, F. (2018) 'Has trust in social media disappeared?', *Policy Options*, Jan. 15. Available at: https://policyoptions.irpp.org/magazines/january-2018/has-trust-in-social-media-disappeared/ (Accessed 6 June 2020).

McKnight, D. (2018) *Populism Now! The Case for Progressive Populism*. Sydney: New South Press.

McLaughlin, D. (2017) 'Ukraine under fire for banning Russian social media', *The Irish Times*, May 17. Available at: https://www.irishtimes.com/news/world/europe/ukraine-under-fire-for-banning-russian-social-media-1.3086397, (Accessed 21 Sep. 2019).

McLuhan, M. (1964) *Understanding Media: The Extensions of Man*. California: Gingko Press.

McNair, B. (2018) *Fake News: Falsehood, Fabrication and Fantasy in Journalism*. London: Routledge.

Media4Democracy (2020) European Media Literacy Week 2020, Review of EU Policies & Activities on Media Literacy Touchstone for EU Delegations' Action to Confront Disinformation. Information Note to EU Delegations.

Menn, J. (2017) 'Exclusive: Russia used Facebook to try to spy on Macron campaign – sources', *Reuters*, Jul. 27. Available at: https://www.reuters.com/article/us-cyber-france-facebook-spies-exclusive/exclusive-russia-used-facebook-to-try-to-spy-on-macron-campaign-sources-idUSKBN1AC0EI, (Accessed 19 June 2020).

Meister, S. (2019) 'Understanding Russian communications strategy: Case studies of Serbia and Estonia', *IFA Edition Cultural and Foreign Policy*. Available at: https://ifa-publikationen.de/out/wysiwyg/uploads/70edition/understandMeistering-russian_meister.pdf.

Metz, C. and Mike, I. (2019) '*Facebook's A.I. Quiz Now Faces the Task of Cleaning it Up*', *The New York Times*, May 17. Available At: https://www.nytimes.com/2019/05/17/technology/facebook-ai-schroepfer.html (accessed 17 Sep. 2020).

Michalchuk, S. (2019) 'Internet communications as a factor of political protests in Ukraine', *Studfiles*, Nov. 6. Available at: https://studfiles.net/preview/8098574/, (Accessed 10 Sep. 2019).

Mill, J. S. (1859) *On Liberty*. London: John W. Parker and Son.

Miller, D. and Slater, D. (2000) *The Internet: An Ethnographic Approach*. Oxford: Berg.

Minich, R. (2018) 'Ukraine's had revolutions, but where is the real evolution? - Atlantic council', *Atlantic Council*. Feb. 20. Available at: https://www.atlanticcouncil.org/blogs/ukrainealert/ukraine-s-had-revolutions-but-where-is-the-real-evolution/, (Accessed 22 Sep. 2019).

Moffitt, B. (2020) *Populism*. Cambridge: Polity.

Morozov, E. (2012) *The Net Delusion: The Dark Side of Internet Freedom*. New York: Public Affairs.

Mouffe, C. (2018) *For a Left Populism*. London: Verso.

Mudde, Cas and Cristóbal Rovira Kaltwasser (2017) *Populism: A Very Short Introduction*. Oxford University Press.

Mueller, R. (2019) 'Report on the investigation into Russian interference in the 2016 Presidential election, volume I of II', *U.S. Department of Justice*, Mar. Available at: https ://www.justice.gov/storage/report.pdf, (Accessed 19 June 2020).

Myers, D.G. (1975) 'Discussion-induced attitude polarization', *Human Relations*, 28(8), 699–714.

Myers, S.L. and Mozur, P. (2019) 'China is waging a disinformation war against hong kong protestors', *The New York Times*, Aug. 13. Available at: https://www.nytimes. com/2019/08/13/world/asia/hong-kong-protests-china.html, (Accessed 17 May 2020).

Nabytovich, I. (2014) 'Narrative shaping power of social media: A new turn of Ukrainian public sphere with #Euromaidan Hashtag appearance', *Spheres of Culture*. Available at: http://www.er.ucu.edu.ua:8080/bitstream/handle/1/745/Sakivska_Narrative%20S haping.pdf?sequence=1&isAllowed=y, (Accessed 30 July 2019).

Nadelnyuk, O. (2018) 'How Russian "Troll factory" tried to effect on Ukraine's agenda. Analysis of 755 000 tweets', *Vox Ukraine*. Available at: https://voxukraine.org/lo ngreads/twitter-database/index-en.html, (Accessed 25 Sep. 2019).

Napoli, P.M. (2018) 'What if more speech is no longer the solution? First amendment theory meets fake news and the filter bubble', *Federal Communications Law Journal*, 70(1): 55–104.

Napoli, P.M. (2019) *Social Media and the Public Interest: Media Regulation in the Disinformation Age*. New York: Columbia University Press.

Napoli, P. and R. Caplan (2017) 'When media companies insist they're not media companies and why it matters for communications policy', Conference Paper, Presented in September 2016 to Telecommunications Policy Research Conference At, Arlington, VA.

National Association for Media Literacy Education (2019) 'Media literacy defined', *National Association for Media Literacy Education*. Available at:https://namle.net/publ ications/media-literacy-definitions/, (Accessed 25 May. 2020).

NATO Strategic Communications Centre of Excellence and Fredheim, R. (2019) 'Robotrolling. NATO stratcom centre of excellence', NATO Strategic Communications, Centre of Excellence, 1–6. Available at: https://stratcomcoe.org/r obotrolling-20191, (Accessed 25 Sep. 2019).

Nayem, M. (2014) 'Protests in Ukraine: It started with a Facebook message', *Opensoc ietyfoundations.org*. Available at: https://www.opensocietyfoundations.org/voices/upri sing-ukraine-how-it-all-began, (Accessed 14 Sep. 2019).

Nesteriak, Y. (2019) 'Formation of Ukraine's media system after the collapse of the USSR | Формирование медиа системы Украины после распада СССР', *Środkowoeuropejskie Studia Polityczne*, 4, 153–169.

Nguyen, V. and Kyumin, L. (2019) 'Learning from fact-checkers: Analysis and generation of fact-checking language', *Sigir*, Jul. 21-25. Available at: https://web.cs.wpi.edu/~k mlee/pubs/vo19sigir.pdf, (Accessed 15 May 2020).

Nicolaou, E. and Smith, C.E. (2019) 'A #MeToo timeline to show how far we've come — & how far we need to go', *Refinery29*, Oct. 5. Available at: https://www.refinery29 .com/en-us/2018/10/212801/me-too-movement-history-timeline-year-weinstein, (Accessed 2 June 2020).

Nicoli, N. (2012) 'The disempowerment of in-house production at the BBC: An analysis of the window of creative competition (WOCC)', *Journal of Media Business Studies*, 9(4), 148–165.

Nicoli, N. (2013) 'Social television, creative collaboration and television production: The case of the BBC's the virtual revolution', in Friedrichsen, M. and Mühl-Benninghaus, W. (eds.), *Handbook of Social Media Management: Value Chain and Business Models in Changing Media Markets*. Berlin: Springer, 603–618.

Nicoli, N. (2014a) 'The role of PSB during a time of austerity in cyprus', *The Cyprus Review, Special Issue on the Crisis, State and Peace: Europe at the Cyprus Border*, 26(1), 205–212.

Nicoli, N. (2014b) 'From digital switchover to austerity measures: A case study of the cypriot television landscape', *International Journal of Digital Television*, 5(3), 207–220.

Nicoli, N. and Komodromos, M. (2019) 'The impact of CSR news reporting in the digital age. The case of the bank of cyprus', in Antonaras, A. and Dekoulou, E. (eds.), *Cases on Corporate Social Responsibility and Contemporary Issues in Organizations*. Pennsylvania: IGI Global, 71–89.

Nicoli, N. and Papadopoulou, E. (2017) 'Building and protecting reputation through trip advisor: A case study for the cyprus hotel industry', *EUROMED Journal of Business*, 12(3), 316–334.

Nimmo, B., François, C., Eib, C.S., Ronzaud, L., Ferreira, R., Hernon, C. and Kostelancik, T. (2020) 'Secondary infektion', *Graphika*, Jun. 16. Available at: https ://secondaryinfektion.org/downloads/secondary-infektion-report.pdf, (Accessed 19 June 2020).

Nordquist, R. (2018) 'Spin: Language that has designs on us', *ThoughtCo.* Available at: https://www.thoughtco.com/spin-communication-1691988, (Accessed 17 Aug. 2019).

Norris, P. and Ingelhart, R. (2019) *Cultural Backlash: Trump, Brexit, and Authoritarian Populism*. Cambridge: Cambridge University Press.

Norwich University (2017) 'Consequences of the collapse of the Soviet Union', *Norwich University*. Available at: https://online.norwich.edu/academic-programs/ resources/consequences-of-the-collapse-of-the-soviet-union, (Accessed 8 Sep. 2019).

Nygren, G., Glowacki, M., Hök, J., Kiria, I., Orlova, D. and Taradai, D. (2016) 'Journalism in the crossfire', *Journalism Studies*,19(7), 1059–1078.

Obama, B. (2016) 'Now is the greatest time to be alive', *Wired*, Dec. 18. Available at: https ://www.wired.com/2016/10/president-obama-guest-edits-wired-essay/, (Accessed 27 Sep. 2018).

O'Conner, G. and Weatherall, J.O. (2018) *The Misinformation Age: How False Beliefs Spread*. New Haven: Yale University Press.

Ofcom (2020) 'Covid-19 news and information: Consumption and attitudes: Results from weeks one to three of ofcom's online survey', Office of Communications, Apr. 21. Available at: https://www.ofcom.org.uk/__data/assets/pdf_file/0031/194377/ covid-19-news-consumption-weeks-one-to-three-findings.pdf, (Accessed 4 May 2020).

O'Grady, S. (2019) 'No wonder brexiteers tried to disown the merkel "Kraut" meme. It revealed their twisted worldview for all to see', *The Independent*, Oct. 9. Available at: https://www.independent.co.uk/voices/angela-merkel-brexit-leave-eu-kraut-tweet -germany-a9149096.html, (Accessed 22 May 2020).

Önal, L. (2015) 'Gezi park and EuroMaidan: Social movements at the borders', *Innovation: The European Journal of Social Science Research*, 29(1), 16–40.

Ong, J.C. and Cabañes, J.V. (2019) 'When disinformation studies meets production studies: Social identities and moral justifications in the political trolling industry', *International Journal of Communication*, 13, 1–19.

Ong, W.J. (1982) *Orality and Literacy: The Technologizing of the World*. London: Methuen Publishing.

Onuch, O. (2015a) 'EuroMaidan protests in Ukraine: Social media versus social networks', *Problems of Post-Communism*, 62(4), 217–235.

Onuch, O. (2015b) 'Facebook helped me do it': Understanding the Euromaidan protester "Tool-Kit"', *Studies in Ethnicity and Nationalism*, 15(1), 170–184.

Orlova, D. (2016) 'Ukrainian media after the EuroMaidan: In search of independence and professional identity', *Publizistik*, 61(4), 441–461.

Osburn, M. (2019) 'New report: Mueller lacks substantiating evidence of Russian election interference', *The Federalist*. Available at: https://thefederalist.com/2019/07/08/new-repo rt-mueller-lacks-evidence-of-russian-election-interference/, (Accessed 21 Nov. 2019).

Panichi, J. (2015) 'EU declares war on Russia', *Politico*, Feb. 2. Available at: https:// www.politico.eu/article/russia-propaganda-ukraine-eu-response-disinformation/, (Accessed 22 May 2020).

Papacharissi, Z. (2010) *A Private Sphere*. Cambridge: Polity.

Papacharissi, Z. (2015) 'We have always been social', *Social Media + Society*, Apr. 17. DOI: https://doi.org/10.1177/2056305115581185

Papacharissi, Z. (2019) 'Forget messiahs', *Social Media + Society*, July – Sep. 1-3. https:// doi.org/10.1177/2056305119849710

Pawlack, P. (2015) 'Understanding hybrid threats', *European Parliamentary Research Service Blog*, Jun. 24. Available at: https://epthinktank.eu/2015/06/24/understanding-hyb rid-threats/, (Accessed 13 May 2020).

Peters, C. and Broersma, M.J. (eds.) (2012) *Rethinking Journalism: Trust and Participation in a Transformed News Landscape*. London: Routledge.

Picard, R.G. and Pickard, V. (2017) 'Essential principles for contemporary media and communications policymaking', Reuters Institute for the Study of *Journalism*, University of Oxford. Available at: https://reutersinstitute.politics.ox.ac.uk/our-res earch/essential-principles-contemporary-media-and-communications-policymaki ng, (Accessed 12 Apr. 2020).

Pickard, V. (2020) *Democracy Without Journalism*. New York: Oxford University.

Pifer, S. (2009) 'Ukraine's geopolitical choice, 2009', *Eurasian Geography and Economics*, 50(4), 387–401.

Pinker, S. (2018) *Enlightenment Now: The Case for Reason, Science, Humanism and Progress*. New York: Penguin.

Placek, M.A. (2016) '#Democracy: Social media use and democratic legitimacy in central and Eastern Europe', *Democratization*, 24(4), 632–650.

Plus One (2019) 'Facebook in Ukraine: The research of Ukrainian internet audience', Plus One. Available at: https://plusone.com.ua/fb/en/, (Accessed 22 Sep. 2019).

Pokrop, J. (2019) 'Facebook users in Russia March 2019', *NapoleonCat*. Available at: https ://napoleoncat.com/blog/facebook-users-in-russia-march-2019/, (Accessed 19 Sep. 2019).

Polyakova, A. (2017) 'The Kremlin's latest crackdown on independent media', *Foreign Affairs*. Available at: https://www.foreignaffairs.com/articles/russia-fsu/2017-12-05/ kremlins-latest-crackdown-independent-media, (Accessed 30 Nov. 2019).

Pomerantsev, P. (2019) 'This is not propaganda', *The Guardian*, July 28. Available at: https ://www.theguardian.com/books/2019/jul/28/this-is-not-propaganda-adventures- war-on-reality-peter-pomerantsev-review (accessed 17 Sep. 2020).

Pond, E. (2017) 'War in Ukraine: Is this the way it ends?', *Survival*, 59(6), 143–156.

Poor, N. (2017) 'Mechanisms of an online public sphere: The website slashdot', *Journal of Computer-Mediated Communication*, 10(2). Available at: https://academic.oup.com/jcmc/article/10/2/JCMC1028/4614448, (Accessed 28 Nov. 2019).

Pop-Eleches, G. and Robertson, G.B. (2018) 'Identity and political preferences in Ukraine – before and after the Euromaidan', *Post-Soviet Affairs*, 34(2–3), 107–118.

Popken, B. and Cobiella, K. (2017) 'Russian troll describes work in the infamous misinformation factory', *nbcnews*, Nov. 17. Available at: https://www.nbcnews.com/news/all/russian-troll-describes-work-infamous-misinformation-factory-n821486, (Accessed 20 June 2020).

Popsters (2019) 'The audience of social networks in Russia 2019', *Popsters.ru*, Nov. 18. Available at: https://popsters.ru/blog/post/auditoriya-socsetey-v-rossii, (Accessed 20 Sep. 2019).

Poroshenko, P. (2017) 'Decree of the President of Ukraine №133 / 2017 | Указ Президента України №133/2017', *Official Website of the President of Ukraine | Офіційне інтернет-представництво Президента України*. Available at: https://www.president.gov.ua/documents/1332017-21850, (Accessed 13 Sep. 2019).

Pospieszna, P. and Galus, A. (2019) '"Liberation Technology" or "Net Delusion"? Civic activists' perceptions of social media as a platform for civic activism in Belarus and Ukraine', *Europe-Asia Studies*, (71)10: 1664-1684.

Postill, J. (2018) 'Populism and social media: A global perspective', *Media, Culture & Society*, 40(5), 754–765.

Postill, J. (2019) 'Populism and social media: A global perspective' updated and abridged version of Postill, J. (2018)'. Available at: https://www.oxfordresearchgroup.org.uk/blog/populism-and-social-media-a-global-perspective, (Accessed 12 May 2020).

Pushkov, A. and Kosachev, K. (2019) 'We told you so: Russian officials react to Mueller report on collusion', *The Moscow Times*, Mar. 25. Available at: https://www.themoscowtimes.com/2019/03/25/we-told-you-so-russian-officials-react-to-mueller-report-on-collusion-a64939., (Accessed 30 Nov. 2019).

Putnam, R.D. (2000) *Bowling Alone*. New York: Simon and Schuster.

Rathi, (2018) 'Effects of Cambridge analytica's Facebook ads on the 2016 Presidential Election', *Towards Data Science*, Jan. 13. Available at: https://towardsdatascience.com/effect-of-cambridge-analyticas-facebook-ads-on-the-2016-us-presidential-election-dacb5462155d, (Accessed 6 June 2019).

Rettman, A. (2017) 'Mogherini urged to do more on Russian propaganda', *euobserver*, Oct. 20. Available at: https://euobserver.com/foreign/139573, (Accessed 7 Jan. 2020).

Rheingold, H. (1993) *The Virtual Community, Homesteading of the Electronic Frontier*, Reading, MA: MIT Press.

Richter, A. (2019) 'Accountability and media literacy mechanisms as counteraction to disinformation in Europe', *Journal of Digital Media & Policy*, 30(3), 311–327.

Ricoeur, P. (2007) *History and Truth*. Chicago: Northwestern University Press.

Risko, E.F. and Gilbert, S.J. (2016) 'Cognitive offloading', *Trends in Cognitive Sciences*, 20, 676–688. https://doi.org/10.1016/j.tics.2016.07.002

Risse, T. (2010) *A Community of Europeans? Transnational Identities and Public Spheres*, 1st Edition. New York: Cornell University Press.

Rosen, G. (2020) 'An update on our work to keep people informed and limit misinformation about COVID-19', *Facebook Newsroom*, Apr. 16. Available at: (https://about.fb.com/news/2020/04/covid-19-misinfo-update/, (Accessed 3 May 2020).

Rosen, R.J. (2011) 'So, was Facebook responsible for the Arab spring after all?', *The Atlantic*. Available at: https://www.theatlantic.com/technology/archive/2011/09/so-was-facebook-responsible-for-the-arab-spring-after-all/244314/, (Accessed 30 Nov. 2019).

Rosenberg, M., Confessore, N. and Cadwalladr, C. (2018) 'How Trump consultants exploited the Facebook data of millions', *The New York Times*, Mar. 17. Available at: https://www.nytimes.com/2018/03/17/us/politics/cambridge-analytica-trump-campaign.html, (Accessed 19 Feb. 2019).

Ross, A.S. and Rivers, D.J. (2018) 'Discursive deflection: Accusation of "Fake News" and the spread of mis- and disinformation in the tweets of President Trump', *Social Media + Society*, 4.

RT (2014) 'Putin signs into force more anti-extremism laws', RT International. Available at: https://www.rt.com/russia/169352-russian-extremism-financing-ban/ (Accessed 30 Nov. 2019).

RT (2019) 'Google & Facebook are meddling in Russia's affairs with political ads on election day – watchdog', RT International. Available at: https://www.rt.com/russia/468364-google-facebook-russia-election/ (Accessed 28 Nov. 2019).

Rutten, E., Fedor, J. and Zvereva, V. (2014) *Memory, Conflict and New Media: Web Wars in Post Socialist States*. Oxfordshire: Routledge.

Ryabinska, N. (2011) 'The media market and media ownership in post-communist Ukraine', *Problems of Post-Communism*, 58(6), 3–20.

Saburov, A. (2015) ИНТЕРНЕТ-ТРОЛЛИНГ НА СЛУЖБЕ У ГОСУДАРСТВЕННОСТИ. *Commons*. Available at: https://commons.com.ua/uk/internet-trolling-na-sluzhbe-u-gosudarstvennosti/, (Accessed 24 June 2020).

Sapolsky, R. M (2017) *Behave: The Biology of Humans at our Best and Worst*. London: Penguin Press.

Scott, M. (2014) 'Mail.ru takes full ownership of VKontakte, Russia's largest social network', *DealBook*. Sep. 16. Available at: https://dealbook.nytimes.com/2014/09/16/mail-ru-takes-full-ownership-of-vkontakte-russias-largest-social-network/?_r=0, (Accessed 23 Sep. 2019).

Shane, S. (2017) 'The fake Americans Russia created to influence the election', *The New York Times*, Sept. 7. Available at: https://www.nytimes.com/2017/09/07/us/politics/russia-facebook-twitter-election.html, (Accessed 16 June 2020).

Shattock, E. (2020) 'As European eyes turn to India's fake news lockdown, Argentina's human rights response should be evaluated', *Internet Policy Review*, Apr. 8. Available at: https://policyreview.info/articles/news/european-eyes-turn-indias-fake-news-lockdown-argentinas-human-rights-response-should, (Accessed 12 May 2020).

Shirky, C. (2009) *Here Comes Everybody: The Power of Organising Without Organisations*. London: Penguin.

Shultz, R. and Goodson, R. (1984) *Dezinformatsia: Active Measures in Soviet Strategy*. New York: Pergamon Press.

Shveda, Y. and Park, J.H. (2016) 'Ukraine's revolution of dignity: The dynamics of Euromaidan', *Journal of Eurasian Studies*, 7(1), 85–91.

Siebert, F.S., Peterson, T. and Schramm, W. (1984) *Four Theories of the Press: The Authoritarian, Libertarian, Social Responsibility, and Soviet Communist Concepts of What the Press Should Be and Do*. Chicago: University of Illinois Press.

Silverman, C. (2010) 'Inside the largest fact checking company in the world', *Columbia Journalism Review*, Apr. 9. Available at: https://archives.cjr.org/behind_the_news/inside_the_worlds_largest_fact.php, (Accessed 20 Feb. 2020).

Similar Web (2019a) 'Top websites ranking Ukraine', SimilarWeb. Available at: https://www.similarweb.com/top-websites/ukraine, (Accessed 23 Sep. 2019).

Similar Web (2019b) 'vk.com August 2019 overview', SimilarWeb. Available at: https://www.similarweb.com/website/vk.com, (Accessed 25 Sep. 2019).

Smith, R. (2013) *Strategic Planning for Public Relations*. London: Routledge.

Snowden, D. (2005) 'Story telling: A new skill in an old context', *Creative Commons*. Available at: http://old.cognitive-edge.com/wp-content/uploads/1999/01/10-Story tellling1---Old-Skill-New-Context-.pdf, (Accessed 12 Dec 2019).

Spencer, S. (2019) 'An update of our political ads policy', *Google*, Nov. 20. Available at: https://www.blog.google/technology/ads/update-our-political-ads-policy/, (Accessed 19 May 2020).

Srnicek, N. (2017) *Platform Capitalism*. Cambridge: Polity.

Srnicek, N. and Williams, A. (2016) *Inventing the Future: Postcapitalism and a World Without Work*. London: Verso.

Stahle, M. (2017) 'The secret Swedish troll factory', ekuriren, Feb. 23. Available at: https://www.ekuriren.se/sormland/the-secret-swedish-troll-factory/ (Accessed 2 Sep. 2018).

State Committee for Television and Radio-broadcasting of Ukraine (2005) 'On April 8, 2005, at 10.00, the state committee for television and radio broadcasting of Ukraine held a roundtable meeting dedicated to the memory of the dead journalists of Ukraine', *Kmu.gov.ua*. Available at: http://comin.kmu.gov.ua/control/uk/publish/printable_ar ticle?art_id=35186, (Accessed 10 Sep. 2019).

Statista (2020) 'Number of active monthly Facebook users worldwide', Statista, Apr. Available at: https://www.statista.com/statistics/264810/number-of-monthly-active -facebook-users-worldwide/, (Accessed 9 May 2020).

Stavichenko, A. (2014) '"Putin is a terrorist!" how did you meet the Russian president in Vienna | «Путин – террорист!» Как встречали российского президента в Вене', *Glavcom*.ua, Feb. 25. Available at: https://glavcom.ua/photo/316067-%C2%ABpu tin-%E2%80%93-terrorist-%C2%BB.-kak-vstrechali-rossijskogo-prezidenta-v-vene .html, (Accessed 25 June 2020).

Steensen, S. and Ahva, A. (2017) *Theories of Journalism in the Digital Age*. London: Routledge.

Stefanov, R. and Vladimirov, M. (2019) 'Russian influence on the media: A case study of Serbia', in Meister, S. (ed.), *Understanding Russian Communications Strategy: Case Studies of Serbia and Estonia*. IFA Edition Cultural and Foreign Policy, 31–50. Available at: https://ifa-publikationen.de/out/wysiwyg/uploads/70edition/understandMeiste ring-russian_meister.pdf.

Stiakakis, E., Liapis, Y. and Vlachopoulou, M. (2019) 'Developing an understanding of digital intelligence as a prerequisite of digital competence', *Mediterranean Conference on Information Systems (MCIS)* 2019 Proceedings, Nov. 15. Available at: https://aisel .aisnet.org/mcis2019/27/ (Accessed 29 May 2020).

Stop Fake (2014) 'About us', *StopFake*. https://www.stopfake.org/en. Available at: https://www.stopfake.org/en/about-us/, (Accessed 6 Sep. 2019).

Stop Fake (2019) 'Robotrolling *2019/1*', *StopFake*. Available at: https://www.stopfake .org/en/robotrolling-2019-1/, (Accessed 22 Sep. 2019).

Stop Fake (2020) 'Homepage', *StopFake*. Available at: https://www.stopfake.org/en/ main/, (Accessed 13 June 2020).

Summers, T. (2018) 'How the Russian government used disinformation and cyber warfare in 2016 election – an ethical hacker explains', *The Conversation*, July 27. Available at: https://theconversation.com/how-the-russian-government-used-disin

formation-and-cyber-warfare-in-2016-election-an-ethical-hacker-explains-99989, (Accessed 26 June 2020).

Surzhko-Harned, L. and Zahuranec, A.J. (2017) 'Framing the revolution: The role of social media in Ukraine's Euromaiden movement', *Nationalities Papers: Journal of Nationalism and Ethnicity*, 45(5), 758–779, doi:10.1080/00905992.2017.12 89162.

Tambini, D. (2017) 'How advertising fuels fake news', *LSE Media Policy Project Blog*, Feb. 24. Available at: https://blogs.lse.ac.uk/medialse/2017/02/24/how-advertising-fuels -fake-news/, (Accessed 2 Sep. 2018).

Tapscott, D. and Tapscott, A. (2016) *Blockchain Revolution: How the Technology Behind Bitcoin is Changing Money, Business and the World*. New York: Random House.

TASS (2018) 'Yarovaya law obliges operators and internet companies to store user correspondence', *TACC*. Available at: https://tass.com/politics/1011585., (Accessed 28 Nov. 2019).

TASS (2019a) 'Russian telecom watchdog urges google to ban promoting illegal rallies on YouTube', *TACC*. Available at: https://tass.com/society/1072945, (Accessed 28 Nov. 2019).

TASS (2019b) 'Foreign forces used YouTube to manipulate protesters in Moscow – senator', *TACC*. Available at: https://tass.com/politics/1072942, (Accessed 28 Nov. 2019).

TASS (2019c) 'The Presidential council for civil society and human rights concerns the criminal code about the insult to the feelings of believers "almost dead"', *Глава СПЧ считает уголовную статью об оскорблении чувств верующих "практически мертвой"*, *ТАСС*. Available at: https://tass.ru/obschestvo/6789200, (Accessed 30 Nov. 2019).

TASS (2019d) 'Laws on inauthentic news and the protection of state symbols entered into force', *Законы о недостоверных новостях и защите госсимволов вступили в силу*, *ТАСС*. Available at: https://tass.ru/politika/6271869, (Accessed 30 Nov. 2019).

TASS (2019e) 'Russian MFA: In the Muller's report there is no evidence of Moscow's interference in elections', *МИД РФ: в докладе Мюллера нет ни одного доказательства "вмешательства." Москвы в выборы*, *ТАСС*. Available at: https://tass.ru/politika/6352689, (Accessed 19 Nov. 2019).

Taylor, M. (2019) 'Combating disinformation and foreign interference in democracies: Lessons from Europe', *The Brookings Institute*, Jul. 31. Available at: https://www.bro okings.edu/blog/techtank/2019/07/31/combating-disinformation-and-foreign-in terference-in-democracies-lessons-from-europe/, (Accessed 20 June 2020).

Techopedia (2019) 'What is tradigital? - Definition from techopedia', Techopedia.com. Available at: https://www.techopedia.com/definition/23831/tradigital, (Accessed 19 Sep. 2019).

Tegmark, M. (2017) *Life 3.0*. New York: Vintage.

Telecriticism (2005) 'Journalistic revolution–2004: Events, people, discussions', 70–72, 151–154, 195–201, 227–234. Available at: https://detector.media/php_uploads/files/ books/revolution_2004.pdf, (Accessed 12 July 2019).

Tenbarge, K. and Perrett, C. (2020) 'Harvey Weinstein found guilty of third-degree rape. Here are all the celebrities who knew about his treatment of women, according to Ronan Farrow's book', *Insider*, Feb. 24. Available at: https://www.insider.com/c elebrities-knew-harvey-weinstein-sexual-abuse-ronan-farrow-catch-kill-2019-10 , (Accessed 2 June 2020).

Thaler, R.H. and Sunstein, C.R. (2009) *Nudge: Improving Decisions about Health, Wealth and Happiness*. New York: Penguin Books.

The Economist (2017) 'Ukraine bans its top social networks because they are Russian', *The Economist*. May 19. Available at: https://www.economist.com/europe/2017/05/19/ukraine-bans-its-top-social-networks-because-they-are-russian, (Accessed 24 Sep. 2019).

The Economist (2018) 'The discord amplifier', *The Economist*, Feb. 24.

The Economist (2019) 'Combating fake news: Lie detector', *The Economist*, Oct. 26.

The Guardian (2020) 'Facebook refuses to restrict untruthful political ads and micro-targeting', *The Guardian*, Jan. 9. Available at: https://www.theguardian.com/technology/2020/jan/09/facebook-political-ads-micro-targeting-us-election, (Accessed 12 June 2020).

The Moscow Times (2018) 'Russia's "Big Brother" law enters into force', *The Moscow Times*, Jul. 1. Available at: https://www.themoscowtimes.com/2018/07/01/russias-big-brother-law-enters-into-force-a62066, (Accessed 20 June 2020).

Tilearcio, T. (2018) '*VKontakte*: Learn about Russia's largest social network | synthesio', *Synthesio*, Oct. 4. Available at: https://www.synthesio.com/blog/vkontakte-russia-largest-social-network/, (Accessed 23 Sep. 2019).

Tiernan, R. (2020) 'OpenAI's gigantic GPT-3 hints at the limits of language models for AI', *ZDNet*, Jan. 6. Available at: https://www.msn.com/en-us/news/technology/openai-e2-80-99s-gigantic-gpt-3-hints-at-the-limits-of-language-models-for-ai/ar-BB14RvVk, (Accessed 2 June 2018).

Timmer J. (2017) 'Fighting falsity: Fake news, Facebook, and the first amendment', *Cardozo, Arts & Entertainment*, 35(3), 669–705.

Titcomb, J. (2017) 'Governments in 30 countries are paying "keyboard armies" to spread propaganda, report says', *The Telegraph*, Nov. 14. Available at: https://www.telegraph.co.uk/technology/2017/11/14/governments-30-countries-pay-keyboard-armies-spread-propaganda/, (Accessed 26 June 2020).

Tomson, D.L. (2020) 'The rise of Sweden democrats: Islam, populism and the end of Swedish Exceptionalism', Brookings, Mar. 25. Available at: https://www.brookings.edu/research/the-rise-of-sweden-democrats-and-the-end-of-swedish-exceptionalism/ (accessed 30 Apr. 2020).

Tregubova, Y. (2017) 'Велике переселення: як з'явився інтернет в Україні та скільки людей уже там? Радіо Свобода', Radio Svoboda, Apr. 4. Available at: https://www.radiosvoboda.org/a/28409877.html, (Accessed 11 Sep. 2019).

Trier, J. (1931) *Der Deutsche Wortschatz im Sinnbezirk des Verstandes*. Ph.D. diss. Bonn.

Turner, S.P. (2003) *Liberal Democracy 3.0*. London: Sage Publications.

Ukrainian Truth (2017) 'The Presidential administration instructed to criticize Sadovoy and praise Poroshenko for the law', Ukrainian Truth (Ukrainskaya Pravda), Mar. 14. Available at: https://www.pravda.com.ua/rus/news/2017/03/14/7138143/, (Accessed 16 Sep. 2019).

Urry, J. (1999) 'Globalization and citizenship', *Journal of World-Systems Research*, 5(2), 311–324.

Van de Beek, E. (2017) 'Press freedom in Russia – Putin as a dog', *Russia Insider*, Nov. 11. Available at: https://russia-insider.com/en/press-freedom-russia-putin-dog/ri21544, (Accessed 20 June 2020).

Van Loon, J. (2008) *Media Technology: Critical Perspectives*. New York: McGraw Hill.

Verkhovna Rada of Ukraine (2014) 'For the period of January 14-17, the Verkhovna Rada adopted 11 laws and 1 resolution', Verkhovna Rada of Ukraine - *Gov*.ua. Available at: https://rada.gov.ua/en/news/News/News/87088.html, (Accessed 16 Sep. 2019).

Vosoughi, S., Roy, D. and Aral, S. (2018). 'The spread of true and false news online', *Science*, 359(6380), 1146–1151.

Vossen, K. (2016) *The Power of Populism: Geert Wilders and the Party for Freedom in the Netherlands.* London: Routledge.

Voyko, D. (2017) 'Lviv student was sentenced to 2.5 years for quoting Lenin on Facebook |Львовского студента осудили на 2,5 года за цитаты Ленина в Facebook', *Strana .ua*, Mar. 15. Available at: https://strana.ua/news/70674-lvovyanina-posadili-na-2-5 -goda-za-citaty-lenina-v-facebook.html, (Accessed 7 July 2019).

Wael, G. (2012). *Revolution 2.0: The Power of the People is Greater Than the People in Power: A Memoir.* Boston: Houghton Mifflin Harcourt.

Wahl-Jorgensen, K. (2008) 'Mediated citizenship: An introduction', in K. Wahl-Jorgensen (ed.), *Mediated Citizenship.* London: Routledge, vii–xiii.

Walker, S. (2014) 'Founder of *Vkontakte* leaves after dispute with Kremlin-linked owners', *The Guardian*, Apr. 2. Available at: https://www.theguardian.com/media /2014/apr/02/founder-pavel-durov-leaves-russian-social-network-site-vkontakte, (Accessed 22 Sep. 2019).

Walker, S. (2017) 'Russian troll factory paid US activists to help fund protests during election', *The Guardian*, Oct. 17. Available at: https://www.theguardian.com/world /2017/oct/17/russian-troll-factory-activists-protests-us-election, (Accessed 18 May 2020).

Walter, E. and Gioglio, J. (2015) *The Power of Visual Storytelling: How to Use Visuals, Videos and Social Media to Market Your Brand.* New York: McGraw-Hill Education.

Wardle, C. (2017) 'Fake news: It's complicated', *First Draft News.* Feb. 17. Available at: https://firstdraftnews.com/fake-news-complicated/, (Accessed 2 Sep. 2018).

Wardle, C. and Derakshan, H. (2017) 'Information disorder: Toward an interdisciplinary framework for research and policy making', *Council of Europe: Report.* Available at: https://rm.coe.int/information-disorder-toward-an-interdisciplinary-framework-fo r-researc/168076277c, (Accessed 18 Nov. 2019).

Way, L.A. (2019) 'Ukraine's post-Maidan struggles: II. Free speech in a time of war', *Journal of Democracy*, 30(3), 48–60.

We are Social (2020) 'Digital 2020: Global digital overview', We are Social, Jan. 30. Available at: https://wearesocial.com/blog/2020/01/digital-2020-3-8-billion-peo ple-use-social-media#:~:text=Worldwide%2C%20there%20are%203.80%20billion ,percent)%20over%20the%20past%20year, (Accessed 6 June 2020).

Website Ranking (2019) 'vk.com', *Website Ranking.* Available at: https://www.similarw eb.com/website/vk.com, (Accessed 30 Nov. 2019).

Weedon, J., Nuland, N. and Stamos, A. (2017) 'Information operations and Facebook', *Facebook Newsroom*, Apr. 27. Available at: https://fbnewsroomus.files.wordpress.com /2017/04/facebook-and-information-operations-v1.pdf, (Accessed 22 May 2019).

Weisburd, A., Watts, C. and Berger, J.M. (2018) 'Trolling for Trump: How Russia is trying to destroy our democracy', *EVI Berger.* Available at: https://foia.state.gov/se archapp/DOCUMENTS/Litigation_Jun2018/F-2017-12795/DOC_0C06513789/ C06513789.pdf., (Accessed 20 June 2020).

Wikipedia (2019) 'List of journalists murdered in Ukraine', *Wikipedia.* Available at: https ://en.wikipedia.org/wiki/List_of_journalists_murdered_in_Ukraine, (Accessed 13 Sep. 2019).

Wikipedia (2020) 'Internet research agency', *Wikipedia.* Available at: https://en.wikipedia .org/wiki/Internet_Research_Agency, (Accessed 20 June 2020).

Winseck, D. (2020) 'Vampire squids, "The Broken Internet" and platform regulation', *Journal of Digital Media & Policy. (forthcoming)*

Woolley, S. (2020) *The Reality Game: How the Next Wave of Technology Will Break the Truth and What We Can Do About It.* London: Endevour.

Wolf, M. (2018) *Reader, Come Home: The Reading Brain in a Digital World*. New York: Harper.

Wu, T. (2016) *The Attention Merchants*. New York: Alfred A. Knopf.

Wu, T. (2018) *The Curse of Bigness: Antitrust in the New Gilded Age*. New York: Columbia Global Reports.

Xiao, A. (2020) 'Responding to election meddling in the cyberspace: An international law case study on the Russian interference IN the 2016 presidential election', *Duke Journal of Comparative & International Law*, (30)2, 349–378.

Yakovlenko, E. (2013) 'More than 60 journalists have been killed since 1991, with about 50 injured this month', *Day (День)*, Dec. 26. Available at: https://day.kyiv.ua/ru/ article/den-ukrainy/s-1991-goda-pogiblo-bolee-60-zhurnalistov-okolo-50-postra dali-za-etot-mesyac, (Accessed 13 Sep. 2019).

Yandex (2014) 'Overview of social networks and Twitter in Ukraine | Огляд соціальних мереж і Твіттера в Україні', Yandex, 1–9. Available at: http://cache-default99v.cdn .yandex.net/download.yandex.ru/company/Yandex_on_UkrainianSMM_Summer _2014.pdf, (Accessed 24 Sep. 2019).

You, D., Vo, N. and Lee, K. (2019) 'Attributed multi-relational attention network for fact-checking URL recommendation', *arXiv*, Jan. 7. Available at: https://arxiv.org/ pdf/2001.02214v1.pdf, (Accessed 22 May 2020).

Zakusylo, M. (2018) 'Liars registry, penalties and social network blocking: How MPs want to deal with fakes | Реєстр брехунів, штрафи та блокування в соцмережах: як депутати хочуть боротися з фейками', detector.media, Sep. 7. Available at: https ://detector.media/infospace/article/135393/2018-03-07-reestr-brekhuniv-shtrafi -ta-blokuvannya-v-sotsmerezhakh-yak-deputati-khochut-borotisya-z-feikami/, (Accessed 11 Sep. 2019).

Zarofsky, E. (2019) 'The deep pathology at the heart of a scandal at Der Spiegel', *The New Yorker*, Jan. 30. Available at: https://www.newyorker.com/news/dispatch/ the-deep-pathology-at-the-heart-of-the-scandal-at-der-spiegel, (Accessed 20 Jan. 2020).

Zerfass, A., Verčić, D., Nothhaft, H. and Werder, K.P. (2018) 'Strategic communication: Defining the field and its contribution to research and practice', *International Journal of Strategic Communication*, 12(4), 487–505.

Zuboff, S. (2019) *The Age of Surveillance Capitalism: The Fight for a Human Future at the New Frontier of Power*. New York: Profile Books.

Zuckerberg, M. (2019) 'The Internet needs new rules: Let's start with these four areas', *The Washington Post*, Mar. 30. Available at: https://www.washingtonpost.com/opin ions/mark-zuckerberg-the-internet-needs-new-rules-lets-start-in-these-four-areas /2019/03/29/9e6f0504-521a-11e9-a3f7-78b7525a8d5f_story.html?utm_term=. 842f5cb21e4e, (Accessed 1 Apr. 2019).

Zuckerberg, M. (2020) 'Big tech needs more regulation', *The Financial Times*, Feb. 16. Available at: https://www.ft.com/content/602ec7ec-4f18-11ea-95a0-43d18ec715f5, (Accessed 1 May 2020).

Zukin, S. (1991) *Landscapes of Power: From Detroit to Disney World*. Berkeley: University of California Press.

INDEX

Note: **Bold** page numbers refer to tables; and page numbers followed by "n" denote endnotes.

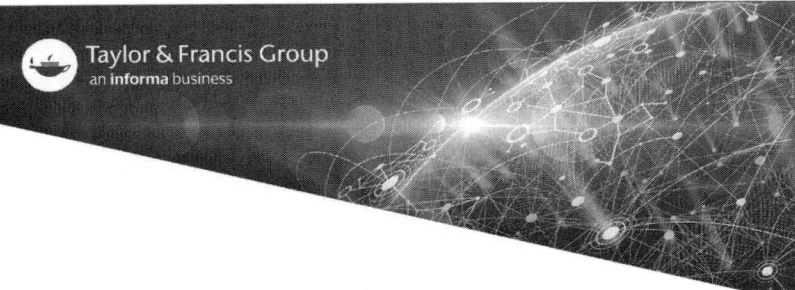

Printed in Great Britain
by Amazon

59199877R00099